LETTERS FROM ALABAMA
1817–1822

By the Same Author

YOURS TILL DEATH:
Civil War Letters of John W. Cotton

HISTORY OF ALABAMA, 1540–1900,
As Recorded in Diaries, Letters and Other Papers of the Times

THE VIRGINIA HOUSE OF BURGESSES, 1750–1774

Southern Historical Publications No. 14

LETTERS FROM ALABAMA
1817–1822

by

Anne Newport Royall

Biographical Introduction and Notes

by

Lucille Griffith

UNIVERSITY OF ALABAMA PRESS

ISBN 0-8173-5034-9 (alk. paper)
Library of Congress Catalogue Card No.: 70–76584
Manufactured in the United States of America

TO

my brothers

Ludwig, William, Ralph,

David, and Charles

and in memory of Edwin

TABLE OF CONTENTS

PREFACE

I first "met" Mrs. Anne Royall several years ago when I was compiling a book of source materials in Alabama history. Up to that time I had been completely unaware of her or her writings; I have since found that most Alabamians share my ignorance. Finding her comments on such diverse topics as revival meetings and injustices to widows, and descriptions of Andrew Jackson and her fellow travelers, to be vivid in detail and earthy in flavor, I read on. To my surprise I found Mrs. Royall was a prominent woman journalist for more than a quarter of a century before her death in 1854, publishing some ten books of travel accounts, one novel, and two successive weekly newspapers in Washington, and sponsoring causes, often unpopular, in the manner of latter-day "muckrakers." She was a well-known habitué of the halls of Congress, looking for news and subscribers, sniffing out irregularities in governmental departments, and pressing claims for a pension which she believed should have been hers from her Revolutionary War husband. For those who helped her she had high, often inordinate, praise; for those who refused her or crossed her path she was a "holy terror," lashing out against them often in intemperate language. Through the columns of her paper she debated such public issues as the Bank, anti-Masonry, Nullification, and the franking privilege; she was forever attacking what she considered a very diabolical plot to unite church and state. There was never a doubt where she stood on any of the issues on which she spoke out; she was no compromiser or "fence-straddler." She has the distinction of being the only woman in our national history who was tried (and convicted) for being a "common scold." She was, in short, an aggressive, intolerant, outspoken, suspicious, meddlesome, nonconforming but patriotic, and fascinating woman.

Anne Royall, we might say, began her journalistic career in Alabama. Although the letters were not published until 1830, some four years after *Sketches of History, Life and Manners in the United States* (New Haven, 1826), they were her first literary effort. Ostensibly written to a young lawyer friend "Matt" in Virginia, the letters are dated from November 28, 1817 to June 8, 1822. The title is somewhat inaccurate because of the fifty letters the first fourteen describe a journey taken in November, 1817, from Cabell County Court House, Virginia, through Mount Sterling, Lexington, and Bowling Green, Kentucky, and then Nashville and Fayetteville, Tennessee, on her way to Huntsville, Alabama. Later she visited Melton's Bluff, Courtland, Moulton, and Florence. The last letter in the collection is dated from Huntsville on June 8, 1822. The letters include, in addition to personal matters and comments on the inconveniences of travel, a considerable amount of description of the country through which she traveled and discussions —often lengthy—of religion, literature, education, social injustices, crops, and important personages she met in her travels. While she is often outspoken, her comments in these letters are more temperate than those in her later works.

It is not certain when Mrs. Royall first thought of publishing the letters. In one of them she playfully threatened to become a writer, but there is no way of knowing whether this was mere jest or whether she had ambitions to publish. Whatever her original intentions, her circumstances after 1823, when her husband's heirs broke his will and she, a woman in her fifties, was left penniless, forced her to make a living. She published this volume, as she did the others, with the hope that they would sell and bring in much-needed money. In the winter of 1824 (or the date may be 1826, since Mrs. Royall's handwriting is almost impossible to read at times), she sent the manuscript to one Carey in Alexandria. Up to that point it had been ill-fated. Two years ago, she said, she had sent the letters to friends in Virginia to have them copied and published. Somehow they ended up in Washington where they remained until her arrival. The package had been opened and the contents "much abused." When she contacted a publisher in Baltimore, that gentleman discouraged her by telling her that booksellers were "fearful of publication for what reason he does not say." The letters, she wrote Mr. Carey, were on coarse paper and in the worst handwriting he probably ever saw, but she believed they had value. Before she left Huntsville, she had some acquaintances read the manuscript, and "it was pronounced a work of some merit," but she had become so provoked about it that if she had it back she "would throw it in the fire." The letters, she said, were not mere literary devices; they were actually written to her friends and the most of them without "any design of being published" until she was advised to do so by some of her "literary friends." (Anne Royall to Carey, Alexandria, Va., February 12, 1824 [or 1826], Library of Congress.)

Mrs. Royall often apologized for her poor handwriting; she could well have done the same for her spelling, punctuation, and sentence structure. Having grown up on the Pennsylvania frontier where there was little opportunity for schooling, she seems to have had little or no contact with world literature until after her marriage to Captain William Royall, who turned her loose in his ample library, where her eager mind acquired many ideas but little discipline. Her writing lacks the polish of the typical early nineteenth-century writing, but it does have vigor and conviction. The letters are here published with *all* of the imperfections of the 1830 edition. Only the letters are used here; the long appendix about members of Congress in the original work, no doubt added to increase the sales, is omitted here because it does not have any value for, or shed any light on, the first part of the book.

The purist may be annoyed by the many errors in composition, but the person looking for lively comments on life on the Alabama frontier in what Thomas P. Abernethy calls the "formative period" will find much that is worth reading. Mrs. Royall's comments on the geography, travel conditions, economic opportunities, local personages and institutions help to fill out the record of the years when Alabama was evolving from a territory to a state, a period about which there is a shortage of first-hand accounts. Mrs. Royall is one of the few women travelers to visit the Tennessee River Valley area, and her views are worth noting if for no other reason than that they are the views of a woman.

Letters from Alabama is of course long out of print and copies are very rare. The University of Alabama has one of the few in existence, and I am indebted to Dr. W. Stanley Hoole, its librarian, for permission to microfilm it. I also gratefully acknowledge financial assistance from the Alabama College Faculty Research Fund, which helped to defray the costs of photocopies of Mrs. Royall's scattered papers and of travel to Washington to read the papers in the Library of Congress. Much of the physical work of this project has been done by student secretaries at Alabama College, whom I again thank sincerely: Jayne Byrd for transcribing the microfilm, Wanda Foster for help with the proofreading, Cathy Woolley and Sarah Wyatt for typing the final draft. Dr. Lorraine Pierson has read the introduction and made valuable comments. Last, but not least, I wish to thank Linda Soest from Seattle, Washington, for sharing her knowledge of Mrs. Royall and for being a good companion while we mined the Royall treasures in the Library of Congress.

Lucille Griffith

Montevallo, Alabama
January 1, 1968

ANNE ROYALL—
TIRELESS TRAVELER
and COMMON NUISANCE

by
Lucille Griffith

ANNE ROYAL
Tireless Traveler and Common Nuisance

The first third of the nineteenth century was an era of travelers and travel books. Travel in America was slow; roads were bad, stages uncertain, and overnight accommodations substandard, even for an age that was far from fastidious. But these inconveniences deterred only the timid. The more hardy and adventurous continued to go west into the unsettled regions, the Ohio Valley, the Mississippi Valley, and the Old Southwest. Most of these travelers were searching for suitable permanent homes, but some were simply looking for adventure with no intention of spending more than a few weeks, or months at most, in the United States. Especially in the decade following the War of 1812, many foreigners, the majority of them British, French, or German, visited the new country to see what there was to see. Most of them felt compelled to record for their friends at home, and incidentally for posterity, their experiences in the American wilds; consequently, books on America abounded during this period. Such books enjoyed wide sale and, even a century and a half later, furnish valuable information about many facets of culture in the new nation.

Because foreign travelers generally followed common routes, we find the same places described again and again; and in the literature of that period we have, in effect, a fairly complete chronicle of several main roads and key settlements.

Travelers in the South usually began their circle tour in Virginia. They would pay their respects at Mount Vernon and, as long as Jefferson lived, spend a few days at Monticello. They would then go to Richmond and Petersburg. Whether a traveler went to Charleston, South Carolina, by land or water depended on his own inclination, but that city was almost invariably a stop on the tour. From Charleston he would go to Savannah, then up river to Augusta, and then by stage to Milledgeville and Columbus. At Columbus he would cross the Chattahoochee River into Alabama and visit Fort Mitchell on his way to Montgomery. At Montgomery he would board a steamboat and proceed by water to Mobile and, finally, to New Orleans. Seldom did a traveler have a destination beyond the mouth of the Mississippi River. On his return trip he could board a riverboat for Natchez, Memphis, Louisville, and Pittsburgh, and then proceed by land to the Atlantic seaboard. Or he could travel by land, following the Natchez Trace much of the way. There were minor variations, of course, but these were the routes most often followed.[1]

Adam Hodgson, an Englishman who visited the United States between November, 1819 and March, 1821, is a good example of the traveler who followed the classic route. On his return he kept to the Natchez Trace but made side trips along the way, visiting Huntsville and Lookout Mountain. He chose to follow the Holston River into Virginia, visiting Abingdon, Salem, Natural Bridge, and Rockfish Gap, before arriving eventually at Richmond.[2] On the other hand, General Lafayette, the most famous, and, consequently, the most feted, visitor in the South for a generation, chose to return by steamboat up the Mississippi, Ohio, and Cumberland Rivers to Nashville for a visit with General Andrew Jackson. He returned to the Ohio, and after making brief stops along the way to visit such prominent people as Mrs. Henry Clay, he left the river in Pittsburgh and proceeded by land across Pennsylvania and New York State to Boston. He returned to Washington before leaving for Europe.[3] In the same period, the German Karl Bernhard, Duke of Saxe-Weimar-Eisenach, followed much the same route but traveled south through the Carolinas by land.[4]

Some travelers, of course, went west to Pittsburgh and followed the rivers south and west; still others chose to travel by land from Washington through western Virginia to their destinations. One unidentified traveler, known merely as "Rambler," followed a route that took him through Tennessee, Alabama, Mississippi, and Louisiana. One of his best descriptions is of Huntsville, Alabama, which most travelers in the territory visited at some time on their journeys.[5]

Many domestic travelers also moved around in the period. They, however, tended to put their observations into guidebooks for the immigrant, and, consequently, much of their writing becomes promotion or propaganda. Nevertheless, there were a few Americans who traveled for personal pleasure or hopes of future gain and wrote letters or kept journals that cannot be called promotional. Such a one was Mrs. Anne Royall, who wrote, among many other things, *Letters from Alabama*, which were published in 1830 though written much earlier.

Anne Royall is generally remembered, when she is remembered at all, as a woman editor of two successive Washington weekly newspapers, a reformer, and an eccentric character-about-town. But it was as a traveler and author of travel books that she first came into public notice. She seems to have been born with a yen to do the unusual and to visit new places. Her first trip into the Southwest, recorded in *Letters from Alabama*, appears to have been prompted by no motive other than a desire to travel. While she was in Alabama, however, a set of unfortunate circumstances thrust her into the business of making her own living. Well past fifty years of age and trained to no vocation, she turned to the activity she liked best—

traveling and sharing her experiences with others in hopes that the sale of her books would earn her an adequate income. For the next thirty years she tried to live by her pen.

When Mrs. Royall made the trip she records in *Letters from Alabama,* her husband had been dead only a few years and, as the widow of a prominent and wealthy Virginian, she traveled in a manner befitting a lady of her station, riding in her own carriage and attended by her personal servants.[7] Before her life was over she would be living in poverty and eking out a bare living by her publications. She was often dependent on the charity of her friends, at times begging for as little as a dollar with which to buy paper for her newsweekly.

Little is known of Mrs. Royall's early life other than the fact that she was born Anne Newport in Maryland. The date of her birth is accepted as 1769.[8] Biographers and feature writers, however, by putting together bits and pieces gleaned from her writing and using a large amount of imagination, have created for her a romantic past replete with noble (possibly royal) ancestry and a childhood as an Indian captive. Some published accounts contain much misinformation and no little nonsense. Many of the blatantly exaggerated stories appeared after her death when she could not refute them, even if she would have wanted to, which is doubtful. Anne's father, William Newport, was rumored to have been the illegitimate son of one of the Calverts, possibly with royal blood in his veins.[9] There is an oft-repeated story that Anne herself had been taken captive by the Indians in her infancy and lived with them fifteen years. The locale of her captivity is reported to be on the frontier of either Virginia or Pennsylvania. One story even suggests that her mother was an Indian maiden whom her father had married after he "fled." It probably adds interest to the story that no one ever seems quite certain from where he fled or why. Having lived as a savage (so the story goes), Anne was totally unlettered and learned to read only after she married the rich and elderly Captain William Royall, with whom she lived happily ever after. There is even one story that in 1802 Captain William Royall, an officer in the Continental Army and a hero at Valley Forge, on hearing that a young girl (Anne would have been past thirty if her birthdate is correct) was a prisoner of the Indians on the banks of the Ohio River, "resolved to rescue her." The story has "the dashing young soldier" (an officer in Washington's army a quarter of a century earlier) marrying the girl, who to all appearances "save in color and the Anglo-Saxon mold of her features," was of Indian blood. According to another legend, after their marriage, the couple moved to Alabama, where the Captain "as a planter dispensed his ample hospitalities" and his wife had to learn not only the English language but also such ordinary things as "mounting the stairs, drinking from a glass or cup, eating with knives, forks and spoons, sitting in chairs, sleeping in beds." "Yet," said one admirer, "she afterward accomplished more than any other woman of her times."[10]

The well-established facts, however, are almost as romantic as the fancies of the imagination. Anne's father, William Newport, was a Tory during the Revolutionary War. Whether or not he was a descendant of the Calverts, he did receive an annuity from the Proprietors until the outbreak of hostilities. He probably lost his property in his native Maryland to the Patriots and, feeling his position threatened, fled to the Pennsylvania frontier near Pittsburgh, where he tried to make a living for his wife and two small daughters. He was an educated man, and he taught Anne to read and write and somehow supplied her with books. Apparently, William Newport did not live long, for Mrs. Newport married a Mr. Butler, who also died within a few years. All we know about Anne's mother is that she had relatives in Virginia named Anderson and (by inference) that she was a hardy soul.[11] The family lived, as every other frontier family did, in a log cabin with the most rudimentary furniture and primitive foods. Anne's companions were Indian children her own age; from them she readily acquired their habits, ideas, and "some of their impulses." The story is told that General George Washington, passing through the settlement on a hunting trip, said that there was not an officer in the Continental Army who could ride better than Anne nor, after he saw her bring down a buck with her trusty rifle, "shoot with surer aim."[12]

The Newport-Butler family was one of the few to escape the Hannah's Town Massacre of July 13, 1782, but the stepfather died shortly thereafter. After his death, leaving the younger daughter with friends, Anne's mother set out on foot with Anne and the baby half brother to seek refuge in Virginia.

What route the refugees followed is unknown. But exhausted and half-starved, with Anne's mother suffering from blood poisoning, they finally arrived in the Staunton area of Virginia, sometime, it is believed, in 1785. It may have been purely accidental that they ended there; on the other hand, they may have heard of the curative properties of the waters at the springs and the mother decided to seek healing there. Whether it was by fortuitous circumstances or deliberate design, the life of Anne Royall was altered radically as a result.

The three waifs found shelter in the home of Captain William Royall, an eccentric and wealthy bachelor who lived in "baronial splendor" on Sweet Springs Mountain.[13] As soon as Anne's mother recovered sufficiently, he gave her work so she could "earn her independence."

Born at Bermuda Hundred, near City Point, Virginia, where his Welsh and French Huguenot ancestors had lived for two generations, William Royall had grown to manhood among such aristocratic neighbors as the Byrds, Seldens, Nelsons, Harrisons, and others.[14]

Where or under whom he received his education is not known, but he was reared as a son of the Enlightenment in the same climate of opinion in which his more famous contemporary, Thomas Jefferson, grew to maturity. In later years, his home at Sweet Springs Mountain contained an extensive library, well stocked with books by Voltaire and other writers of the age.[15]

In 1774, his father, Richard Royall, died, leaving to his son William all the lands he had in Chesterfield County and "the rest" of his estate. His will did not mention a wife or other children; however, later court records show Richard's wife, Elizabeth, claiming dower rights in her late husband's estate, "Hundred Neck Land," and mentioning another son, Richard. There seem to have been other children who were ignored in the will. Thus, the favoritism shown to William may have been the basis of a later suit through which his family regained the Royall property.[16]

Shortly after the elder Royall's death, hostilities between England and the American colonies erupted into open warfare. William entered the war as a captain and remained in Washington's army until the end of the conflict. He was listed as one of the "heroes of Valley Forge" and saw action under General Lafayette. One of Anne Royall's prized possessions was a handwritten note from Lafayette praising her late husband as an officer and a gentleman.[17] According to her account, he raised the first company in Virginia, which under Patrick Henry captured the gunpowder that Governor Dunmore had stored in Williamsburg. Most of the war he spent in Virginia and North Carolina, where, as a generous man of wealth, he performed many services for the American Patriots. He served as judge advocate to both his regiment and the brigade and took the Continental troops from Virginia to Guilford Court House, North Carolina, at his own expense after the defeat of General Gates. His personal losses included two fine horses, a servant, and a portmantau containing one hundred pounds specie.[18] For all his services and losses Royall never received a cent of pay; even the bounty land in Ohio to which he was entitled as an officer was not granted until after his death.[19]

In the years immediately after the Revolution, Sweet Springs Mountain was still largely frontier, but already many families from the Tidewater counties of eastern Virginia were moving into the area. Jeffersons, Carters, Fairfaxes, and others were seeking fresh lands to replace old ones exhausted by more than a century of tobacco culture. William Royall was among them. His decision to "desert his eastern Virginia and go live among the mountaineers" was based not only on economics but also on admiration for the hardy folk. During Tarleton's raid the residents of the Charlottesville area had impressed him with their patriotism when "old grayheaded men and little boys" marched forth to meet the foe. Within a few years, keeping a promise to return, he moved west and settled at Sweet Springs Mountain, where he lived out his life.

Anne Newport, who was probably about sixteen years of age when she arrived with her mother at the Royall's home, attracted the attention of the "very learned and very eccentric" master of Sweet Springs. Her "agile brain" captivated him, and he took it upon himself to educate her. In view of his background, breeding, wealth, and education, he was able to open up a whole new world of learning to the frontier lass.

Anne Newport and William Royall were married November 18, 1797, some twelve years later, in a ceremony performed by the Reverend William Martin in Botetourt County. There is no way of knowing whether Anne and her mother had remained under his roof during all the preceding years. What evidence there is seems to indicate she was not at Sweet Springs Mountain at the time of her marriage. For instance, Botetourt County, where they were married, is miles away from Royall's home. Mrs. Royall's story of the occasion also indicates she was living elsewhere. "I was in the garden sowing seeds," she remembered, "when the messenger came with a saddle horse for me to go and get married." The marriage certificate states clearly that the wedding date was November 18. Long afterwards, however, Anne "could swear" that it was May and the dogwood was in bloom when she was summoned to her wedding. There is no way of knowing whether the autumn date was a clerical error or whether Anne's memory played her false.[20]

But married they were, and Anne, obeying "her old master's command with truly feudal willingness and submission," became the mistress of the house in which she once was a servant.[21] The marriage was to last sixteen years until her husband's death in 1813.

Captain Royall, as described by one of his wife's biographers, was "a good husband of the bluff British Squire type." He was both wealthy and generous—and sentimental. On her birthdays and other festive occasions, he made his wife gifts of valuable property. All her life Anne looked upon her husband as master and judge; she had great reverence for him, and not a little awe.[22] He respected her and had a way of including her in conversations when company was present. And there was often company at their home. Since Sweet Springs was the site for court sessions, local leaders were often guests in the Royall household. The story goes that both Washington and Jefferson passed that way more than once, and there is strong evidence that dignitaries, even some foreign ones, were frequent guests. Royall shared the ideas of Thomas Jefferson, Thomas Paine, Voltaire, and other deist political writers. He had only contempt for pompous ignorance, but great respect for learning and devout faith in the future of the new republic. Anne read every book in his considerable library, some of them again and again. She borrowed books from her neighbors, and sometimes forgot to return them. All her later life she was given to quoting appropriate passages from her reading.

Thus, through books and conversation, Anne Royall acquired knowledge of a world very different from the one she knew as a child. It is not surprising that the ideas she learned, (at her husband's feet, it might be said) stayed with her as long as she lived. She herself was a deist and had little patience with denominational narrowness and bigotry. She had great contempt for sham and crookedness and was forever stripping off disguises and exposing fraud. She learned from her husband that the Masonic lodge could be her best friend in time of trouble. Like her husband, she had great patriotic hopes for the future greatness of their United States.

How much the death of her husband in 1813 changed the life of Mrs. Royall can only be surmised. She may have stayed on at their home for the first few years, although she speaks of trips to Ohio.[23] The Captain had provided well for Anne, so that she had no financial worries. His will, made in 1808 and recorded at the spring court of 1813, presumably soon after his death, is simple, direct, and worded like the usual early nineteenth-century will. In it William bequeathed to his wife Anne for the duration of her widowhood all of his estates, both real and personal, except one tract of land which went to Ann Malvina Cowan, the daughter of Anne's sister, who may have made her home with the Royalls.[24] Anne and Captain Royall's nephew, William Archer, were named executors. Archer was the son of Royall's half brother, John Archer. Making provision for disposal of his property after his childless widow's death, Royall left it to William Archer. Archer was not a Royall, and not a cent of money or an acre of land went to the other Royall heirs.[25] These heirs soon started litigation to break the will and get control of the property. They had succeeded in their objectives by the summer of 1823.[26]

There is a great deal of mystery surrounding the breaking of William Royall's will. There is no record of the litigation, and even the name of the Royall nephew who allegedly was responsible for doing so is known only by inference. It is a matter of record that there was a court case involving William R. Roane, in which Mrs. Royall sued him for libel in 1812–1815.[27] Libel, so the record says, was contained in letters written from two widely separated Virginia counties, Fincastle on the frontier and Charles City in the Tidewater. Allegedly, they were written to William Royall in Monroe County as "friendly warning" about his wife's actions. In later years, Mrs. Royall wrote, "Mr. William R. Roane, who was once rich—now not worth a cent . . . William Royall's nephew and a great fool."[28] While these incidents may not prove that Roane was the nephew involved in breaking the will, he is the only one to whom evidence points.

Nor is it clear on what grounds the will was broken. It is strongly hinted that there was scandal. Some people doubted that a marriage between Anne and William had ever taken place. This sounds a bit absurd, and anyone wishing to find out could have seen the marriage certificate at the courthouse. There were also claims that either the will was forged or it had been obtained under pressure from a man in the state of possible senility. Mrs. Sarah Porter suggests that there was personal scandal involving the young lawyer, Matt, to whom the *Letters from Alabama* were written. Whether Mrs. Porter had access to records no longer available, or simply was citing rumor, and drew on her imagination is not known.[29]

The marriage undoubtedly was legal, and the will had every evidence of being valid, and yet Anne lost the suit. Why? We simply do not know. She seems not to have fought hard in the case. Such behavior was so uncharacteristic of her that it adds to the mystery of the whole episode.

But whatever were the circumstances under which the will was broken, Mrs. Royall at an age past fifty was left without money or property and was forced to make her own living from this time forward. Had it not been for this event, the country might never have heard anything about her. She might have done extensive traveling, but it is doubtful whether she would have published books about her journeys; she certainly would not have edited a newspaper. For the next eight or so years she spent her time on the road, writing and publishing books in quick succession. Between 1826 and 1831 she wrote and had published ten volumes of travel and a novel.[30]

Anne Royall as Traveler

Mrs. Royall began her first extensive trip in the late fall of 1817, four and one-half years after her husband's death. On this trip she traveled in style, riding in her own carriage and attended by her personal servants. She had no deadline to meet, so she traveled leisurely and prolonged her stay where she chose. It took her about six weeks to make the journey from Monroe County, Virginia, in the extreme western corner of what is now West Virginia, to Huntsville, in the Alabama Territory. There is no adequate explanation for the length of her stay in Alabama. She remained there from December 1817 to July 1823, except for an absence of several months in 1819 when it is believed she was trying to defend her property rights in Virginia. She often met former acquaintances, but in her *Letters from Alabama* there is no indication she ever stayed in their homes. Instead, she lived at taverns or the equivalent of modern boarding houses. There she received callers, wrote letters, and passed the days pleasantly with fellow travelers or other interesting boarders. In Huntsville, Moulton, Melton's Bluff, and Florence she called on the most prominent families and was invited to their social gatherings. Sooner or later she met nearly all of the leading citizens and many of the rank and file.

Why did Mrs. Royall prolong her sojourn in this Alabama area? She had no relatives there and no close friends, at least close enough to live with. She never explained her reasons, and we are, therefore, left to guess. An answer that seems as good as any is that she was waiting for a conclusion of the suit against her husband's will, and North Alabama was a good place to spend the time. There is little indication of anxiety in the letters she wrote "Matt," but she does refer to her unfinished business affairs from time to time, indicating that she was aware of the situation. She may have liked the Huntsville–Melton's Bluff–Florence area because it provided a life somewhat like the one she had lived earlier in western Virginia: speculators were surveying and selling land; settlers were arriving from the East in an almost constant stream; young professional men sought opportunities in the new country. Likewise, interesting travelers from abroad contributed to the social and intellectual atmosphere. The land was rich and the country full of life and optimism. It was an exciting place to be. There is no record of all the places she visited, but it is known that in the summer of 1822 she went to visit friends at Blakely across the bay from Mobile. She seems to have made acquaintances in the port city and kept a lively interest in the place the rest of her life. Up to this point, traveling and writing were only diversions.

Beginning on July 1, 1823, however, Mrs. Royall became a "serious traveller." She began her first book with a simple preface stating that

> Having been advised to try the mineral waters in Virginia for my health, I set out on horseback from St. Stephens in Alabama, July 1, 1823, intending to take the stage at Huntsville with a view to divert my mind from melancholy reflections, to which it was disposed from ill health. I resolved to note everything during my journey worthy of remark, and commit it to writing, and to draw amusement and instruction from every source. In doing this I shall not imitate most journalists in such remarks as "cloudy or fair morning," and where we stop dates &c.[31]

In this manner and spirit she began a battle against melancholy, boredom, and, above all, poverty.

Accurate chronology for Mrs. Royall's activities is hard to establish. In the next eight years or so she visited many parts of the United States and interviewed hundreds of people. From 1823 to 1826 she went from South Alabama through

Tennessee and Virginia to Alexandria, where she arrived so ill she sought help from members of the Masonic lodge. M. E. Clagget, "the friend of the friendless and pride of mankind" and also proprietor of the City Hotel, took in the penniless woman and, according to her own testimony, kept her from December 15 to April 6, providing her with an elegant parlor and bedchamber plus a servant to wait on her. Under these conditions Mrs. Royall recovered and readied her first book, *Sketches*, for a publisher. After she was well enough to travel, she went to Washington, New York, and southern New England. During the next two years (1827–1829) she traversed Delaware, Pennsylvania, New York, all of New England, and even part of Canada. *The Black Books* and *Mrs. Royall's Pennsylvania* are the products of these years of travel. Her final trip, which she called her "Southern Tour" (1829–1830), took her through the South by the usual route to New Orleans. She returned to Washington—where she had been between trips since 1824—by St. Louis, Illinois, Indiana, and Ohio. Thereafter she seems to have stayed near home, making only short journeys away from the Capital City.[32]

There was no such thing as easy travel in those days. Mrs. Royall jolted and bumped over roads alternately dusty or muddy in summer and frozen in winter; she even trudged many miles on foot when a stage broke down, which was a frequent occurrence. Stagecoaches kept schedules with departures long before dawn and often only three or four hours after their arrival. There were times when stage drivers and tavern keepers tried to cheat her of what little money she had; there were other times when she was refused lodging because the reputation of her sharp tongue had gone before her. She was often at odds with drivers and mailmen over her trunks, which contained books she hoped to sell. There were even times when she had no money at all and lived on charity provided by the Masons or even by complete strangers. But nothing stopped her.

She seemed to enjoy most of what she saw. At Crawford Notch in New Hampshire she was so taken with the beauty of the scenery that she forgot about her threadbare coat, much too thin for the wintry blast. She took an almost childish delight in walking through Cumberland Gap, the hike made necessary by the fact that the stage could not carry its passengers in the heavy mud. She found much she did not like, but she took keen delight in sights of nature—a sunset, a hanging vine, a colorful flower—as well as in good conversation on almost any topic and in the many types of people she met on the way. Before Mrs. Royall had finished her travels she was more than sixty years of age. Probably no woman of her time was so indefatigable a traveler.

Mrs. Royall had two specific purposes in her travels: to collect material for a new book and to sell the ones already printed. She had definite ideas of what would appeal to her reading public. She gave full and methodical descriptions of what she saw. She commented systematically on public buildings, hospitals, colleges, prisons, almshouses, museums, schools, theatres, and libraries. She listed and described leading citizens, often with a frankness that makes one wonder why she was not sued for libel. All her writings are filled with character sketches, some complimentary, others damning.[33] It was often said that the people who treated her well, and especially those who bought her books, were given the kind treatment. There may have been some truth in this accusation. She made a practice of interviewing people of both political parties, leaders of rival groups, and representatives of different shades of religion. She had definite likes and dislikes about places: Alabama was her favorite state; Lynchburg, Virginia, she liked, but everyone breathed a sigh of relief when she had left; Boston had an appreciation of her literary work; Mobile was a nest of hoodlums and rogues; New Haven was the Eden of the Union.

Throughout her life Mrs. Royall took a lively interest in

people. To call her a name-dropper would be unfair, because some of her best sketches are of unimportant folk she met on her travels. Nevertheless, the fact remains that she was impressed with celebrities and gave long descriptions of them; probably no woman in her day met more of them. Her meeting with General John Coffee, companion of Andrew Jackson at Horseshoe Bend and New Orleans, is a good case in point. She had expected Coffee, whom she met soon after her arrival in Huntsville to be a "stern, haughty, fierce warrior." She was surprised to find the thirty-five year old, six-foot Coffee "with ever so fine a figure." His face was full and round, his features handsome, his complexion ruddy, his black hair "carelessly thrown to one side in front displaying one of the finest foreheads in nature—high, smooth, and retreating." His countenance showed much animation while he talked and his black eyes sparkled, but the moment he stopped speaking his face resumed a "soft serenity" and "its wonted placidness."[34]

Years later she called on the venerable John Adams at his home.

I found the dear old man [she wrote] sitting up before the fire. He would have risen but I flew forward to prevent him. He pressed my hand with ardor and inquired after my health. . . . In answer to my several inquiries relating to himself he replied that he was then [April 1825] eighty-nine years and six months old—"a monstrous time," he added, "for one human being to support." He could walk about the room, he said, and even down stairs. . . . His teeth were entirely gone and his eyesight very much impaired. . . . But he retained his hearing perfectly. His face did not bear the marks of age in proportion to his years, nor did he show the marks of decay in appearance except his teeth, and his legs which were very much reduced. He was dressed in a green camblet morning gown, and his head uncovered, except his venerable locks were perfectly white. The most childlike simplicity and goodness appeared in the sunshine of his countenance which when speaking or listening became extremely animated, but when left to itself, subsided into unclouded serenity.[35]

Of the unpleasant incidents in her travels, probably the most traumatic happened in Burlington, Vermont. There can be no doubt that it was the result of her attitude toward organized religion. In even her earliest writings she showed her distrust of "Evangelicals" and "blue skins" to the point of fanaticism; time did not make her any more tolerant. Their zeal for lost souls and missions was pure hypocrisy, she believed. She seldom met a preacher for whom she had one iota of respect; she saw only sexual implications in the interest these "priests" had in the "unconverted," most of whom she noticed were women. She never let an opportunity pass to attack or berate the clergy and the lay leaders of the church. Although there is little printed evidence now to indicate how widely known her views were, her "fame" often seems to have reached her destination before she did. She said that the church papers denounced her. Whatever the reason, there were many places where she met open hostility and, as in Burlington, actual bodily harm.

There was nothing unusual about her arrival in the Vermont city. The following day several prominent men, including ex-Governor C. P. Vanness, called at the tavern where she was staying. This was customary. During the interview, they talked about "the state of society in Vermont, the various denominations, and the missionaries' schemes." One of the gentlemen observed that there were many enlightened people in Burlington and among the sects, but there were also many "blue skins." Mrs. Royall told them that in getting a general description of any place she always called on both parties, "the Orthodox and the Liberal Party," though, she wryly observed, she had never yet sold a book to the former. She felt it was her duty to include both, and if she got nothing else from an interview, she "always got something" to put in her book. One of her callers told her that a "good specimen of the blue skins" lived across the way if she wanted to talk with him.

A heavy snow had fallen the previous night and she knew

she should stay indoors but, feeling the pressure of time, she began making interviews. She called first on two editors, one a Jackson man and the other an Adams man. Both men received her politely, but the Adams man told her, "We do not know what to say about you, Mrs. R. So much has already been said that nothing is left for us to say." There is no record of her reply.

She next went to the store where the "blue skin" was to be found. The steps to the building were high, about ten feet, from which the snow had been cleared away. Inside she found a gloomy-looking man and one she described as "fierce and savage . . . stoutly built . . . his face looked of iron hardness and seemed as though he had lain out on a frosty night." When she asked if he were Mr. Hecock, he said yes but without raising his eyes or otherwise acknowledging her presence. Mrs. Royall's reaction was to wonder if he took her for a daughter of Baal or Ashteroth or one of the wanton women of Tyre and Sidon! When the man had finished going through the papers before him, she introduced herself and asked for his patronage.

> Yes, he replied, "I'll patronize you, I have heard of you before." "And now you see me." "Yes, I see you ought to be put in the workhouse instead of being suffered to run over the country." "Is this your religion, sir? Is this the language of a Christian? And, pray sir, what have I done to confine me to the workhouse . . . mind who you speak to you hypocrit!"

While Mrs. Royall was opening her bag to produce some papers that would prove she was not "a fit subject for the workhouse," Hecock opened the door and, walking behind her, took her by the shoulders and pushed her out of the room and down the steps into the street. Had it not been for the snow, she firmly believed, she would have been "dashed to atoms" on the pavement. As it was, she suffered a dislocated ankle and a broken bone on the same leg, "the whole limb bruised and mangled in the most shocking manner." To add insult to injury Hecock insisted to a gentleman who had answered her cry for help that "she was not hurt, she only pretends she is hurt." Furthermore, the other man in the store joined with Hecock in spreading the report that a dog had pushed her down the steps! It is surprising that Mrs. Royall did not seize the story and turn it to her advantage by agreeing that it was indeed a dog—a two-legged one! Nevertheless, she described him in terms that to her were as damning—he was a "missionary, . . . a black Presbyterian" who went to church three times on Sunday—and goodness only knew how many times at night—and made "long faces and long prayers." She was told that he, like the Puritans of early New England, was wrestling with Satan and that this was "the first trial of his courage."[36]

The day, as she specifically recorded, was December 17, 1827; she did not walk again until June, 1828. During her confinement in Burlington she suffered the "most excruciating pain," partly because a doctor did not reach her until her leg was badly swollen. In the five weeks she was there she battled with four physicians, three of whom refused to treat her further either because she had no money or because she would not follow instructions and insisted on her own treatment. The pain was relieved, she found, if she took off the splint and immersed her foot in a bucket of warm salt brine. Deciding that she would never recover in the climate of northern New England, she determined to go to Washington. And go she did, but even by easy stages she suffered every kind of pain "a description of which baffles the English language." If the pain was beyond description, so also was her annoyance at the delay in finishing a volume of *The Black Book.*

This was Mrs. Royall as a traveler—traveling, writing, and selling by day and night, interviewing people she felt had something to say, describing places in a manner that is of interest even a century later, working under hardships, meeting opposition but letting nothing detain her.

Anne Royall as Novelist

Mrs. Royall's second book was a novel, *The Tennessean.* While she was in Moulton, Alabama, she met a Mr. Burlison whose life story somewhat resembles the plot she used in the book. Burlison had moved west to Tennessee with his parents, they had fought the British and the Indians during the Revolutionary War, and had survived the rigors of life on the fringe of civilization. He entertained Mrs. Royall with long tales of how he and his brothers outwitted the Indians, carved out a farm from the forest, and engaged in many other adventures. His life would make a novel, she wrote her friend Matt. At the time this may have been only a chance remark with no particular meaning, but faced with the problem of making a living, she used his stories as a basis for the novel she wrote some half-dozen years later.

The story, told in the first person, is hung loosely around the adventures of two young men who were roommates at Princeton: Burlington from Boston and Wilson from New Jersey. Young Burlington's father had suddenly lost all his entire fortune through the trickery of a man whom he had befriended and taken in as a business partner. Forced to leave college because of his father's debts, Burlington and his friend decided to go west to Tennessee, where they set up a store in Nashville. Almost immediately they became involved in an expedition into Mexico, their destination being (as they learned after they were well into "enemy" territory) some silver mines, and experienced a series of misadvantures. They were captured by the Spanish authorities, thrown into a dungeon, and condemned to execution, but were rescued from the gallows, with only minutes to spare, by the beauteous wife of the local officer. Boston was their destination when they fled, but on the way they ran into more mishaps. They endured torture, shipwreck, and capture by pirates (one of whom was the villain who had defrauded the Bostonian out of his substance); they met with immeasurable and incomprehensible complications before they got back to the United States. But all ended well, with Burlington marrying the lovely creature who had freed them in Mexico. Probably no novel ever had so many relatives who were thought to have been lost at sea or in some other disaster but reappeared at moments of crisis; nor more lives saved in the nick of time; nor more improbable extremes of poverty and wealth, disaster and good fortune.

The book has all the faults of the long-winded, gothic, romantic nineteenth-century romance, plus those of the dime thriller or penny dreadful. The plot is rambling, the conversation stilted, the villains the blackest, the heroines the fairest, love the purest, poverty the deepest, and charity the most generous. In short, as George S. Jackson says, it ought to have been the American novel to end all American novels! It is easy to understand why Mrs. Royall never made any money from it.

Anne Royall as Petitioner

Mrs. Royall spent long frustrating years in an effort to get a pension as the widow of a Revolutionary War soldier. Even in the end she had only partial success, and she died as impoverished as she had lived for thirty years.

From the American Revolution until 1818 there were no general pension laws in the United States; only men disabled in service were entitled to benefits. Before the war, however, considerable aid had been allowed to victims of wars. For example, widows of men who fell in colonial wars had been able to petition general assemblies for relief, but each case seems to have been handled individually. Later, states having large amounts of lands, like Virginia, compensated many of their petitioners with land grants in the West. Even before the end of hostilities, Virginia passed legislation giving every man who had served in one of the services for at least three years a tract of land varying in amount from 300 acres for enlisted men up to 15,000 acres for a major general.[37]

An 1818 law of Congress declared every needy man—from officer to private—who had seen at least nine months' service during the Revolution to be eligible for a pension, which ranged from twenty dollars per month for officers to eight dollars for others. This law was changed many times, but it was not until 1836 that every widow of a veteran was eligible for a pension, and even then only if she had been married to the serviceman before the end of his service. In short, in most cases this meant that the marriages had to have taken place before 1783. Two years later (1838) the law was liberalized to include widows who married servicemen before January 1, 1794. Not until ten years later was any modification made in the policy toward widows; in 1848 the law was changed to include widows whose marriages were performed prior to 1800. It was through this labyrinth of legislation that Mrs. Royall sought from Congress financial relief as the widow of a veteran.[38]

Mrs. Royall began her campaign early, possibly as soon as she reached the Washington area in 1823 or 1824.[39] There is no existing printed evidence of her campaign until 1832, but it appears that at that date the case was far from new. In a front-page article in her weekly newspaper, she deplored the fact that "while millions are squandered in various ways upon inanamate stocks and stones, human beings imbued with life and blood and feeling are left to struggle, with hunger, sickness, scoffs, insults while millions are paid to sly cheats for statues, monuments, books, and pictures to perpetuate the achievements of the Revolution." She praised Senators Freylingheuysen, Webster, and Silsbee for their efforts to get widows in the bill. They "strove hard" to this end, but to no avail.[40]

The fact that Mrs. Royall was not married to William Royall before 1794, as required by the Act of 1838, did not keep her from sending petitions to Congress for a pension. Ex-President John Quincy Adams, then in the House of Representatives, regularly handled them for her. The Committee on Revolutionary Pensions, to which the petitions were sent, just as regularly rejected them. In May, 1842 Mr. Fornance of the Committee made a summary report that shows something of the history of the case:

> . . . the Committee have carefully examined the claim of the petitioner, who is the widow of Major William Royall, an officer in the army of the Revolution. This claim, with all the papers and evidence, has been before Congress for some years, and has been reported against several times. At the 26th Congress there was an adverse report; and at the 25th Congress, Mr. Bond, from the Committee on Revolutionary Pensions, reported that "the evidence submitted to the Committee fully establishes the alleged services of the said William Royall, and it is satisfactorily proved that the petitioner is his widow. The marriage of the parties, however, was not solemnized until the month of November, 1797, and consequently is not embraced within the provisions of the present pension laws, which do not include, cases of marriage after 1794. The committee deem it inexpedient to extend the provisions of the law thus referred to and therefore report against the prayer of the petitioner."[41]

Nevertheless the new committee, in view of the fact that the captain had served his country throughout the war and that there were many other widows falling into the same category as Mrs. Royall, recommended that she be given a half-pay pension for ten years.

Great was the rejoicing in the Royall household! Mrs. Royall would get an entirely new wardrobe; her faithful friend and companion, Mrs. Sally Stack, would see Niagara Falls! The boys who ran the printing press would get a half-day off, and all of them could stop worrying about the future. But their joy was premature. Congress, believing it would set a dangerous precedent if it made an exception of Mrs. Royall, rejected the recommendation of the Committee.[42] The two poor women must have been heartbroken.

Finally, under the Act of July 20, 1848, Anne Royall, seventy-nine years of age, was granted an annual pension of $480. Although there is nothing in the official papers to show it, Mrs. Porter says that Mrs. Royall was given a choice between taking a half-pay pension for ten years or full pay for five years in one lump sum.[43] Very foolishly she chose the lump sum; the act had been amended so that other legal heirs were allowed to share in money that was granted to widows. Mrs. Royall's sad summary of the case was: "The heirs of law took half our commutation money and every dollar of the remainder we owed to those who had trusted us (the dear people). We kept three dollars and Sally got seven out of the $1200."[44] Another biographer, George S. Jackson, states that Mrs. Royall's chief competitor for the pension was a Mrs. Elizabeth Roane, "quite evidently one of the same group which brought about Anne's poverty and need of a pension in the first place." Mrs. Royall did not give up, however. In spite of her advanced years, she made futile attempts to collect interest on the debt the government owed her dead husband. When she died, she left "thirty-one cents and a debt of six dollars back rent."[45]

One writer has observed that two significant points were proved beyond doubt in these pension proceedings: the validity of her husband's military service and the legality of their marriage. Mrs. Royall, if she were aware that there may have been any doubt about either, may have wondered if a quarter century of struggle with Congress was not a high price to pay for these two facts, however important.

Anne Royall as Defendant

Anne Royall has the distinction of being the only woman in our national history to be tried and convicted of being a "common scold." The trial, which took place in the summer of 1829, left its scar on her and haunted her the rest of her life. It colored her writing and hardened the lines between her and her foes.[46]

The complaints that led to her arraignment were filed by the leaders of a Presbyterian Church on Capitol Hill known as the Engine House Congregation. There seems to have been a running feud between Mrs. Royall and this group that dated back to her arrival in Washington some four or five years earlier. What had been smoldering ill will and mere bickering erupted into open contempt and actual name-calling on her return from New England early in 1829. It was just over a year since her unfortunate "accident" in Burlington, Vermont, which she described in the second volume of the *Black Book*. She wrote a friend that in New England she "drove the scamps" [the missionaries] before her like a ship until she "got into Vermont the land of Arabs. There they faced about and intended no doubt to put an end" to her and the *Black Book* together. And, as she added ruefully, they actually came very near it.[47] This and other incidents had brought forth some of her choice epithets for church people, whom she called variously "blue skins," "Evangelicals," and "missionaries."

She had a publisher's deadline and time was running out for the next volume of the *Black Book*, and in order to lose a minimum of time she wrote the young woman who occasionally worked for her to have the house in readiness when she returned to Washington. But to Mrs. Royall's astonishment nothing had been done—no fire, no wood—and the neighbors could tell her nothing about the young woman.[48]

This was the first indication that the smoldering feud was erupting. Relations became worse between Mrs. Royall and her neighbors in the church and some kind of an open break came on June 1. Anne said that they kept trying to "convert" her (to her annoyance), that adults prompted boys in the congregation to throw stones through her windows, and that disorderly people stood outside her window and called out obscenities to her. Most of these events took place at night, she said sarcastically, when "the outpouring of divine goodness is most powerful." She remained a hardened sinner, however, in spite of "the praying in the Engine house, or the pious stone throwing, Holy Willy's visits or even Preacher Thunder." Whether it actually happened or Mrs. Royall invented it, she reported a meeting of the leaders of the congregation at which they discussed what could be done about her. The "usual methods" had admittedly failed on her. Supposedly, a friend told her what transpired there but, "being elbowed out," he heard only fragments of sentences. They were using the words "cart-tail-ducking stool—Sabbath School—fine and imprisonment—outpouring—nuisance—we'll tie her neck and heels—glorious gospel—virago—only let me get hold of her—vital religion—I wish we could hang her—The Holy Bible—drowning will do as well—Judge Holt, page 326—revealed religion—Statute, Henry VIII—refreshing revivals." "I was pleased the gospel spreaders were so deeply interested in my soul," she remarked bitterly. "My body was to go to pot."[49]

Whether this meeting actually took place is not known, but it may have. To members of the Congregation the woman was a nuisance. They brought charges against her, and Mrs. Royall was called before the court of the District of Columbia. After examination she was dismissed on the technical grounds that there was no law to punish her for the alleged offence. But not to be thwarted, the plaintiffs brought considerable pressure to bear on the civil authorities and she was arraigned again.

The indictment read in part:

> . . . Anne Royall . . . widow, being an evil disposed person, and a common slanderer and disturber of the peace and happiness of her honest neighbors, on the first day of June in the year . . . one thousand eight hundred and twenty-nine, and on divers days and times

as well before as afterwards, was and yet is a common slanderer of the people of the neighborhood in which she . . . resides. . . .

There were three charges against her: that of being a public nuisance, a common brawler, and a common scold. She was tried only on the last count.[50]

Judge William Cranch presided, and in spite of the experience, Anne retained a liking and respect for him. The witnesses for the state, all from the Engine House Congregation, were nearly all members of the family of John Coyle whom she invariably called "Holy Willy." Mrs. Royall's witnesses were few in number and most of them somewhat timid in testifying in her behalf. Even her friend Waterston, Librarian of Congress, paid her compliments but said she called all Presbyterians cutthroats. Her best witnesses were Secretary of War John Eaton and a few ladies. Their testimony, she wrote, was "clear and unequivocal, and directly opposed to that of the prosecution." Her lawyer was a Mr. Cox, who ruefully observed that "yesterday" there was no law to punish his elderly client but that "today" they seemed to have found one. The law, thus conveniently discovered, was of medieval English origin and there was need of much translation and interpretation of the Latin and the early English to make it apply to Mrs. Royall's case, but it was done. The defendant made a short but spirited address to the jury. But it did not help her cause; she was found guilty. The next time she was to be tried, she wrote later "summon twelve tom-cats" for jurors!

The whole trial was a farce, and few people seemed to take it seriously. In fact, the courtroom seemed to have been in an uproar most of the time. Once during the testimony, the judge had asked a witness, a senator, what Mrs. Royall had said to him. His reply was that she had asked him one Sunday afternoon if he was "not ashamed to be seen walking with them old maids." When the judge said that perhaps they were old maids, his spirited reply was "no, they wasn't for one of them was my sister." This struck the spectators as very funny. One of Mrs. Royall's witnesses put an end to the business of the day—everyone was so convulsed with laughter—when he testified that he never knew her to slander but two people and that was when she had said he and Mr. Waterston were "the two cleverest and handsomest men in Washington."[51]

But this was no laughing matter to Mrs. Royall. She had been found guilty and sentenced to be ducked in the Potomac River. There was no New World precedent for such a sentence, but the navy yard was ordered to prepare a proper instrument for the execution of the verdict. They actually constructed such a device and brought it to the court room.[52] But wiser counsel prevailed and the sentence was commuted to a fine—ten dollars and costs. However, she was forced to put up fifty dollars as assurance she would keep the peace. Two young friends, probably newspaper men, paid the sum for her. The trial was over, but for Mrs. Royall, "all the water of the Potomac will never wash out the foul stain of this infamous prosecution."

What was behind this unique episode in our history? Mrs. Royall and her earliest biographer, Mrs. Porter, were sure that there was a deliberate plot to "get" her. The latter refers to the "formidable host" against her—the evangelical ministers, politicians whose election depended on the congregations of these ministers, the anti-Masons who would "gladly have torn her to pieces," the office holders who resented her "nosing through their departments," the money power (represented in the United States Bank), and many others she had attacked or exposed.[53] Other students are not so sure that there was a formal plot.[54] She had offended all these groups, certainly, but many of them had only slight cause for grievance by 1829. Her attack on the Bank, for example, came later, when that institution became a campaign issue between Clay and Jackson. But the fact remains that in her travel books she had denounced many public people with vehemence, and the members of this particular church constantly. We are not sure what she called them to their face, but we do know the names she used in print. Technically, she may be correct when she insisted she never swore at them as she was charged with doing. But certainly she had abused them often and violently, and they refused to take her diatribes any longer.

Shortly after the trial she started on the last long journey she would take. This trip she described in a three volume *Southern Tour.* Not long after her return to Washington she founded her first newspaper, which she used as a vehicle to reach a wider audience and in a sense to vindicate herself before the public.

Anne Royall as Writer

Anne Royall's writing is undisciplined but vivid. She often apologized for her penmanship (and well she might!), but she seems to have been unaware that her punctuation, spelling, sentence structure, and coherence were also poor. To be sure, she was writing in a period before spelling had been standardized. Noah Webster did not publish his dictionary until 1828, and Mrs. Royall's writing habits had been formed long before then. But even for her time, her spelling is original and inconsistent. It is not especially phonetic except when she attempted to reproduce a dialect for which she had a great liking and a considerable deftness at composing. She often doubled a consonent where it should have been single or vice versa. She likewise often uses a wrong vowel in one or more syllables. However, her spelling merely annoys. It does not make her writing difficult to read. But her punctuation does. Her excessive use of commas and dashes, colons for semicolons, and periods in the middle of a sentence after which she continues writing without using a capital letter are among her frequent errors. Consequently, some of her sentences are less than clear.

She constantly capitalized the first part of a combination like "Tennessee river," but not the last. There is no way of knowing how many of these errors were her own and how many were the printer's, but her extant letters lead one to believe that most of them were her own.

Furthermore, at times she was "carried away" (to use her own phrase) with a subject and produced some very uninhibited and florid prose. She also had a gift for mixing figures of speech. A prime example is a comment she made on several fires in Washington, two of them at stables. "This is singular," she wrote in *The Huntress*. "Perhaps they are getting into practice to burn down the Augean stables by way of killing two birds with one stone."[55] Her long series of descriptive words can be overwhelming; for example, she called the witnesses at her trial ". . . the evangelical-tractical-biblical-Sabbath School-prayer meeting-good, honest, pious, sound Presbyterians of Capitol Hill."[56] She was inclined to give too much detail, especially when describing her own personal injuries or insults. In her character sketches, although she was often very accurate, she was at times overly free with the use and abuse of personal names; she could be as unrestrained in praise of her friends as she was in denunciation of her foes. And her attempts at wit could be rather crude. In Utica, New York, she was told that the tavern keepers were "bucktails." "Let them be bucktails or cowtails," she wrote in the *Black Book*, "the nether end of any animal fits them well."[57] In short, her work was undisciplined and amateurish.

But these negative qualities should not blind one to the fact that there were compensating strengths. When Mrs. Royall had something to say, she said it. Her vocabulary was strong and telling. Except when she was castigating her foes, she was generally in good humor. Her writing has accuracy of fact and description. She did not hedge; there was never any doubt on which side of a question she stood. It must be said to her credit that her opinions were based on honest, though perhaps mistaken, convictions. She was patriotic and intolerant of fraud and corruption. Her writing is energetic, and her personality is felt on every page.

An unidentified reviewer recognized some of these last qualities when he wrote in the *Boston Commercial*,

> She marches on, speaking her mind freely, and unpacks her heart in words of censure or praise as she feels. Sometimes she lets fall more truths than the interested reader would wish to hear, and at others overwhelms her friends with a flattery still more appaling. At any rate, hit or miss, the sentiments she gives are undoubtedly her own; nor will it be denied that she has given some very good outlines of character. Her book is more amusing than any novel we have read for years.[58]

Since mention has been made of her efforts at playwriting, a further word on that is appropriate. There is no existing copy of her one play, and what is known of it is contained in the pages of her weekly, *Paul Pry*. As early as March 10, 1832, Mrs. Royall was "happy to apprise the public that her play, *The Cabinet, or Large Parties in Washington*, would soon be ready for the stage." Just when the first performance was scheduled is uncertain, but it was within the year. Apparently, this first presentation was to be given at a theatre, and tickets sold fairly well, but when the audience arrived the theatre was dark. An agent appeared and told them that no performance would take place and that their money would be refunded. Mrs. Royall and her friends were thunderstruck. She had authorized no such statement. However, she soon discovered that the "evangelicals and antimasons" had pressured the owner of the building to forbid the production of a play written by "that old infidel, Anne Royall."[59]

The Masons, however, came to her rescue. A company of young men volunteered as actors, and Mr. Joseph Gales, of the

National Intelligence, obtained for her the use of the Masonic Hall. The play was given at least twice, but both performances were plagued by stormy weather.[60] Some eight years later she decided to revive the play as a benefit for herself. She was waiting only for "pay day and good weather."[61]

The contents of the play can only be surmised from the dramatis personae and a letter to the editor. Of the colorful names she gave her characters, Caperkite, Parson Sneak, Mrs. Foolscap, Roughhead, and Rattle Robin head the list.[62] A letter from one signing his name "Cosmopolite" gives some indication of the theme of the play.

> Respected Madam: [he wrote] I cannot refrain from expressing to you extreme gratification that I received on last evening from the presentation of your very excellent and truly unique play of The Cabinet. The masterly manner in which you have handled the subject is above all commendation. And I am but expressing the opinion of a large majority of the highly respectable and intelligent auditory of the evening when I assure you that an intellectual treat was afforded such as this city has long been a stranger to. There are so many excellencies running through the whole piece that I find it impossible to particularize. Suffice it to say that the pungent strain of wit never flagging, still increasing . . . reminds me more of the dazzling cord of gold running through a fissure of silver than of all else. The religious hypocrit was held up to merited scorn, and I could not but reflect that if one of that description had been present, he would with fright have bathed his heart with sweat.[63]

The writer hoped that Mrs. Royall would "favor the world" with *The Cabinet* in pamphlet form so that it could be in the library of every person in the district.

The play was reviewed in Boston and Philadelphia by the "first literary and dramatic gentlemen." Citizens of Washington "as well as distinguished visitors" had "called loudly"— for the play to be brought to the stage. It was printed. Mrs. Royall was inclined to think that Mr. Joseph Jefferson, the leading actor of the day who seems to have agreed to play in the initial stages, was to blame for the failure of the whole project. The author had excluded everything that might sound like "party spirit," yet she judged she was to be "sacrificed to party purposes or rather party revenge." Both Jefferson and Mr. Seaton, whom she considered gentlemen and personal friends, "sighed" and seemed opposed to a comedy that might offend the general will. Mrs. Royall's retort was that "if the exertions of an aged female who has no other dependence to sustain life is to be rested from one of any party or to my injury" she prounounced it a "pitiful subterfuge" unworthy the character of any gentleman.[64]

In view of the fact that Mrs. Royall knew nothing of playwriting, one may surmise that Mr. Jefferson's sighs may have been over the form and quality more than from any offense it might give political figures. There is little doubt that the play was less than a masterpiece.

Anne Royall as Newspaper Woman

From 1831 until a few weeks before her death in the autumn of 1854, Anne Royall edited a weekly newspaper in Washington. She first called it *Paul Pry*, but decided that the name gave the impression it was a scandal sheet. Consequently, in 1836 she changed it to *The Huntress*. Whether this gave any more favorable impression as to purpose is open to question.

Her motives for editing a paper probably included a desire for a wider audience than her books provided and the need of making a living. There is little question that the first motive was strong, but there is more evidence to support the latter. She seems never to have made much money from her travel books and, being ineligible for a pension under the existing laws, she simply had to find means of adding to her meagre income. Shortly after she founded the paper, she wrote: "From serious loss by sea and fire, I was forced to establish a paper and to meet a few debts due to honest and deserving men.

Paul Pry was a four-page paper. In the prospectus in the first issue she stated her purpose and editorial policy:

> Our course will be a straight-forward one as heretofore. The same firmness which has ever maintained our pen will be continued. To this end, let it be understood that we are of no party. We will neither oppose nor advocate any man for the Presidency. The welfare and happiness of our country is our politics. To promote this we shall oppose all and every species of political evil, and religious frauds without fear, favor or affection. We shall patronize merit of whatever country, sect or politics. We shall advocate the liberty of the Press, the liberty of Speech, and the liberty of Conscience. The enemies of these bulwarks of our common safety, as they have shown none, shall receive no mercy at our hands.[65]

Up to this point her approach had been dignified and worthy of a Washington newspaper. But, losing a sense of balance, she lapsed into nonsense and wrote pure drivel. She promised "extermination" to "cannibals, the Anti-Masons, the co-temporaries of negro insurgents," and castigation to all "pious" army and navy officers who made "war upon old women." She threatened "pious booksellers who take pious bribes," "pious young ladies who hawk pious tracts into young gentlemen's rooms," and admonished "all old bachelors and old maids to be married as soon as possible." This kind of writing was not becoming, but it did foreshadow some of her less admirable productions.

In addition to the prospectus, the first issue of *Paul Pry* had a long discourse on "The true dignity of manners and deportment," articles on a statue of George Washington which was proposed by Horatio Greenough, an extract from an English paper on the speed of the horse, a news item about a trip to Naples which Sir Walter Scott proposed to make, a notice from the Vigilante Association of Columbia, South

Carolina, offering an award of $1500 for the apprehension and prosecution of any white person distributing or circulating the *Liberator*. There was editorial comment on anti-Masonry, missionaries, post office reform, and possible removal of postage on newspapers. The column devoted to poetry was filled with verse taken from the *Young Ladies Journal*, *Atlantic*, *Souvenir*, and *The National Republican*. There were also anecdotes about Davy Crockett. Mrs. Royall probably considered an article berating Congress as the heart of this issue, her first newspaper effort. In it she accused, among many other people, the doorkeepers of both the House and Senate, the chief clerk and messengers of the House of not fulfilling their duties, and the personnel on Capitol Hill generally of being guilty of nepotism. This general arrangement of content, with some variations of course, would remain essentially the same throughout her journalistic career. There were no advertisements in the first issue but three weeks later, on December 24, the editor included some.

She was little given to "chitchat, table talk, city anecdotes and all that sort of thing" which she knew would "humor and amuse" her friends, and which she later professed she had hoped to include when she took hold of her paper. But open criticism of her early statements compelled her "to gird on the sword and take the field to defend our country's civil and religious rights." Instead of recording the "mirth and gaity and good old stories" of her numerous friends, she found herself "on the battle field" and in the "van" of the men editors of the city, too many of whom were hiding behind the institutions of the day, like the Bank, rather than fighting them. So if *they* would not fight them, *she* would![66]

Very soon the contents of the sheet fell into a pattern it would keep. Many of the stories and news items were taken from other publications. The new material was mostly of two kinds: letters to the editor which Mrs. Royall answered at great length, and editorial-type essays or discourses on various questions and abuses of the day. The student of American humor will be interested in a column of jokes she included from time to time. *The Huntress* contained more fiction than its predecessor, and the diatribes against Congress became longer, but there were few essential differences between the two publications.[67]

How widely her weekly circulated outside Washington can only be guessed. There were letters from readers in widely separated parts of the country—Ohio, Virginia, Alabama, Connecticut, and others—which indicate that at least an occasional issue reached friends at distant points.

How well the paper was received is again a matter of conjecture. Mrs. Royall chose to print only a few of the letters that came in, and we have only her word for the contents of the others. Soon after *Paul Pry* began publication, she noted editorially that her table was loaded with "letters of every different sort," but she had "foreborned" to publish any of the "more encouraging" letters, although she had received "hundreds breathing the same cheerful encouragement." An editor from Richmond, Virginia, called the style of *Paul Pry* "original and laconic" with more of the true American system in it than in any of the high-sounding dailies and semiweekly papers that were so much under the "influence of our beggarly, aristocratic manufacturers, bankers, brokers, and their political adjuncts."[68] One of the ablest letters, she said, was from "one of the first gentlemen of the South." In it he praised her useful "exertions in reforming the abuses of government." Inaccessible to the corrupting influences of a "corrupt and degenerate age," holding to her republican virtues, she had come to be more dreaded than loved by the "venial minions of political favoritism." He favored letting the people know that the authority they had delegated to their representatives was being abused in Washington. "Let Paul Pry follow them," he wrote rhetorically, "with a watchful eye through their public and private walks and expose their most secret conduct to the views of a constituency whose confidence cannot be abused with impunity. Let the people only have knowledge and they will do right." After pontificating about ignorance being the first step toward despotism and a muzzled press being a prelude to utter darkness, he ended with a ringing challenge:

> Do not permit Paul Pry to slumber for one moment. Leave no place unexplored. And spare no one from his inquisitive and searching gaze. Should Paul become weary in doing well, let me say one word by way of encouragement. Fear not, tire not, and spare not.

The editor hardly needed this advice, but she followed it, enthusiastically, and unflinchingly.[69]

Even in an age when journalism was a personal matter, Mrs. Royall's methods and techniques were decidedly individual. Never financially able to purchase first class equipment nor hire competent workmen, she faced even more problems than the average publisher. Consequently, when she considered the printing substandard or delivery slow, she openly explained why. The foreman, an Irishman, had had a wedding in his family and had celebrated too well and too long; the building that housed the press was so open that during a bitterly cold spell the paper froze as it went through the press, slowing production to a snail's pace. Her beloved Sally Stack[70] was sick, and Mrs. Royall had to deliver the papers in addition to her own work. The orphan boys who in later years furnished most of the help were very young; and while she was very fond of these fine boys, they lacked the maturity to print a paper. As she once apologized—the foreman was, after all, only thirteen years old.[71]

We get glimpses of Mrs. Royall as a newspaper woman cornering Congressmen and other public men for their views on current issues, ferreting out corruption and irregularities, and making thinly veiled threats of exposure if things were not straightened out. She interviewed innumerable people on Capitol Hill and reported their views in the columns of her paper.

Her visits were not always welcome, and men often chose to dodge her, flatly to refuse interviews, or simply to be absent from their offices or boarding houses when she called. Many of these rebuffs she took in her stride, but when she was sure some dishonesty was afoot, she blasted the perpetrators. These blasts were not unexpected for she had a reputation for a sharp pen but she also warned her "victims" ahead of time. In one issue alone of *Paul Pry* she indicated whom she would attack next: Colonel Steen whom she would "dish up in our next," the postmaster of Winchester, Pennsylvania, and Judge Darlington whom she would put "before the public" in such a way that would do them little credit.[72] She unfailingly followed up her threats to "take care of" individuals with a double blast of denunciatory rhetoric!

She did her own interviewing and resorted to the usual tricks of the trade to get entree with the people she wished to see. There is even one story, in all probability pure fiction, that she wished to talk with President John Quincy Adams about a certain public issue. After he had consistently refused to see her, she looked for some other opportunity to get to him. According to the story, she learned that he often swam in the Potomac River at a certain place so she simply went and sat on his clothes on the bank of the river until he agreed to talk with her. This is undoubtedly an apocryphal story because Adams was her constant friend and talked with her on many occasions, but it does indicate that Mrs. Royall had the ingenuity and tenacity associated with modern reporters.[73]

But these are only glimpses. The one full look we get of her as a newspaper woman was recorded by Phineas T. Barnum, the great American showman. He visited her in 1836, at what probably was the best period of her life as an editor. He said that she was "quite a celebrated personage." He had exchanged copies of *Paul Pry* for his own *Herald of Freedom.* She strongly sympathized with him in the persecutions he had to endure and was delighted to see him; in fact, "she was even boisterous in her assurances of the fact." He reported that

Anne was the most garrulous old woman he ever saw; her tongue ran like "wildfire." They talked about congressmen and possible candidates for the forthcoming presidential election, and he received an "awful explosion of tempestous passion" when he jokingly told her he expected to "go for" Van Buren. She raved on for half an hour before she "talked herself out of breath." He had heard that she was "monomanical upon political subjects" but, nevertheless, she was a goodhearted, generous woman. Lowering her voice to a calm, ordinary tone, she apologized for her tirade, saying she was sorry he mentioned politics for she was "so nervous" on that subject. Sally announced that the papers were ready for mailing, and Anne invited him to go along to the printing office where they could talk and work together. Barnum's description of the operation is worthy of a full quotation:

We proceeded to a small brick building, near the house, and after experiencing some difficulty in climbing up a dirty pair of stairs, and groping our way through a dark passage in the second story, we reached the printing-office of "Paul Pry." The whole force of the establishement consisted of one man and one boy. A pile of newspapers in wrappers, and all directed to their places of destination, lay upon the middle of the floor.

"Now, Barnum," said Anne, "I am going to sort these papers for the mails, for our lazy officials in the post office would not do it in a week, and you can help me; so sit right down on the floor by my side, and we can work and talk together."

Anne then seated herself upon the dirty floor, and as there was no chair in the room, I sat down beside her, not daring even to spread my handkerchief or in any way remove the dust, lest she should construe it into an insult.

In this way I spent another half hour with Anne, aiding her in assorting her papers, and keeping up with her a very agreeable conversation. . . .

Before he left, however, he tried to hire her to make "a dozen or twenty" public lectures on government, but for some reason he could not tempt Anne with pecuniary reward, although he was sure the venture would have been profitable.[74]

Anne Royall was not a bad editor. From the meagre evidence still available, it appears that fellow editors, although they publicly feuded with her, felt kindly toward her and found her entertaining. One Louisiana editor wittily offered to back for the presidency every congressman who had befriended her during an illness.[75] Certainly, the general reading public enjoyed watching her pillory public figures. Her style was explosive and hard-hitting, and she could get tiresome when she piled insult upon insult, but her serious editorials were lucid and to the point. She had a definite and unmistakable point of view. When she accidentally failed to make herself clear or was accused of some misinterpretation, subscribers never failed to call her to task.[76] She had a good eye for news and often passed on to her readers bits and pieces she picked up in exchanges.

Not that she pleased all her readers all the time. They were free with their advice on what she should ignore or attack. "Let these Bible Societies alone," some said; others, "church and state men, give it to them." "Mrs. Pry, it takes you to do it." "Throw in some more cayenne, Mrs. Royall. We want something relishing!" Following a policy of "more cayenne," she thrashed out at what she considered to be plots and irregularities. She was no society editor, writing about subjects of interest to women alone. She was a knight in shining armour out to find and attack fraud and corruption wherever she found them. "Our paper is small," she once wrote, "the weather is cold, times are hard, our fire is low, our candle is dull," but she might have added, the nation is in danger and she must save it![77]

Anne Royall as Reformer

Anne Royall has been called the "grandma of the muckrakers." Journalists writing at a later date easily saw Mrs. Royall as the newspaper woman who started the practice of exposing persistent abuses in hopes that an aroused public would see that remedy and reform followed.[78] This militantly independent woman may have rebelled at any classification, but on the other hand she may have liked the recognition that she was doing what she professed to do.

In one collection of Mrs. Royall's papers there is a note worthy of attention as furnishing a key to her career as a reformer. "Mrs. R.," the anonymous note reads, "did not intend to write more than two lines when she took up the pen but her blood boils to see her country degraded below the savages—as to independence there is none."[79] These lines are in Mrs. Royall's handwriting but whether she wrote them originally or copied them from some publication is not known. The envelope is addressed to Peter Force, Esquire, editor of the *National Journal*. In light of the vast amount of writing she turned out in her life, one may doubt whether she ever intended to write so briefly on any subject. But in this case, as in many others, circumstances aroused her ire, and as a "virago errant in enchanted armor," as John Quincy Adams once called her, she went forth to do battle.[80]

She began her career as a critic of society long before she became a newspaper editor. In her very first literary production, her *Letters from Alabama*, she found many conditions and causes on which she made very definite comments. She berated injustice in whatever form she found it; and it made no difference whether the victim was an Indian, an unfortunate woman, or any other person mistreated in man's inhumanity to man. As she traveled and wrote in the 1820's, she was even more convinced that there was too much fraud, corruption, and plotting for the good of a free nation. Her travel books are filled with incidents to prove her contentions. Her reputation was, therefore, well established by the time she became an editor. Soon after she launched *Paul Pry* a correspondent wrote, "And permit me to say that your useful exertions in reforming the abuses of government have long since received the sincere homage of your admirers." Her travel experiences proved to be a valuable foundation when she set out to attack these abuses in a systematic and more or less orderly fashion in her weekly paper.

Like Patrick Henry, she was concerned with her country's dying liberty; her causes were patriotic, at least as they appeared to her. She did not confine her attacks to political abuses, but most of them were tied to public officials or public questions in some way. She fought for public education with the unbounding faith of a child of the Enlightenment, sure that more schools and better dissemination of knowledge would cure most of society's ills. On the masthead of *The Huntress* in 1837 appeared this sentence: "Education—'the main pillar which sustains the Temple of Liberty.' Johnson."[81] In opposition to the "nativist" groups she favored liberal immigration laws—a stand that was not popular in all circles. One reader of her weekly wrote that he was sorry to see "an old matron of the Revolution"—and the widow of one of the renowned patriots of that day who "nobly defended the rights of the natives and established native liberty"—take the position she did. She was now denouncing the new patriots who dared defend their country from the onslaught of "foreigners" who threatened soon to outnumber the native Americans and to cause the pillars of liberty to crumble and fall.[82] In a long reply Mrs. Royall taught her "ignorant and dogmatical" correspondent a lesson in early American history. It was true, she said, that her husband fought for independence—but independence of American liberty. He fought for the rights of every citizen, foreigners and natives, who, she believed, were about equal in number in the 1770's. There were not enough to fight the British, so the Americans had to send for more foreigners. General Lafayette came, bringing with him men, ships, and money. Her husband was instructed in military tactics by a foreigner, Baron von Steuben, and he had had a company of foreigners under his command, and no men fought better. Had it not been for these foreigners "the natives would have been even to this date British subjects." She simply did not believe that the Almighty ever gave "a fee simple to this country to any set of men to the exclusion of another."[83]

While she deplored drunkenness as one of the great evils of mankind, she looked on temperance societies as part of a great scheme of the "tyrannical priests [the clergy of any denomination] to subdue our country."[84] She favored Sunday mail because it was prohibited by the Blue Laws that were strangling the freedoms of the American people. Furthermore, the men opposed to Sunday mail seemed to be the ones who "lost" her shipments of books and who pilfered money sent to her and were, therefore, her personal enemies. She hated slavery, but had no patience with the abolitionists. She said that in opposing abolition she did not oppose the movement but the uses made of it. Free men cannot be forced into measures; every individual and every state must "take their own time and their own mode."[85] As it appeared to her, the abolitionists were merely the "blue skins" in a different guise and therefore enemies of freedom.[86] Had she lived to the eve of the Civil War, she would have suffered great agony. She opposed slavery and abolition alike and favored "states' rights," but she strongly opposed nullification. The union "now and forever" was as much a part of her being as anything in the world, and one of her last public wishes was that "the union of these states may be here eternal."[87] Throughout all her career she deplored the double standard of morality and justice applied to the two sexes, yet she was no feminist. She seems to have had little, if any, interest in the women's rights movements that were fermenting in her time. In fact, she was even opposed to the practice of hiring women clerks in certain departments of the federal government. To be sure, she seems not to have opposed the clerks because they were women but because they were relatives of officials in Washington, and the whole practice of nepotism she considered a part of the corruption in the federal government.[88] These and many other causes received her attention from time to time, but four big and important issues held her neverfailing concentration for long periods of time: the church-state controversy, anti-Masonry, the United States Bank, and corruption in government. Of these the church question absorbed her energies for the longest time.

She feuded with the church throughout her adult life. This was not because she was personally irreligious or opposed to religion. According to her own standards she was a sincerely religious person, if "loving God and doing good to one's neighbors" was religion. However, she was called an "enemy of religion," and "enemy of God," and the epithet of "infidel" was often hurled at her. In reply to such an accusation Mrs. Royall once wrote: "I am not an infidel; that is, I do not say the Bible or the Christian religion is untrue. All I say is that I do not read the Bible—and I will tell you why. I was raised . . . amongst the heathens where I learned nothing but virtue." When she was introduced to civilized people and before she had read the Bible that had been placed in her hands, she watched the conduct of those who did read it and found they committed murder, robbed, stole, got drunk, betrayed their friends, and were guilty of "all the abominations"—and she was afraid to read it for fear she might do all these crimes, too.[89] More than once she challenged her critics to point out even one sentence of hers in which she did not uphold the Christian virtues. Church people, she observed, professed religious principles but neglected the human courtesies of looking after the needy and unfortunate. They collected large sums of money for the "missionaries," but did not practice their professed beliefs. In short, Mrs. Royall did not oppose "Bible religion," but "money religion."[90]

Mrs. Royall fought back at the church people in varying ways. In her milder moods she told humorous tales in which they were the butt of the joke. For instance there was the anecdote involving a woman at Moulton, Alabama, with whom she was trying to carry on a conversation. When she asked what religion she professed, the good woman replied, "Ne'ere one. I'm a Cumberland presbyterian."[91] Again, there was the story about young Mr. Beecher, a nephew of Dr. Lyman Beecher of Boston, who solved the problem of distributing the religious tracts his uncle sent him. Catching some of the many goats in Montgomery, Alabama, he stuck a tract on each horn and "sent them forth to spread the gospel," much honester missionaries, she observed, than the two-legged variety.[92]

This was a period of rampant pioneer evangelism, and the many movements that came out of it—the temperance crusade, the Sabbath crusade, the Sunday School movement, Millerism,[93] and abolition—formed a hydra-headed monster that Mrs. Royall was convinced boded no good for the public. In her more violent moments, she denounced all of these, reserving some of her most severe criticism for the "evangelicals," a term she used to include practically all Christian churches except the Roman Catholics. Of all these she hated the Presbyterian clergy the most; her favorite term for them was "the holy willies." They were the ones who had been back of her arraignment as a common scold. Sarcastically she called the witnesses at the trial ". . . the evangelical—tractical—Sabbath school—prayer meeting—good, honest, pious, sound Presbyterians of Capitol Hill."[94] When the *New England Religious Weekly* wrote that "the old hag [Anne Royall] publishes a weekly paper at Washington . . . which is a strong Jackson print and contains all the scum, billingsgate and filth extant," she added, "Wonder what part of the Bible he found that?"[95] Priestcraft, she believed, "destroys every noble feeling and even human nature itself and changes those who are cursed with it into Democrats. . . ."[96]

The efforts of the Holy Willies to convert women was nothing short of immoral, and the tracts which were flooding the land were an abomination, "scandalous impositions, void of decency and common sense, a libel on religion and morality."[97] She made something of a point of destroying these ubiquitous tracts, throwing them overboard when she found them on boats or out the windows of hotels.

Mrs. Royall was fully convinced that there was a deep diabolical plot to form a union of church and state in this country. "She appears . . . dreadfully alarmed at the progress of Christianity" a fellow editor observed. "She is vociferous against those whom she is pleased to call The Church and State Party."[98] Whenever Protestants introduced a bill or she saw those "sniveling priests" in the Capitol, she felt she had evidence to prove her fears. Nearly every issue of her weekly contained a tirade on the subject. Stationing herself under the very dome of the Capitol, as it were, for thirty years she watched Congress to see that the Evangelical lobbyists made no breach in the Constitution.

In her frequent rambles through offices on Capitol Hill seeking subscriptions and sniffing irregularities, she often observed a half dozen or so "orthodox parsons" employed in reading temperance tracts and, she suspected, even writing them. These were men who were employed at good salaries but were lazy drones who should be turned out "to obey their master whom they pretend to worship, who bids them go and spread the gospel without money and without script." Parsons, she said editorially, had no right to public office; nevertheless, there were several clergymen holding important positions in the government. The Chief Clerk and Superintendent of Mail Contracts in the general post office was the Reverend O. B. Brown, and no doubt there were "lots of priests stowed away in the nooks and corners of the departments." This was further evidence of the existence of the Church and State Party.[99] The "missionaries," who were behind this whole movement were one of those two great absorbing tyrants which had "drained the whole country of their property" and men consequently had to "sell their consciences or starve."[100]

Reaction to these attacks varied. There were some who were so offended they cancelled their subscriptions; others advised her to "lay off" the Church, Sunday Schools, and tract societies; still others encouraged her to "put it on" even harder, insisting that she was the one who could do it most effectively. She believed, and probably correctly so, that most of the clergy were opposed to her and warned their parishioners and other acquaintances to beware of her. In many places she visited she was greeted with, "we have heard of you, Mrs. Royall," in tones less than friendly. This was the work of the priests, she was sure.

In this matter of the church, there is little doubt that she was prejudiced, suspicious, and at times unreasonable, but at the same time honestly patriotic, trying to save the Republic from what looked to her as a great curse.

To understand Mrs. Royall's campaign against anti-Masonry, it is necessary to remember that there was once a movement to wipe out all secret societies as being "un-American." Only Phi Beta Kappa was able to survive and, it did so by becoming an honor society. The Anti-Masonic Party, for there was a formal organization, grew out of an incident that happened in upstate New York in 1826. One William Morgan, a resident of Batavia, New York, and allegedly a former Mason (although no one ever learned where he took his degrees), published a pamphlet in which he claimed to have revealed the secrets of the order. Shortly afterwards, he disappeared under circumstances that indicated foul play, and the Masons were held responsible. In a lengthy series of inquiries and court trials that threw no light on the fate of Morgan it was revealed that virtually every office holder in the state of New York was a Mason. There was a popular outcry at this finding, and the contagion spread as far west as Ohio and east to Massachusetts. For a time anti-Masonry was a merely social upheaval, but its leaders were soon to make it serve their political purposes. When a year later a badly mangled body was washed ashore on Lake Ontario and there was much speculation about its identity, Thurlow Weed, one of the leaders of the party, said, "It's good enough Morgan for me until after the elections."[101] The anti-Masons appealed to religious prejudices and even saw in the small number of Catholics arriving on American shores a menace to the liberty of the Republic. In many states the party opposed Andrew Jackson and endorsed many items in Henry Clay's American system.[102]

Anne Royall had every sentimental and practical reason to favor the Masons. Her husband, an ardent Mason, once told her that if she was ever in real need to turn to his fraternal brothers for help. And she found this to be true. They had befriended her at many crucial points in her life. They took her in when she arrived in Virginia in 1823, sick and destitute, and kept her until she recovered and readied her first book for the publisher; they subscribed to her various works, provided a hall for the production of her play, and in places where she needed protection, acted as a welcoming committee and bodyguard. In gratitude she praised the Masons openly and often. One of the characteristics she mentioned whenever she could in her personal sketches was that the man was a Mason. She often said, "He is a Mason. That is enough." Something favorable about the Masons appears on almost every page she wrote. Having this firm attachment to the order, she had little sympathy for anti-Masonry. Anti-Masons and the "blue skins" often acted in unison and caused her real trouble in several places.

She gave a good summary of her views on the subject in a lengthy paragraph:

These silly opponent's [she wrote] might as well attempt to pluck the sun and the moon out of the heavens as to destroy Masonry—old as the deluge. And, to give my opinion of it in a few words,—if it were not for Masonry the world would become a herd of savages. Like the fire on the altar, Masons are the only class of men that have preserved charity and benevolence alive—that sacred spark which came down from heaven, has been preserved by Masons. What more it consists of I do not know (for I have never looked into Morgan) this was enough, and more than any other institution can boast. Masonry can boast of the best Christians since the world began. My husband, well known to have been one of the most respected men, and descended from one of the most respectable families in America, uniformly told me that Masonry was the greatest institution in the world, and that if I was ever in destress to call on them. This I have found to be true. When Christians, so-called, the godly missionaries, have shut their doors upon me, the Masons have opened theirs.

As a result of the anti-Masonic campaign Masonry was at a low ebb, probably its lowest ever in America, and Anne had to save it and the nation from the prejudice, bigotry, and savagery that would follow if the foe succeeded. She was not one to be neutral.

For Anne Royall the question of Masonry was all-important and the whole question became politically acrimonious. But while there was some national interest in it, it was concentrated in the Northeast with New York State as a focal point. The Bank, on the other hand, was of such national importance that few could ignore it.

The Second United States Bank was chartered for twenty years in 1816. Following a wavering policy, the presidents of the Bank had overextended credit or tightened it too rapidly to please people in all parts of the country. Andrew Jackson, with the typical westerner's distrust of banks, had little faith in it. Even in his first annual message he questioned the constitutionality of the Bank and asserted it had failed to establish a sound and uniform currency. When it became clear that the President was intent on eliminating the Bank, its president, Nicholas Biddle, who had done much to make the institution serve the nation, embarked on a policy of opposition. Following a speech by Thomas Hart Benton attacking the Bank, Biddle and Henry Clay decided to apply for recharter, although the old charter still had four years to run. A bill for recharter was introduced in February, 1832. They thus threw down the gauntlet to Andrew Jackson in an election year. Congress passed the measure, but in a masterly message the President vetoed it. Henry Clay, running for president, needed an issue and ran on a pro-Bank platform. What had been merely an important question became a burning issue. Jackson interpreted his overwhelming victory as a mandate to kill the Bank before it expired naturally.[103]

Anne Royall always insisted she did not take sides with any party, but she was a Jacksonian at heart and supported the Jackson position on the Bank with all the fervor of a zealot, writing long front-page articles about it. She reported many of the current criticisms and denounced it as one of the great evils of the day. The Bank facilities had "a powerful and irrisistible attraction" which drew some of the best men to Philadelphia.[104] It was too powerful. "The United States Bank not a political machine!" she exclaimed in horror. "It is a despot. It is the rack. It is the inquisition. It is a monster of corruption." "Not political?" she asks. Then, she wanted to know, what wields the power in Congress and governs Pennsylvania and owns the press? The Bank was everything but a friend of the people. She was accused of maintaining that the Bank was the cause of all the corruption in the country. She had to admit that the men in the Bank party always treated her with gentlemanly courtesy—which was more than she could say about the Pious Party—and even at times could joke with her about her stand on the Bank.[105] One fellow Washington editor wrote a long, florid article about her and her stand on the Bank, ending with the mock plea, "Kill, if you please Mrs. Royall, the U.S. Bank, upset their whole concern, leave not one stone upon another" but snatch him from the great bonfire. "You have said the Bank will not be rechartered. Don't you perceive the Bank is a dead duck when you say the word?" He had lost Mrs. Royall's friendship because of the

Bank. "Oh, horrible, how horrible!" "He is so witty and comical, one cannot hate him" was her comment.[106]

Jackson's veto of the Bank she believed raised him to the "highest pinnacle of honor" and placed him among the "most magnanomous sons of America" and proved the "most sterling integrity of the man." For her the question was at an end. The President had saved liberty, which had been on the very brink of destruction. He had thus endeared himself to every virtuous American and won the admiration of Europe.[107]

In December, 1832 Mrs. Royall "flattered" herself that she "would get leave to breathe at last." With the election over and the Bank question settled she could relax without a great cause to fight. Not so! She began "casting an eye" over the vanquished and found them far from conquered.[108] There was corruption everywhere. Every place she went she saw nothing but fraud, violence, and oppression, distress of all kinds and vice of the most abandoned kind. In Washington she saw clerks idling away their time, money being squandered on worthless projects, the honest poor being neglected, congressmen abusing their franking privilege, postal clerks stealing from the mails, minor officials accepting bribes, and practically everyone guilty of nepotism. Almost all the local news in both *Paul Pry* and *The Huntress* was confined to irregularities in the different departments of the government. She made frequent tours through the State Department, Treasury, and Post Office and other buildings, spotting corrupt officials who ought to be turned out of office. It was said she could "sniff corruption a mile away." Following her policy of naming names, she told who the criminals were and what they were guilty of. To be sure, at times the "crime" was that of being an anti-Mason or an evangelical, but she did point out many cases of overt dishonesty. Many readers, of course, enjoyed these castigations and approved of her methods, which were generally conceded to be effective. "You have stopped the wheels of government because your remarks are generally so very true and you are so quaint and querulous that your paper is more in regard than the proper work of the office." Thus spoke a representative of one of the departments the editor was castigating.[109] Her opinions were respected or feared; people listened to her, and it was important to public officials that they appear well in her columns. Therefore, many of them shunned her or bought her works to avoid a damning, or at least unflattering, image that they were sure she would picture of them if they openly criticized or defied her.

In the last issue of *Paul Pry* (before the name was changed to *The Huntress*), Mrs. Royall wrote at length of the services that she had performed through her paper for her country at large and for Washington in particular. *Paul Pry* had been the first to "sound the note of alarm that there were traitors in the camps." It first exposed frauds in the Post Office Department. It was the first to challenge the frauds in the handling of Indian lands in Georgia and other southern states. She had been the first to detect changes in official policies. Through her paper she had pointed her finger at certain pious rogues who were swindling the government out of millions.[110]

Anne Royall espoused an impressive list of causes. Time has proved her remarkably correct (or, as she might have said, "right-headed") about them. To these causes she gave herself unstintingly. A cause to her was not a transitory item to be picked up and discarded as soon as its popularity waned, but a principle to be followed persistently and doggedly through a lifetime.

She was best known for her exposures and adverse criticisms. But there was another Anne Royall who was consistently trusting, optimistic, and patriotic. She exhibited these qualities in what proved to be her valedictory in the last issue of *The Huntress*. "We trust in heaven for three things," she wrote. "First, that members [of Congress] may give us the means to pay for this paper. . . . Second, that Washington may escape that dreadful scourge, the cholora. Our third prayer is that union of these states may here be eternal."[111] Mrs. Royall was eighty-five years old.

Anne Royall as Anne Royall

For all her notoriety and publicity during her lifetime, her death received very brief notice. A Washington paper carried this short announcement:

Mrs. Anne Royall died at her residence in Washington on Sunday morning, October 1st, 1854, at a very advanced age. She was the widow of a revolutionary officer, Colonel William Royall, and she published a newspaper in Washington for many years, first as "Paul Pry" which name afterwards was changed to "The Huntress."[112]

The *Washington Evening Star* published a somewhat longer article on her.

Mrs. Anne Royal Dead

This venerable and eccentric lady died at her residence on Capitol Hill in this city yesterday morning. She must have been well nigh 90 years of age. Ever since the publication of the famous history of her perigrinations throughout the country, fighting the presbyteria, she has made her residence here, first editing *The Huntress* and subsequently living by its proceeds published by others in her name. For the last four or five years she has been out and about very little owing to her increasing infirmities. When about, however, her tongue went on as before, always to attract wanderers around her. Vehement and violent as her antipathies, and expression of them, she was equally as warm in the friendships for those she favored, though from her peculiar way of manifesting her likings few indeed courted her affectionate regards. To the hour of her death she preserved all the peculiarities of thought, temper and manners which at one time rendered her so famous throughout the land.[113]

Her funeral was held the following day from her home on B Street and Capitol Hill, the site on which the Library of

Congress now stands. Her friends had been invited to attend without further notice. One can only wonder how many of them went to the Congressional Cemetery where the bodily remains of Anne Royall were interred. Other papers, including ones in the South, picked up the notice but little more information appeared at the time.[114]

For a while there seems to have been little interest in her. In her middle eighties at her death, she had lost some of her earlier fire. She evidently was becoming somewhat senile. The last issue of *The Huntress*, written about ten weeks before her death, contains articles on several of her favorite topics, but it is noticeably the writing of an old woman. For months she had been plagued with rheumatism and had not been about much. Her Sally had been sick, and they had lost touch with many activities of the outside world.

Anne Royall was not forgotten, however, and before long people began to reminisce about her, mostly recalling her eccentricities. It is not surprising that not everyone remembered her kindly; some of them, like Amos Kendall, had felt the sting of her criticism. He wrote:

> There was living in Washington at that time [the Jackson administration], a singular woman named Anne Royall, the widow of Captain Royall of the United States Army. She was homely in person, careless in dress, poor in purse and vulgar in manners. But she had a tolerable education, much shrewdness, and respectable talents. She procured her subsistence by publishing books in which she praised extravagantly those who bought her books or gave her money, and abused without measure those who refused or in any way incurred her displeasure. Some, through love of flattery, and more through fear of abuse, contributed to her support. . . .[115]

There were others who remembered her. Colonel James Tait, later a magistrate, recalled her as a little woman with a rough though not homely face. She dressed plainly, "having little regard for the wide hoopskirts and big sleeves of fashion."

One venerable gentleman described her as a "holy terror"; others agreed. John W. Forney, for example, said of her:

> She was the terror of the politicians, and especially of Congressmen. I can see her now tramping through the halls of the old Capitol, umbrella in hand, seizing upon every passer-by and offering her book for sale. Any public man who refused to buy was certain of a severe philippic in her newspaper . . . She was a woman of great industry and astonishing memory. . . .[116]

John Quincy Adams' famous description of her as going about "like a virago errant in enchanted armor, redeeming herself from the cramps of indigence by the notoriety of her eccentricities, and the forced currency they gave to her publications" is probably as much an example of the love Adams had for turning a clever phrase as it was an accurate picture of Mrs. Royall.

An elderly newspaperman who had known all the great and near great of Washington for a half-century and was familiar with all the editors and writers of the period considered Anne Royall the most interesting of them all. She was a "character for a Dickens or a Thackery to deliniate."

> What a stir Mrs. Royall made [he wrote at a much later date], whenever her royal presence was made known, especially among a lot of the representatives. Her sharp, strident voice cutting the atmosphere like a knife. She wore thick grey, worsted mitts, through which her claws protruded, and grasped a green cotton umbrella, a bundle of newspapers, a subscription book of the *Huntress*. Her soul was in arms and she was always eager for a fray. Henry Clay, Daniel Webster, Lt. Gen. Scott, John C. Calhoun, and lesser lights who infested Congress and newspaper offices fell over each other in vain efforts to escape. They all failed and were held up one by one and compelled to subscribe. Let anyone refuse or become delinquent and the next edition of her paper would erupt with a stream of venom and abuse with the mention of names as would put the lava flow of Vesuvius . . . to shame. Both houses of Congress bowed down in fear of her.

He added that "Congress felt a weight lifted when she died." He also gave more description of her physical appearance. In the summer she wore a green calash, a hood generally worn in a carriage; in the winter several shawls, dark and shabby or sometimes a cloak with a hood, closely covering her head. Her face was swarthy, raw-boned, and "traversed by a thousand wrinkles."[117]

In spite of her eccentricities, she was good-hearted and harmless. Others agreed that while many regarded her as a "horrid creature," others knew that she possessed kindliness and charity to a surprising degree.[118] She visited the sick, she shared her substance with the less fortunate, and she gave a home to several orphan boys who ran her printing press.

It was impossible for Anne Royall to be neutral or indifferent on any topic, and apparently it was as difficult for her contemporaries to judge her objectively. People either approved of her and found her interesting, or hated her and could not tolerate her. After a hundred years it is somewhat easier to evaluate her.

On the negative side she lacked balance, especially on religious questions, and calm judgment, culture, tact, and good taste. She could be disagreeably insistent, and was too fond of name-calling. Furthermore, there seems to have been an element of paranoia in her makeup; she always suspected a plot of some kind against the Republic, liberty, or herself. Whenever she had a reverse, she was sure that her enemies (either the Pious Party or the anti-Masons) had a hand in it. She was forever suspecting that she was being spied upon. She, also, could be as inconsistent as anyone, loudly supporting the right of every man to his own opinion but bitterly denouncing people whose views differed from her own. She was meddlesome and nonconforming. In short, she was what is often called "a character."

On the positive side, she was forceful and straightforward. Her descriptions are accurate and her evaluations honest. No one can deny that she was patriotic and that her ideals were moral. She was a positive character who made her presence felt and, fortunately, in most instances for the right causes.

A real understanding and appreciation of Anne Royall is possible only when one begins to evaluate her in relation to her time. She was living in a man's world, doing a man's work, competing with men in the newspaper world on the same terms. Many of the characteristics people criticized in her would have gone unnoticed in a male editor. In other words, she had prejudice against her sex to overcome in addition to a long list of problems that were peculiarly her own.

Critics of her appearance seemed not to consider the grinding poverty she lived in all those years she was in the public eye. She was always beset with problems. She may have been careless in handling her finances, but she often had financial troubles that were not of her making. Regardless of how well her books sold, she found it almost impossible to collect from many of the booksellers, especially those in distant cities She must have written literally hundreds of letters in trying to collect the money due her. Doubtless people on Capitol Hill learned to dodge her, but she considered Congressmen and other public officials as the most interested in the contents of her paper and, therefore, the best subscribers. Consequently she spent much time in the halls of public buildings, selling new subscriptions and collecting delinquent ones—at the same time getting news items and other material for the next issue. She may have been tiresome in her persistence, but she had little choice. This was her method of making a living. If she actually begged money from her friends (which she did many times in her later years), she was asking for small sums only to keep the press going. The paper was her means of making a living and also the mouthpiece through which she could speak to save the country. It was vitally important that she keep it operating, and if it took additional help from her friends, they shared in the work she was doing. To keep the paper going, therefore, was vastly more important than dressing fashionably or even neatly.

According to any standards, Anne Royall was a remarkable woman, but when one considers her age she becomes truly phenomenal. Born in 1769, she started making her own living in her middle fifties, at an age when most American women of the time were considered old. When she started her newspaper, she was sixty-one; when she died she was eighty-five.[119] While her contemporaries recognized the fact that she was elderly, few of them seemed to feel there was anything unusual about a woman of her age still editing a newspaper. Nevertheless, it is truly remarkable that an octogenarian was still mentally alert and physically active enough to keep a paper going, especially since she did it almost single-handedly, acting as reporter, editorial writer, and every other writer on the staff. Even her contemporaries recognized the strength of her mind. Not until near the very end of her life did her writing begin to lose its vigor and even then only by comparison with her own earlier work.

Anne Royall was not only poor and old, but she was alone. She had a sister and a half brother, but they lived in distant states, and since she never mentions them in her paper, one may assume there was no close relationship between them. Certainly, they did nothing to provide for her in her later years. Her one close friend and companion was the faithful Sally Stack, who lived with her some twenty-five years, sharing her successes and failures, delivering the papers, and probably making their abode livable and providing the companionship Mrs. Royall needed. Any crusader by very nature is lonely, cut off from most of his contemporaries, and this may be one of the reasons Mrs. Royall was so suspicious, seeing a plot at every turn. Her causes were right and anyone who opposed them or her had to be considered an enemy—not only her enemy but also an enemy of freedom itself. She was always an independent thinker—rebellious against the bigotry and dogmatism of any creed, whether religious or political.

And her causes *were* right; the evils she fought are the ones keepers of the twentieth-century conscience are still trying to eradicate. They are just as contemporary in the 1960's as they were in the 1840's. While there now seems little fear of an established Church, the whole question of relations between Church and State is far from settled. Public leaders still differ on such matters as the use of school busses for parochial schools, grants from public funds to church colleges, and tax exemption of church property. Corruption in government and, especially, the misuse of public funds that Mrs. Royall exposed and denounced with such vehemence are still with us. She had perception to recognize evils that continue to be evils.

Except for the years of her marriage, her life was hard. Reared on the frontier, far from the amenities of cultured society and largely isolated from civilization, she had her first contact with the world of culture and of ideas only when she was already a young adult. For a time she lived as a menial in the household where she later was mistress. It may be that much of her later trouble with her husband's family stems from the fact that they considered her beneath him socially. From the early 1820's on, her life was one constant struggle. Traveling, writing, publishing, fighting against evils as she saw them consumed her years. In spite of these hardships, or perhaps because of them, she accomplished, as one of her admirers once said, "more than any woman of her time." A remarkable woman, surely, and one who deserves our continuing respect and admiration.

LETTERS FROM ALABAMA
1817–1822

LETTERS FROM ALABAMA

Letter I.

Cabell Court House, Virginia, 28th Nov. 1817.[1]

Dear Matt,

I LAMENT your absence from Charlestown, at the time my setting out; yet perhaps it is better so, expecially as it was not in your power to transact the business with S——. On my arrival here, I sent for Mr. Ladely, who very politely undertook to execute the business without delay; but how you are to get the papers in time, Heaven only knows. I must leave it to chance. You say you are going to Ohio to spend the winter —for your health, I presume—better go to North Carolina, or any southern climate. Go to bed early, and rise betimes in the morning. You ruin your health by setting up late. Hang the cards, they are to be your ruin: I never knew any good come of them. They will, if you persist in them, cost you your health, reputation, perhaps your life! Cards subject you to bad company and bad hours. What is worse? Oh, M. quit them—pursue something more worthy of yourself.

But I see I must quit writing. Mr. L. and myself are both sitting at one table, and trying to write; but we shall have to give it up. The room we are in, which is the family apartment, was occupied when I came in, by two or three rough looking men. They had been drinking, and were disputing on politics when I entered. When Mr. L. and myself sat down to write, I thought they would take the hint; but no! here they sit. I suspect they must be some of the *consequentials* of the neighborhood, as they are suffered to occupy the "sactum sanctorum" of the landlady, to the greast molestation of the guests. They have begun on the scriptures now, and a fight, I suspect, will break up the debate. Strange! how the sacred writings are abused by the misguided vulgar. How absurd! and yet how common! You will scarcely see two or three persons together who do not engage in disputes about the scriptures; and yet no subject is so little calculated to sustain contradiction. One party always, and often both, fall into a rage. Were the scriptures given for this? But some will say "it is our privilege to talk in a free country." True—but not to quarrel! I never knew any good, but on the contrary much harm, flow from these disputes: neither is this practice confined to drunkards over their cups: sober, but narrow minded religious sects are addicted to it; and it is always found to prevail most amongst those who practice the duties of the Christian religion least. As there is no surer mark of an evil disposed female, or want of virtue, than to hear her defame her own sex; so there can be no stronger evidence of a hypocrite than to hear him rail at other sects than that to which he belongs: and I should want to better proof of his being every thing but a Christian. The Christian religion does not consist in vain disputes and idle talk, but in the practice of its precepts. I have never heard any of these sectarians dispute the privilege of relieving the distressed. The idea of such a dispute never entered their heads or hearts.

I find Mr. L. a man of much patience. I confess I must yield to him the victory. He is certainly a modest as well as a very pleasant man. Dear M. I must retire to rest. God bless you! Pray take care of your health.

Yours, truly.

N. B. You shall have the papers by Tuesday, if possible.

Letter II.

Mount Sterling, Kentucky, 2d Dec. 1817.[2]

Dear Matt,

HERE I AM, safe and sound, in defiance of wind and weather, bad roads, and all. To use the common phrase, very little worth your attention has occured since I wrote to you from Cabell. I had not proceeded a mile on my way the next morning, before I was met by a gentleman riding on horseback, and alone. This was the thing I wished, provided he was going so far as your town; but from the stranger's appearance, I had little hope of that. He was without any thing that might indicate a journey of any distance. He was thinly clad, without portmanteau or saddle bags, and even without a great coat, although it had snowed during the night, and the morning was intensely cold. He addressed me with the easy politeness of a gentleman, and inquired how far it was to town, meaning Cabell Court House, and also how far it was to Charlestown? My heart leaped for joy on hearing the last interrogatory. After giving him the desired information on each of his inquiries, "Are you going to Charlestown, Sir," said I, drawing forth my packet from my pocket. He replied in the affirmative. "Will you be so good then," I asked, "as to take charge of this packet and deliver it there?" He kindly assented, observing that he would execute my commands with pleasure. All this was the business of a moment; but no sooner had he disposed of the packet, and we were about to separate, than I repented my rashness in confiding so much in a stranger, and thought it might not be amiss to inquire for his place of residence. But what was my astonishment, when he told me he lived in Scotland; but that, at present, he was going to Canada. "At any rate, Sir," said I, "you have the deportment of a gentleman, and I will venture to trust you." "Fear me not," said he, "I will not deceive you." We bowed to each other and separated. You are in a poor trim, thought I, for a journey to Canada at this season, as he parted from me shivering with the cold.

At the distance of a mile from the place of our meeting, I met three men riding with led horses, heavy laden. They were muffled up in great coats, cloaks, &c. I concluded they belonged to the gentleman ahead, probably his *suite;* which I found to be the fact. You will have heard, ere this, that this great personage was *Lord Selkirk.*[3] On the second night after parting with his Lordship, we—I say *we*, for the companions of my journey found me at Big Sandy River—we stopped for the night at an Inn kept by old Mr. Clack. Here I learned the name and quality of the Scottish Lord; and I could not but blame myself for the liberty I had taken with his Lordship. Yet what the plague could he be poking about our wild hills and mountains for? And how was I to know that he was a foreign dignitary? Indeed, he had more the appearance of an out-rider, in the way I met him, than any thing else.

Old Mr. Clack informed us, that Lord Selkirk put up at his house, as he went on—that he was on his return from a tour of three years, which were spent in exploring the western country bordering on the Pacific—and that his *suite* consisted of his Physician, his Secretary and his servant. These were the three men I met in the rear of his Lordship. These particulars Mr. C. collected from the servant, without the knowledge of his superiors, who maintained the strictest silence on the subject of their journey. Mr. C. stated, that his Lordship's domestics behaved with the greatest humility towards him, never presuming to sit in his presence, nor to eat until he had finished his meal—for the rest, he ate a great many eggs, ten or fourteen at a meal; wrote to a late hour at night; and slept under a great many blankets between his own sheets.

The fears of Mrs. Clack, on account of the Earl, afforded us much amusement. She said he must harbor some bad design againt the country—that was certain: "for," said she, "he must be a Jew, or a Turk, or a Tory, or some outlandish animal; for, because, whenever my old man would go out, he would always be a axin me how many neighbors I had, how many were in each family, and how far distant the country was inhabited around us; but, whenever my old man came in, he would just be as still as a mouse!" We endeavored to remove the old lady's fears, by assuring her that little danger was to be apprehended from his Lordship. I have since learned that his motive in visiting the west, was to seek an asylum for his poorer countrymen.

Yours, &c.

Letter III.

Lexington, Kentucky, 8th Dec. 1817.

Dear Matt,

I INTEND to spend a few days in this town, or city, whatever it be called.[4] I have seen but little of it yet. Should I describe it to you, it would be too much like repeating "a thrice told tale." The country around it is well situated—beautiful in the extreme, and in a state of high cultivation. The first three days of my journey, after entering Kentucky, presented no varity, the soil and face of the country being nearly the same from Big Sandy River to Mount Sterling, about ninety miles. The surface is very uneven, covered with heavy timber, and thinly inhabited; but on approaching Mount Sterling, you are suddenly transported, as it were, into another world. The face of the country assumes a new appearance, the soil and its productions differing entirely from the preceding. It is not in the power of imagination to paint the contrast, which you behold on emerging from the gloomy, lonesome woods into open day. The light, which was hitherto excluded by the lofty timber, rushes upon you in an instant; and you find yourself in a soil, rich indeed, but the growth of timber, which principally consists of locust, cherry-tree, and black-walnut, is low and small, and the trees universally terminate abruptly from a large base to a diminutive top, although they have wide-spreading branches. The fruit trees on the Kenhawa equal them in height: they are thinly scattered over the ground. Such is the face of the country from Mount Sterling to this place, and it is said to extend to Danville in this state. The farmers give their attention chiefly to the raising of Indian corn and tobacco, though other vegetables are produced in plenty and in great perfection. But with these subjects, as well as most others, relative to the manufactures and produce of Kentucky, you are much better acquainted with than I am.

You have often heard it stated, that a solid rock of lime-stone runs beneath the surface of the earth here. This is not generally the fact; it only exists in what is called old Kentucky, meaning that part of the state, which extends from Mount Sterling to Danville, and which, I presume, was the first settled. This rock is said to be at unequal distances from the surface, from two and a half to four feet. To this circumstance may be ascribed the diminutive growth of the timber. As I rode through the country from Mount Sterling to this place, I observed that the sugar trees were dead. Upon inquiry into the cause of this novel appearance, I was informed that they were killed by a worm, which attacks the leaves and boughs with such avidity, and in such numbers, that they succeed in destroying the tree; and having despatched the sugar trees, it had begun the same process on all others, except the walnut, which it has never yet been known to touch.

Dr. Claud has called to see me, and I must conclude.

Yours, &c.

Letter IV.

Lexington, Kentucky, same day, 1817.

Dear Matt,

IF YOU ARE a rich man, says Goldsmith, you may enter a room with three loud hems!—march deliberately up to the chimney—and turn your back to the fire. If you are a poor man, shrink into the room as fast as possible, and seat yourself, as usual, on the corner of a chair in a remote part of the room. I omitted the relation of an anecdote of a poor Irish traveller, whom we met at Licking: it will cure you of the *hypo.*

It was dark, it was cold, it was raining—when we entered a tolerable Inn on the bank of Licking river.[5] We had scarcely seated ourselves by a welcome fire, when some one hailed the house from the opposite shore. The landlord stepped out, answered the call, and in a few minutes returned, ushering in a man all dripping with water. We made room for him to approach the fire; but he declined seating himself amongst us, and retreating into the chimney corner, seated himself, not on one corner, but on the edge of a chair. All eyes were turned towards him. How common, and yet how ungenteel—nay, how uncivil—to embarrass a poor, unfortunate stranger! How apt we are to do the very thing we would wish not to have done unto us! It is cruel to stare a poor creature out of countenance only because he is a stranger, and differing from ourselves only in his outward appearance, while his modest, downcast look, tacitly disclose his superior manners.

Poor Paddy, for an Irishman he was, replied to the inquires of the guests, respecting his unpleasant trim, "that his horse was after trowing him in the wather: by the powers he niver was witter in his life. And I wish," continued he, "I wasn't safe at ome, in old Patrick O'Brian's to night, I wouldn't be here, so I wouldn't. Do, if you plase, landlord, give us a gill of whiskey." By this time, the landlord, of his own accord, had appeared with a glass of spirits. "Och! long life to your honor," cried Paddy; "here's wishing you may live all the days of your life, so I do." On being urged to change his clothes, he replied—"indeed, and I havn't a clean rag at all, at all; and so I will just sit here and dry myself by this good fire, and never mind—and I ought to go and see that Gin has her meat, poor bayst! She is the swaytest craycher in the world, for all she trow'd me in the pool; but 'twasn't her fault, for the saddle fill in first, and then you know, she couldn't help that." The landlord begged him to make himself easy, and he would see that Gin should have a plentiful supper.

One of our party asked him, if he had travelled far: "Och! indeed, I have then," said he; "I've been all the way to the Orleans among the agues, and the fayvers, and the miskeetoes, where they make sugar out of dare cane, and grind it in dare mills, wid dare nagurs. It is mesilf that had the ague, tree long monts and nine days; an all the time I lay flat o'me back, an the fayver shakin the skin traugt the bones, an not a christian craycher anigh me to give me a drink, but the doctor, and an old woman to wait on me. And there I lay spaychless, all the time talkin all the nonsense; an if I ever live to get home to Ireland again, it will never be me that will come to this here country again—if I do, my name isn't Dennis O'Brian. Many's the time I'd say to the doctor, doctor, says I, I can't stand it much longer, so jist lit me alone, an lit me die in payce, for the miskeetoes is aytin me up, any way. Says the doctor to me, "Dennis," says he, "have patience, you'll be well by and bye, and so—" He would have run on till now, had he not been interrupted by the entrance of two more travellers; and in a short time afterwards supper was announced.

We all arose to go to supper. Poor Dennis arose very slowly, apparently hesitating whether he ought to advance or not. One of our party tarried behind the company, waiting for him. Finding he was about to decline the summons, he asked, if he would not walk in and take supper with us. "Och! may the blessings attend you for that, for I havn't broke my fast on mayt to-day, but I hated to be afther aytin wid gentlefolks; an I have but little money too, for I give the last dollar I had away to a poor woman that I met in the road a walkin." "Come along, sir," said the gentleman, "You are as good as we are." The kindness of this address made his eyes sparkle, and he took the precedence, which the gentleman gave him, in walking before him to the supper room—exclaiming, "God forbid I should ever be half so good as your honor."

During supper, and long after, he entertained us with a history of his travels from New York to Pittsburg, thence to New Orleans, and last of all from Ireland to America; not, however without the assistance of another glass of whiskey and a great number of *says I's and says he's*. Long before he closed his narrative, I went to bed, and fell asleep; and I know not how long it was before I was awakened by some one who was singing. It was our Hibernian, beguiling his sorrows with a song. Happy man! Is he not to be envied? thought I. In my opinion, much more than he who possesses thousands.

Yours, &c.

Letter V.

Lexington, Kentucky, 9th Dec. 1817.

Dear Matt,

I SHALL leave Lexington after breakfast. In the mean time, you will expect to hear something of this town.

Although I have been here two days, I have learned but little concerning it, having been confined most of the time. In size and population, it is such as it has been described; and is the largest town I ever saw.[6] The first thing that strikes the eye of a stranger, is its white houses, gates, and posts (which last are very large) and the great activity in the streets—many people, carriages, &c. moving in all directions. Here are, also, very extensive Rope Walks. I have not visited any of the manufacturing houses in Lexington, but I have been told they are in a flourishing condition.[7] Of the market, I say nothing, as the cheapness, variety, and abundance of its supplies have been so often proclaimed by others.

I am informed that the citizens of Lexington are remarkable for their benevolence and humanity to the distressed of all descriptions, particularly to poor emigrants, who pass through their town. In no part of the United States, perhaps, do the unfortunate meet with more compassion than in Lexington. This is a noble trait in their character. I found, however, one exception in the person of Mr. Keen (I think his name is,) a vain, impertinent upstart. It contains about 5,000 inhabitants, who are genteel and hospitable. But my horses are ready, and I must conclude abruptly.

Yours, &c.

Letter VI.

Bowling Green, Kentucky, 13th Dec. 1817.

Dear Matt,

We arrived here without meeting with any accident. This place is situate in the barrens of Kentucky, and is a handsome village.[8] These barrens are almost destitute of timber. The soil, however, is very rich, and produces crops equal to any in the state: it is of a black color, tinged with red. Black Jack abounds on these barrens, and serves the inhabitants for fire wood; but it is not sufficient to defend them against the beams of the sun in summer, nor shield them from the cold blasts of winter—neither can it furnish rails for fencing; and the inhabitants are obliged to procure timber for this purpose, and also for building elsewhere at considerable expense. These barrens are but poorly watered, being destitute of springs; and the inhabitants have to supply the deficiency by digging wells. I an informed that the scenery, in summer, is beautiful, being varigated with flowers of the richest hue, and clothed with a coat of most luxuriant grass.

I was considerably amused this evening, in listening to a conversation which took place in the room where I was sitting. There were present five persons—I made the sixth: two doctors of physic, one lawyer, one old farmer, and one of your dandies. For myself, I sat a silent spectator. The subject of disputation arose from the circumstance of a burning coal of fire flying, by accident, into Doctor E's bosom, as the servant threw a log of wood with much force on the fire. This instantly called up the two great properties of all bodies, denominated by philosophers the power of attraction and repulsion. After dwelling some time on these points, they glided, imperceptibly, into the proofs of chymical affinity, by exhibiting in full array the different experiments—such as exposure of phosporus to the action of the atmosphere, muriate of ammonia and carbonate of magnesia, muriate of soda and sulphate of magnesia, ardent spirits and a solution of salt and water, the attraction between mercury and oxygen gas upon being exposed to the common temperature of the atmosphere.

The conversation (which was all Greek to me) was interrupted by the old farmer, who exclaimed, "Oh, d——n your *oxen* and *grass*, Dick; its all nonsense—better come and take some grog, gentlemen, and let us go to supper. What do you think your aunt Patty will do to night, Dick; hey!" "I suppose, sir, she will guess at the truth, and conclude that you could not accomplish your business in time to return home.—I think you may make yourself easy, uncle, and enjoy yourself with your friends." We discovered that one of the young champions was the old gentleman's nephew; and that modest and respectful deportment, which he manifested towards him, inspired the guests with an exalted opinion of his merit.

The old gentlemen having drank his grog and recommended his example to the other guests, supper was announced, and we arose and followed the landlord to the supper-room. After we were seated, the old farmer, who had listened attentively to the illustrations of chymistry, without attempting to join in the conversation, was the first person, who spoke, delivering himself as follows: "I tell you what, Dick, I don't understand none of your high flowing words, see, about this chymistry, nor your *poresses* and *rats*, and magnitudes, and all that are stuff. I don't see that any of you can get along any better than I do, with all your *larnin*, and I never knowed nothing about 'em." The young gentleman's face colored with a deep blush, and he replied: "You deserve much credit, sir, for that success, which has distinguished your industry and skill as a farmer, which has not only secured to yourself an easy independence, but has furnished you with the means of gratifying that liberality and benevolence, for which you are so justly celebrated." "Oh, now hold your tongue about them things, and let us go on about these chymistries. Why, d——n it, I don't understand a word of the confounded stuff at all. I suppose we shall have the sun, moon, and stars, and Joe Graphy next. What do you think of these thinks, friends," said the old man, turning to the dandy?

Mr. Fop, who had evinced his restiveness in a variety of ways during the learned discussion before supper, in which he took no part, being now appealed to, delivered himself thus: —"The rotundity of the earth's velocity, and the humidity of hydrolics, and their specific gravity, *ar* quite ridiculous in the abstract. I *ar* astonished to hear some folks *purtend* to have *larned* the infinities of tractions, when that *ar* a thing that *ar* out of the question!" This rhodomontade was uttered as it were, in a breath. If you had seen the old man, with his mouth and eyes wide open, staring at our dandy, while he was blending the different properties of bodies in a mass, and then hurling the whole to destruction, you would have stared, I believe, far more than the old man himself. "D——n your *ars* and your *finities*," said the farmer. The company could contain themselves no longer—a general burst of laughter from all, even from the servants, put an end to further conversation. The lawyer, who was a pretty clever fellow, I thought would have gone into fits. He laid down his knife and fork, clapped his hands on his sides, and continued to repeat the old man's *ars*, and laugh, till I expected he would drop. The gravity of the nephew was constrained to give way; and, in short, we were compelled to quit the supper-table. My young fop moved off, and I have not seen him since. Have I not taken some pains to amuse you, instead of going to bed? which last I shall now do, however, in a few minutes. Good night.

Letter VII.

December 15th, 1817.

Dear Matt,

AT LENGTH I have reached the state of Tennessee, the land of Heroes. I have been in the state about three hours, and already I seem to tread on sacred ground. As I rode to the Inn, where I now am, I was informed, that I was in *Tennessee*, and I immediately fell into a train of pleasant musing. The victory of New Orleans, the battles of Tallushatches, Talladega, and Emuckfau, all passed, in retrospection before me—

the brave, the intrepid, the invincible JACKSON, and his brilliant achievements engrossed every faculty of my mind. I shall see him! thought I. I shall now be gratified with a sight of the brave Tennesseeans, whose valour has secured forever the honour of their state![9]

After the necessary attention to ourselves, horses, &c. the landlord appeared to be at leisure, and I began a desultory conversation with him on the subject of his state. He informed me, that he had been only two years an inhabitant of the state, having removed hither from Kentucky. I found him disposed to bestow no very favorable encomiums upon the Tennesseeans: in fact, he endeavored to impress me with an opinion, redounding very little to the honor of their moral character. He related the story of a robbery, which had lately been committed at the next house of entertainment, in that direction in which we were travelling. I am amongst the few that do not credit evil reports upon slight grounds, and concluded that in the present instance, rivalry, or something else that the landlord thought proper to conceal, was the cause of this ill-natured calumny; which I found in the end to be true. I was however gratified this evening in becoming acquainted with one of the subaltern officers, who served under General Jackson as a volunteer. He came to the inn for the purpose of passing the night there; and, finding he had been in the army, I attached myself to him the residue of the evening. He bestowed the highest praise on General Jackson, and related many anecdotes of that great man, among which were the two following—one of which concerns his deportment whilst he was a judge.[10]

One day, when he was sitting on the bench at Jonesborough, the sheriff came into the court and informed him that the man (charged with the commission of some offence) would not be taken. Summon every man in the court yard, said the judge. The sheriff did so, and approached the man a second time; but the notorious offender placed his back against the stone wall of a house, and, with arms in his hands, set his pursuers at defiance. Hereupon the sheriff once more complained to the judge, that the man would not be taken. Did you summon all the men in the court yard? asked the judge.—I did, replied the sheriff; but he is armed, and none of the men will approach him. But summon *every* man you *see*, said the judge: and the sheriff, taking the hint, answered—"I summon *you*, then, sir,"—whereupon the judge arose, came down from the bench, approached the man, took him, and delivered him to the sheriff.

The other anecdote relates to his conduct towards *Witherford*, the Indian Chief, who commanded at Fort Mims, the scene of a then recent inhuman butchery by the Indians. After the battle of the Horse Shoe, the Indians sued for peace; and Jackson, to prove their sincerity, ordered them to bring Witherford, bound, to his camp. Learning what Jackson demanded, Witherford determined to go and surrender himself voluntarily. He gained Jackson's camp without being known, and desired admittance to the General. Jackson, astonished at his presumption, asked him how he dared to appear in his presence, after acting such a part as he did at Fort Mims? Witherford replied—"I am Witherford: I am in your power. Do with me what you please. I am a soldier still. I have done the white people all the harm I could. I have fought them, and fought them bravely. If I had an army, I would fight them still. But I have none! My people are no more!! Nothing is left me but to weep over the misfortunes of my country."[11]

Jackson, admiring the firmness of his address, told him, that if he rejected his (Jackson's) terms, although he (Witherford) was completely in his power, he (Jackson) would take no advantage of his situation—that he was at liberty to return to his own camp. "But if, said Jackson, you choose to try the fate of arms once more, and I take you prisoner, your life shall pay the forfeit of your crimes. But if you really wish for peace, stay where you are, and I will protect you."

"Well may you speak to me in this style, now!" replied Witherford. "There *was* a time, when I *had a choice*. I have none, *now*—even *hope* is ended! Once I could animate my warriors; but I cannot animate the dead. Their bones are bleaching on the plains of Tallushatches, Talladega, and Emuckfau; and I have not surrendered myself without reflection. While there was the *smallest hope*, I remained firm at my post, nor supplicated for peace. But, my warriors are no more! The miseries of my nation affects me with deepest sorrow!"—His voice was lost in emotion for some minutes, and then he added—"But I desire peace for the few that are left. If I had had none but the Georgia army to contend with, I would have raised my corn on *one* bank of the river, and fought them on the *other*. But your people are a brave people—you are a brave man; and I rely on your generosity. You talk a good talk: my people shall listen to it." Here all the world might stand up and say, "this was a man!" No wonder the magnanimous soul of Jackson felt for him. Does he not remind you of Logan?

Yours, &c.

Letter VIII.

Nashville, 18th December, 1817.

Dear Matt,

NASHVILLE, like every thing else, sounds louder at a distance than when it draws near. At the distance of a mile from the town, you see a board, with a hand painted on it as large as life, and the fore finger pointing with the following inscription, in large letters, underneath—"*Look and see the*

Town!" Upon looking down the road, you see the town, sure enough. It has a beautiful appearance, when viewed from this point. As you approach it, you are so much engrossed by its lofty looks, from which it is difficult to avert your eyes, that you would be apt to plunge into the narrow Cumberland, which flows between you and "the Town." We, however, did happen not to do so; but preferred a boat, which met us in good time.

Nashville is built on a high bluff, and the houses look very much like tumbling on your head, as you cross the river in a small boat at what is called the middle ferry. The citizens have, with much labor and expense, cut a passage through this bluff, large enough for carriages to pass and repass.[12] This passage, which is cut through a solid rock, turns abruptly down the river as if to seek a more commodious place to land the passengers, who receive no sort of hospitality or attention from the high minded gentleman, who looks down upon them while crossing the Cumberland. I was much disappointed in the size of this far famed Cumberland river. Although the large barges on it seem to indicate that there is much water, yet it is very narrow and steals softly along, its blue smooth waters making not the least noise.

The soil of West Tennessee, north of Cumberland river, is very rich and equally as productive as any in Kentucky or on the Kenhawa—it is an open plain of uninterrupted good land; and the farmers raise corn, tobacco, and pumpkins, in great abundance. They rear great numbers of hogs and horses, and have a great many distilleries in operations. In this way they convert their surplus produce into cash. But neither their hogs nor horses are so large as those of Kentucky; nor can their cattle be compared, in size, with those of that state.

I am afraid my brave Tennesseeans indulge too great a fondness for whiskey. When I was in Virginia, it was too much whiskey—in Ohio, too much whiskey—in Tennessee, it is too, too much whiskey! But I must relate an anecdote of a blind man, before I take leave of the north side of Cumberland river.

We slept, last night, about ten miles north of Nashville. When we stopped at the stile in order to dismount, we observed a gentleman of middle age and decent dress, standing in the yard with a cane in his hand, apparently giving direction to a servant, who was feeding cattle: as soon as we stopped our horses, he pointed his cane towards us and told the servant to go and take those horses. When we had crossed the stile, this gentleman saluted us very politely, and asked us to walk into the house. After giving directions relative to our horses, he also came in, took a seat, and entered into conversation with us. It was now dark. Some men, whom we found there, when we stopped, asked "how much is there to pay?" The landlord, who was no other than the gentleman whom we first saw in the yard, told them the amount; they gave him some money, and he walked to his desk, took out the requisite change, and gave it to them. He then walked out of doors, was gone sometime, returned, took a chair, sat down by the fire, and continued to converse with us till bed-time. But gess my astonishment, upon being informed, that this man was totally blind! and had not distinguished day from night for ten years. His wife, who is one of the finest women I have seen, says, that most travellers who spend the night there, go away without discovering that he is blind—that he could change specie to any amount correctly, but in changing notes, or bills, she had to tell him the amount of the bills.

Nashville is principally built of bricks, and is very handsome, and does much business. In size it is nearly as large as Lexington. It commands a handsome view, both of the river and of a beautiful cedar grove, which is rendered more beautiful by art, being trimmed and cut into cones and pyramids. The citizens of Nashville in their dress and manners exhibit much taste and opulence. About ten years ago cotton was raised in this part of Tennessee in considerable quantities, an acre of ground yielding from ten to fifteen hundred pounds;

but strange as it may seem, it does not succeed here now. It grows as high as ever, but will not open. This defect is said to be owing to the seasons growing colder.

I am sorry I am obliged to leave Nashville so soon; were it not for this I might write you again from this place. Take care of your health, and take care of Tray.[13]

Yours, &c.

Letter IX.

19th December, 1817.

Dear Matt,

AFTER LIMPING along about fourteen miles from Nashville, I was compelled to stop, my saddle horse being foundered; and here I am left alone, and *more*—but no matter! All things happen for the best. I will try to beguile the time in amusing myself with "mine host" and hostess, who I dare say, expect to make their Jack out of me—"Old Feginny begging!" Did you ever see one of your low-bred Virginians—I mean what we call Tuckahoe? The Blue Ridge, you know, as well as I do, separates Virginia into Eastern and Western Virginia, or Tuckahoe and Cohee.[14] Foreigners often distinguish it by the terms Old Virginia and New Virginia. In Old Virginia the lower class of citizens are the most ignorant, presumptuous people in the United States. Well, then, it was one of these bold, arrogant, ignorant, self-important, purse-proud females that constituted the character of my hostess. The old man had not made his appearance, being, as she said, out in the field to look after his hands, (meaning his slaves) for he is rich. My landlady is not homely: she is about forty, low, corpulent, and has a countenance that sets one at defiance. She was all bluster, bustle and anxiety, as if she actually intended to give the lie to the old proverb, that "Rome was not built in a day." She would go out, come in, sit down, get up, and walk to the door and call as loud as if the house were on fire—"Luke, an't you done totin them taters yet?—I 'spose you at the fire again. Sal, you brush them tables off, you hear; take up them ashes, you hear: make up a good fire, you hear[15] An't Rich'd come with some good water yet? Tha, now, you dun it! What's that? [A servant girl had broken a glass—the landlady runs to see.]—Well, my lady, nev'r mind, I'll pay you fow that—pick um up."

In the midst of the scrape a lad came in, who, it seems, was the landlady's son, and had just returned from one of the neighbors. "Well! is it true, that—massey upon me, I bin so hurried I an't had time to pull off my night-cap to-day!—Yond's the old black ho's come up. Sal, go and put him in the stable, and give him some con[corn.] Is it true that Billy's married shoo nuff?" [sure enough.] "Yes!" drones out the boy, no way concerned for his mother's flurries, nor for the passion it was about to throw her into. "Well, now, did every any body hear the match o' that. Go and tell your daddy to come here. I reckon he'll make him pay the ten dollars he borrowed —he shall smack him with a wan't, [warrant] this very night! Well, it doesn't signify, the sharance some people have. I've wocked [worked] hard for my 'state—but yonders your daddy and Betsy too."

The landlord entered. He was one of your tall, dark-skinned, smooth-tongued, sly-looking fellows, that manage matters softly; and quite as low-bred as his spouse. "Fine spot of work! Billy's married, shoo nuff!" Betsy, an awkward lump of mortality, apparently about seventeen strode across the room to dispose of her bonnet; and finding a stranger in the house, she frisked back, and began to adjust her Feginny cloth dress. Not so, the old lady; but before she opened the flood-gate of her tongue, I made my escape to my chamber. The apartment, however, being on the same floor, I heard the whole lecture distinctly, like a torrent, over whelming the new married pair. You know how quick those negro-raised Tuckahoes speak: just so did she, never finishing one sentence before she began another.

"Well, it's just as I thought. Wha-t," says the old man? "Oh, it's a fact—John seed'um together." "I wish," replied the wife, "I may never stir, if he oughten to be hanged. I wish I may die!—a good-for-nothing, stinking, lazy—I 'spose you'll lend him ten dollars again. I bound 'twas to pay for his license—well, it don't signify; you will fool away all your 'state—I'd put him in jail, this very night, before he sleeps, that I would. I'll tell him a piece of my mind. Nev'r mind! fa' to have the inshoince to cote [court] my gal! This comes o' larnin gals to write! A darter o' mine shouldn't lan to write, to save her life!—Nev'r mind—I 'spose he thought I was sich a fool I didn't know what all them letters was about. Tha, now—thar's your thanks faw lett'n him eat here! And so my darter is to be scandalized by sich—."

On a sudden she stopped; but soon she exclaimed, "No! you may go some wha, else—I takes so *sich* trash as you is, into my house!" The person, whom she addressed, was a female, who spoke so low that I could not distinguish her words clearly. It was a bitter cold evening; the sun was setting; and I framed an excuse of asking for water, to go into the apartment to ascertain whether she was such a savage as to turn the woman out of doors. When I entered the apartment, I beheld a poor, but decent-looking woman, with a child in her arms, standing in the door—the wretch had not asked her to the fire, nor offered her a seat. Poor woman! thought I, you have happened to fall in here in a bad time. I ventured to soften the brute of a landlady, and expostulated with her very mildly upon the cruelty of turning a fellow-creature out of doors on such a night! The poor woman turned her eyes upo me in grateful silence. It came into my head to try the effect of money upon this she-imp. I offered to pay her double the poor woman's expenses—but no! oceans of grace would not melt *her* heart to pity. I might as well have attempted to stop the mouth of a roaring lion as to soften her more than savage heart. "Let her go long, wha ever she's goin—I 'spose she's bin with the sojers: how came she by herself? I'm not goin to have my house scandalized by no sich trash—I got nuff of um last fall, stopp'n here; and when I come to find out, nothin 'tall but strumpits come from camp. I 'spose you the same—so you may clear yourself."

The poor woman, during this speech, was struggling to suppress the big tear, which, in spite of her efforts, rolled down her cheeks—she was alone, on foot, and carrying a child. I asked her how far she had to travel. She answered, that she believed it was fifteen miles; that she was going to see her husband, who was lying sick on the road; and that he was returning home from New Orleans, when he was taken so ill he could travel no farther. I endeavored to comfort her, giving her a trifle at the same time. The sun was now in the horizon, and I told her she had better proceed, lest night should overtake her, since the landlord said the nearest house was two miles distant. "It's not a great distance," said I; "keep a good heart—it cannot be possible that there are many such people as these," darting a look of contempt at the landlord at the same time, who must be a pusillanimous wretch to suffer his wife to usurp his prerogatives to the great dishonor of his head and heart. The woman departed. Had my horse been able to travel, I could willingly have left this house with her, sought another lodging. I stood in the door looking after her and for some minutes. To that God, "who tempers the wind to the shorn lamb"—even to him, who says to the wicked thus far shalt thou go, and no farther, did I breathe a supplication in behalf of this distressed female.

Adieu.

Letter X.

19th December, 1817.

Dear Matt,

I HAD BEEN in my apartment but a short time when I was called to supper, which was excellent, considering the eternal clatter of this woman's tongue. I was silent, all her obsolete politeness notwithstanding; and, it was "would I be *hope* to this, and would I be *hope* to that?" During our repast, I showed, by my looks, as much as possible, my abhorrence of her conduct; and the moment I had finished my supper, I retreated once more to my chamber. I called for more wood and stirred up my fire; and having given orders relative to my horse and dismissed my servant, I fell into the following train of reflections on the nature and character of woman! "Yes, I knew that would come next," you will say. Very well; you guessed right, for once.

It is said that woman is the last—best—gift of the Creator. She is celebrated by poets—praised by historians—extolled by travellers—and by all authors, both ancient and modern, is allowed to excell the other in every virtue that dwells in the human heart. Women are renowned for wit, learning, taste, and talents. Park, Ledyard, Weld, Liancourt, and many others, have proclaimed aloud to the world the obligations they are under to women, who at the hazard of their lives flew to their assistance in the hour of danger.[16] When abondoned to despair, afflicted with disease, famine, and in death—woman, "lovely woman," stood before them; and, like an angel, dispelled their fears, relieved their wants, and soothed their sorrows. The Duke of Liancourt, who narrowly escaped the guillotine in France, and who owed his life to the friendship of a woman, has drawn their character with a master's hand. "Their friendship," he says, "is inviolable, their fidelity unshaken, their courage invincible. They are intimidated by no difficulty, and bid defiance to dangers. Amiable woman! When man desponds, she animates him with new hopes—when he is sick, she ministers unto him—when in distress, she comforts him, bids him live, and makes him in love with himself. And well can she soothe and comfort him: she is all patience, she is all fortitude. The endearment of her smiles, the melting accents of her voice, and her bewitching softness, beguile him of his sorrows and makes his prison a palace!" In short, it would be endless to enumerate examples of that decided superiority of women over men in acts of benevolence.

But, fair and softly—who are the objects of this divine excellence?—Man—*not* woman—not their own helpless, friendless, cheerless, forlorn sex—but *men*, who by their nature and constitutions are every way better calculated to bear misfortunes. "But this preference, which is manifested towards man, almost to the exclusion of their own sex in redressing their grievances, is founded in nature, from which they cannot deviate." I admit it—I make every allowance for that immutable law that pervades the material world. I would not dissolve it if I could, and particularly that mutual predilection that the sexes have for each other, independently of moral obligation. In my judgment it is the basis of all our social happiness. The result, then, from this view of the case is, that this irrisistable influence, flowing from necessity, reflects neither praise nor blame on the female character. But does it follow that this impulse, which discovers itself in acts of such noble generosity towards men, should dispose them to a contrary course of conduct towards their own sex? I presume not. At most, it leaves them free to avoid doing them harm. If they choose not to relieve their sufferings, they could pass on as the Priest and the Levite did of old.—But no—cruel woman does not imitate those holy men, and much less the good Samaritan. When woman is the subject—woman is all hostility, either directly or indirectly, in public, in private, in adversity, in prosperity, in the palace, in the cottage; in all alike a deep rooted malignity seem to prevail! In the most civilized nations, in the most civilized age, in the most polished circles of society, history affords us a lamentable evidence that the *general* tenor of woman to her own sex, is envious, deceitful, malicious, haughty, bitter, insolent, revengeful, treacherous, implacable, However specious they may carry themselves, while in each other's presence, no sooner do they turn their backs, than *most* of them indulge more or less in some species of detraction, from the sly insidious hint to broad assertion.

I never in my life witnessed an assembly of women, great or small, but indulged in that most hateful of all vices, slander against her own sex!

What a picture you will say of woman—yet my dear sir, all this your candor will admit![17]

Were you *not* present once when the news of the unfortunate ______ ______ was announced?—I think you were. It was then you saw the true character of woman. It is needless to repeat the peals of artillery discharged from their tongues upon the unfortunate. I recollect well, and so might you, the whole posse, with rage (instead of pity for the frailty of the sex) in their looks; they hunted down their prey, more like blood hounds than human beings, and the forlorn sufferer was spurned from society! This is a pretty general case.

Whither was this unfortunate to go?—seduced!—betrayed!—abandoned!—by whom?—By man—by man who was designed to protect her. Inhuman villain! He robbed her of that "which not inriches him, and makes her poor indeed." Poor, forlorn, and friendless as thou art, thou needest not go to thy own sex for shelter. As well might thou apply to the savage beasts of prey—What then?—Go to man?—O no. He is the cause of all thy wo! An outcast must thou roam, unpitied and forgot.

All this time not a word of reproach is uttered against the

seducer: This is strange. "But he is a wicked profligate, unworthy of respect, and ought to be banished society." No such thing!! He is received into company—he is invited to all our parties!—Nay, he is a *greater* favorite than ever with the ladies. Oh, fie! not for his virtue I presume; but for what all thinking people will concur in, viz: a similarity of taste—depravity of heart—and, above all, that secret something which is paramount to all motives and resists education.

But I deny that this innate principle, which is involuntary, acts as an incentive to cruelty to their own sex, which is voluntary. Does it bind them hand and foot? Does it control the faculties of the mind? Thousands of females come to a miserable end, not by the cruelty of man, but by the savageness of their own sex. These unhappy sufferers, without house or home!—without friends!—destitute!—driven out from society!—doomed to roam through winter's storms!—perhaps without clothes to put on or bread to eat! I weep for you!—it is all I can do! May the God of mercy have mercy on you. Long, long, heavily will ye have to suffer in a world where repentance is vain! Your sorrows are without hope!!!

But you will say, what would I have ladies to do? Take such persons into their houses, associate with them? They would be thought no better[18]—"Every one is known by their company." Yes—if they repent, I would not only take them into my house, but into my bosom. I would wipe the tears from their eyes—I would soothe their sorrows, and support them in the trying hour; I would divide my last morsel with them!!

For those who would not repent,—if they were hungry I would feed them; if they were naked, I would clothe them; and much more, if they were sick, would I minister unto them; I would admonish them, and I would then have done. What did our Saviour? I would not revile them; I would not persecute them. Good night! I beg pardon, once more, for troubling you with a long letter. I was led on by my feelings.

Letter XI.

Reynolds' Tavern, 21st Dec. 1817.

Dear Matt,

I FOUND my horse better this morning, and with no other company than my servant, I bade my entertainers adieu. The family, when I left them, were preparing to attend preaching—for with all the old lady's good qualities, she is in the Church! None attending it but the mother and her daughter! Mighty good Christians, thought I. Of what denomination, I inquired? A Methodist. I suspect that one of the same is here now, a guest, with two others beside myself. The Inn is kept by Mr. Reynolds, and looks very well.

The parson looks very holy; sighs very often and loud; so there is no mistake. His dress is a black, sleek, broadcloth coat, blue pantaloons and vest, with short skirts (domestic;) his cravat is white, and tied on very closely. He is about the middle size, young, ignorant, and very important. He scarcely deigns to cast a look at us, poor sinners; and when he does, he withdraws his eyes with conscious triumph! The other guests are a good natured Yankee pedlar, and a gentleman of genteel appearance. I shall let them rest till after supper.—I promise myself much amusement with the parson and the pedlar.

Prepared with my pencil, I waited some time: nothing to do—all set mute. At length the pedlar, throwing his sparkling black eyes around upon the company, addressed his holyness with, "be you travelling Mister?" The parson, turning his gloomy face towards the speaker, as if his immaculate purity was now about to be tarnished by this vile pedlar, answered him with a look of contempt; and after an interval of some seconds, he said, "I am travelling the *circuit*."[19] "I guess, if you travels the *circle* I bin, you'll have bad travelin on't," said the pedlar. The third gentleman whose name, I find is K——, asked, if "the road was worse towards Huntsville?"—"I guess you'l find purty much so—tarnation swamps and cedars and mud, takes one a'most up to hub sinkin into that are mire grounds 'tall most killed my cattle.[20] I guess if I gets to hum agin I'll stay there." "Have you made good sales, sir," said the gentleman." "I guess I'll spend more 'an I makes—knows no more a tin ware in that are Huntsville than if they had no sense; guess they'll know more on't when I tak't to 'um."

While he was speaking, the hostler made his appearance to know how much oats each traveller wished to give his horse. The pedlar was the first to reply. He said, he "won to have his horses have two gallon a piece" "I have fed yours, sir." "You hadn't ought to fed 'um; I guess you'll gi'um too much."

It appeared the pedlar was direct from Huntsville, and had put up for the night long before I arrived. Mr. K. is travelling that way, and so also is the preacher. The preacher, I suspect, thought the Yankee below him, (but so thought not I,) and Mr. K. above him. I made some remarks on the country, addressed to Mr. K. who is a man of intelligence. We descanted upon the progress of society, agriculture, &c.

Supper being over, Mr. K. and myself dipped a little into the sciences, merely from mutual curiosity. Could we have drawn the pedlar and the preacher in, it would have been worth repeating; but, as you hate *learning* (and so do I, between familiar friends,) I pass it over.

The people generally, through this state, so far, are about the middle grade as to information. If you ask how far it is to the next house?—"Well, I don't know"—Does such a man live on the road? "Well he does." They have the "*well*" to every thing, just as they do with us. There are a great many Methodists in Tennessee, and in the new settled part of Kentucky.[21] I have frequently seen them, and *heard* them, as I rode through the country. It is strange to observe how their preachers draw the women after them.

Yours, &c.

Letter XII.

21st December, 1817.

Dear Matt,

In my last, I forgot to inform you we passed the woman on the road who was turned out of doors. She informed me, that after walking two miles, she obtained lodging, but with difficulty. She had overtaken a wagon on the road, and was riding in it when I passed her, yesterday, about twelve o'clock. The story she related I found was correct, having passed the house, to day, where her husband was confined. But, alas! no wife, nor home, nor children, will he *ever see more—He is dead!* I slept last night in a room adjoining to the one occupied by the preacher mentioned in my last; and, whether sitting up or in bed, I could not ascertain, but a long dialogue passed between him and some other person. This person was a man, I think one of the neighbors, as one came in after dark, who called the preacher *Brother*,—the person, whoever it was, was likely to bring disgrace on the *church*, in violating some of the rules, by intemperance, and something worse: the man spoke so low that I could hear but a word now and then.

Preacher. But you bring reproach on God's people, brother; you ought to be holy and blameless before God; you ought to take up the cross, brother, and deny yourself the things of the world, the pleasures of the world, and the sins of the world, and the e—vils that are in this wicked world; walking in all holiness before Go—d and his holy angels, and blameless and ho—ly.

Neighbor. But, brother, I am tried. [A groan.]

Preacher. Brother, they tell me, that you will drink a little too much.

Neighbor. Brother, I only got a little lively at brother I's shucking; and brother W. were there, and brother D. was there, and brother S. and I thought no harm, and it was a cold night, an' we all drank a little—No, what makes um parsecute me above the rest—I didn't take but three drams since; and because I happen to stump my toe against a little bit of a stump and fell down it was norated over the whole country. [You see he is a little bit of an Irishman.]

Preacher. Oh, brother, you have hurt the cause of God. I hear you have ruined one of the prettiest sisters; that she is with ——— by you. This is wicked.

Neighbor. Oh! brother, it's all a flam. Do you think I would offer to go and be guilty of the like—and what if I did talk to her about the state of her precious soul—sure where's the harm? [The conversation at this part of the story I was unable to hear, except now and then a groan.]

Preacher. Brother, you ought to pray to the Lord to strengthen you, that the d——l may have no power over you while you are travelling through this vale of sorrow and temptations; and ———

Neighbor. Now I'll jist tell you the naked truth, brother, before God, and I've prayed nightly to him—with wrestling, sare wrestling have I wrestled in prayer, that he would save me from sin, and forgive me. Now, this here is the truth—I was jist walking along, not thinking—well, I hope the Lord will forgive me; but as I was saying, I was going to brother Wilson's to see if he had any work for to do; for you know, brother, that Saint Paul labored with his hands. Well, who should I meet, right in the road, walking the self-same way that I was going myself—you may be sure, that auld sarpent, who is always troubling God's people, begun for to tempt me. But, as I was saying, who should I meet, but sister ———. Good morning sister, sez I; good morning brother, sez she: and so we fell to talking about the things that God had done for us, in shedding abroad his love in our hearts—in saving our immortal souls from sin. I sez to her, sez I, sister, how is the state of your precious soul, to day?—Oh, brother, sez she, I feel bound for glory; and so—but the devil put it into my head, I'm sure———. [The rest was spoken low for some time.] And so, we talked about the things of God, till we got very happy.

Preacher. O! brother, you ought to pray to God for that sin, that doth so easily beset you. You have wrought evil in Israel. [The rest past in whispers, and I fell asleep.]

A Preacher here again as I hope to live! The people must be very pious in this place—and he is going to preach too. Here is the house filling fast; great many women—few men—and I shall put this away and join them in worship. I shall leave my prejudice behind with my pen, ink, and paper. Be he Jew or Turk, fool or fanatic, I care not. In the firm belief, that the worship of God is paramount to all other duties, I spurn the narrow mind, which is attached to a sect or party, to the exclusion of the rest of mankind. Can *I* not implore the Divine mercy? Can I not praise that fountain of all excellence, as sincerely with these people as with others?—You may laugh, and think I am jesting; but, I assure you, my friend, I am serious. I am far from being among the number of those, who set at nought the worship of the Deity, however I may deplore the abominable prostitution of that religion which is pure and undefiled. Go thou and do likewise.

Yours, &c.

Letter XIII.

Fayetteville,[22] Tenn. Dec. 22d, 1817.

Dear Matt,

I REMEMBER when you and I, sitting by my fire-side, in that easy familiar frankness, indulged in our remarks on Priests—that they are always the same, let them be of what persuasion they may. I retain that opinion still! Hitherto I have only learned mankind in theory—but I am now studying him in practice. One learns more in a day, by mixing with mankind, than he can in an age shut up in a closet.

But the Priests, I perceive, are precisely the same they were centuries passed—they all aim at power. Their drift, I see, is to gain as many proselytes as possible, without regard to the *conduct* of their flock—they will not suffer them to possess any will of their own—perfect despots. No potentate is more despotic, and no subjects more submissive, whilst in the presence of their Priests, but the greatest rogues in the world when out of sight. I perceive, too, they are very jealous in controversy. They seem to me as though they would fight in defence of their principles, while they leave the practice of religion to the sinners who make no fuss at all about religion. —Between you and I, Matt, this world is most abominably wicked. I have seen such sights—nothing but preaching and praying—and not one to relieve the poor. No! not one steps forward. Can this be Christianity?

Christ says, if you love me, keep my commandments—and this is my commandment—that you love one another. This was our preacher's text last night. I should like to have this text indemnified for the depredation committed on it by his Reverence. His discourse was nothing but a hop, skip, and jump—from one thing to another. Nothing but "hardened sinners you will go to hell and be d——d." Why, the man swore outright. "The wickedness of this world; and the pleasures of this world; and the temptations of this world." *Mem!* thought of the affair of "Brother," the Irishman, and his devout sister.

Now for the righteous: "Press on ye mourners to the end, and—to that glo—riuns [loud as a trumpet] place, prepar—ed for you," &c. &c. He stamped—he roared! Not a word on the subject of love to our neighbors.

I never but once in my life heard a sermon to please me;

and that was preached by a Mr. Sargent, sometime of Ohio.—But this preacher (as he is called) poured out a torrent of nonsense. The men groaned—the young ladies cried—the louder the preacher bawled, the louder they cried—at last they screamed!—Did you ever hear wolves howl? It was more like their howling than any thing else I can name. Is *this* religion? These would, like their sister, turn the poor friendless females from their door. But let facts speak. A gentleman removed to this country last year. He came on sometime before his family, in order to engage provisions for their arrival. Through some oversight, he forgot his money. The neighborhood consisted chiefly of professors of religion. He went to a man, who, as he was told, had a large quantity of bacon and corn for sale, and withal was very religious. He told him his situation: that he had a large family, both black and white, coming on, and he wished to purchase provisions sufficient for them till he could raise a crop; and that, when his family arrived, he would pay him. No!—He would not trust him. The applicant went to another and another, and still received the same answer. Thus discouraged, he at length inquired for the wickedest man in the neighborhood. He was told where to find him. He went to him, and related his situation, and what he wanted. "There," said this *wicked* man, without any hesitation or inquiry, "there is my *crib*, and there is my *smoke house;* use them as your own, whilst their contents last." Which of all these was neighbor to him, who fell among—thieves, I might say.

Yours, &c.

Letter XIV.

Well's Tavern,
5 miles South of Fayetteville, 23d Dec. 1817.

Dear Matt,

I AM now within a short day's ride of Huntsville. I have travelled slow, on account of my horses, the roads being deep and heavy, such as the pedlar described them. The *cane* has made its appearance for some days past, and my servant has been breaking whole arm's full of pipe stems, and throwing them away alternately, as he finds they increase without end. Having never witnessed the growth of the cane before, I was much gratified to meet with it. It first appears scattering, very *slender*, but tall, from eight to twelve feet high. It has blades like Indian corn, and some resemblance of a tassel on the top. It grows every where through the woods; but, as you proceed, it is larger and higher, and *tons* of it lie on the ground, on each side of the road, broken to pieces and rotting; and where this is the case, the green cane is extinct forever, doubtless. The cause of this I cannot learn. *These* stalks are larger than corn stalks, and must have been twenty feet in height![23]

The land increases in fertility as we advance; and this fertility extends a vast distance on each side of us. The land at this place, and Fayetteville, resembles that north of the Cumberland, as black as your hat, and level.

I have travelld a south course since I left Nashville, from which Huntsville is distant 100 miles. Pony, (15 hands high!) is a horse of great patience and slow to anger, or he would have testified his displeasure at this same road: but he tugs along without a murmur. We are now to have a change for the better.

This inn is kept by a bachelor. His mother lives with him, and attends to the cooking department. The tavern is a separate building from the one occupied by the old lady, which is also the kitchen. I was shown into the latter by the landlord, and was pleased to find the house large, neat, and warm; but the lady looked old, cold, and crusty. Being very hungry, (not having dined,) my appetite was no little increased by the savory smell of bacon and cabbage, which Mrs. W. had sitting by her, very snug in the corner, for the family dinner.

I knew from her looks, it would be a cross and pile chance whether she would condescend to set a part of it on the table for me till she saw her own time. But, setting my wits to work,

I prevailed finally, and made a hearty meal, cunningly, by the fire.

There were two good beds, with curtains, in the room, and being weary, my next court to Mrs. Wells was, for liberty to repose on one of the beds: this was also granted. Thus every wish was gratified. Upon inquiry, I learned that the guests, should any arrive, dined in the kitchen, or what you choose to denominate it. Night was drawing on, and I was quite delighted with a place of concealment, should travellers arrive; and, drawing the curtains of a princely bed close, I lay still and snug out of sight.

It was hog-killing day at Wells', and dinner was delayed till the business was over, and the table was sitting for dinner as I lay down, when, as I expected, word came "that two travellers had arrived and wanted supper." The lady returned for answer, "that the table was setting for her own family, and if they thought proper to accept of such fare as she had ready, they were welcome, but that she would prepare nothing more to-night." The Negro woman, who was charged with the message, remonstrated with her mistress, and said "coffee, or tea, ought to be made." "No, I will make none to night; if they don't eat such as there is, they may go without." "Very well!" replied the woman; "you may do as you please, but I know, very well, Massa Tommy won't like it." "Who cares for your Massa Tommy, or you either," said Mrs. W. Accordingly, the bacon and cabbage was placed on the table, with milk, in tin cups—plenty of corn bread—a small plate of butter, and all placed upon a table hard by your humble servant.

Highly delighted with my situation, ensconsed behind the curtains, I awaited the entrance of Mr. Tommy and the travellers. The candle was lit, and our guests summoned to supper. I took a sly peep at them as they were sitting down. One was lame, and a small man, but had a genteel and manly appearance; the other was still less, with a small sallow face and a perfect dandy, or fop, who looked over the table with sovereign contempt.—Mean time the genteel looking man asked if he should help him? The fop hung back some time, but at last said, "yes, sah," [sir,] a Tuckahoe, by the way [a citizen of Virginia, below the Blue Ridge.] This was nuts for me. Tommy, who had likewise taken a seat, paid no attention to the strangers. He was a good looking man, rather swarthy, and about forty years of age.

After eating some time, the little Tuckahoe erected himself on his seat, and observed, without addressing any one in particular, "I believe you have no tea, no coffee in this country." The old lady, with great composure replied, "sometimes," "You dosen't have any flower hea' neither." The lady sung out "sometimes," again. "I b'lieve you' all savages in this country." "Savage enough," said the lady quite in a good humour. Both gentlemen sat in my view, and the face of the other gentleman colored deep at foppy's remarks; who asked, with great spirit, "what country may you call yours, sir?" "I *ar* from Norfolk, Virginny, su'!"[24] "And how do they live there?" "Why, su', they live, su', like gentlemen, su'; I hasn't seen a bit of victuals fit to eat since I left Norfolk, except in Nashville." "That is a great pity, sir," said the other. "But we, of this country, do not rate ourselves by eating: we rate ourselves by fighting. Would you like to take a shot?"

Yours, &c.

Letter XV.

Huntsville, December 24th, 1817.

Dear Matt,

HERE I AM, landed safe and sound, and in high spirits. This will go by the same mail with yesterday's adventures. I broke off short last night, being sleepy: but, taking up the subject—The little man dropped his feathers quite low, upon the departure of his friend, who, immediately arose and walked out of the house. The Tuckahoe, after asking the girl for mo' milk, and mincing awhile, left the table likewise, and walked into the tavern. Had the latter as much spunk as he had impudence, they certainly would have fought—but I heard no more of it. The old lady said, "if my Billy had been at home he would have slapped his jaws."

This morning very early, upon sallying forth, I found my little fop inquiring for his *mar*, [mare,] and it was laughable enough to hear him insist upon sending his *mar* to water, the very self-same way we were going. "I always has my mar *wartered* befo' I starts."

They were both going to Huntsville, where the fighting gentleman lived, as I found in the course of the day. We will have a merry time of it, thought I; and, taking leave, we all set out.

Having every prospect of a rainy day, we whipped on pretty brisk. I found the land high and dry after leaving Wells', and another change in the growth, which is very light, and in many places none at all. The land is of a redish black, light as ashes, and very rich.

I attached myself to the Tennesseean, (he of Huntsville,) being pleased with his manners, and, above all, with his spirit. He related many anecdotes of the recent battles, and was very communicative on the situation and prospects of the territory.[25]

We had taken up more company, and at length the conversation turned on the renown of General Jackson. My little Tuckahoe, not pleased that he was overlooked in the conversation, would some times be alongside, often before, but never behind. His hat stuck on the top of his head, to the hazard of falling off. He twisted and turned, his head now on one shoulder, and now on the other; and again elevated, and next bending forward to look at his stirrups. Finding all his evolutions failed to attract attention, after displaying all his fine parts, and the fine parts of his *mar*, he could brook the indignation no longer.— "By G——d, I suppose, you think General Jackson is a G——d almighty about here." "By G——d, sir, I think he is next to him," said the Huntsville man; "and none but a d——d fool would have made the remark." Now thought I, they will fight. "You, nor no other man, Sir, shall speak disrespectfully of General Jackson, in my presence." This spirited reply, rather cooled the little gentleman's *ire*. He ventured, however, to draw a comparison in favor of General Washington. The other said he "was disposed to acknowledge all possible praise to General Washington, but, at the same time, Sir, the man who dares to impugn the name of Jackson in my presence, does it at his peril." I begged the gentleman to resume his good humour, and turn the little gentleman over to me. Thus he fell out of the pan into the fire. "That ar a fine mar of yours, Mr. Jones," said I, that being his name. "How far have she toted you?" "She have toted me a thousand miles, and she could a toted me a thousand miles mo'." I then inquired after the lobster family, at Norfolk; said I understood "they were a numerous and respectable family." "Humph!" he replied. "I ar astonished to hear some folks talk: the lobsters ar a fish."[26] Thus, I continued to torment him, to the great amusement of the party. He had the only umbrella in company, and the Huntsville gentleman, who could scarcely sit on his horse for laughing, asked, "if he would not compromise with the lady, by giving her the umbrella?" which I would not accept, though it rained moderately fast. He had the most scornful lip I ever beheld.

The cotton fields now began to appear. These are astonishingly large; from four to five hundred acres in a field!—It is without a parallel! Fancy is inadequate to conceive a prospect more grand! The cotton, as it now stands, has the appearance of buckwheat when ripe, being divested of the cotton, (as my friend informed me,) which is picked out. Although the land is level, you cannot see the end of the fields either way. To a stranger, coming suddenly amongst these fields, it has the appearance of magic. He is lost in wonder, and nothing but the evidence of his senses can persuade him it is reality. In laboring to do this, I was forced to abandon my ideas of human industry, which I could not accommodate to this novel appearance.[27]

We arrived in Huntsville about 2 o'clock, P.M. and met another wonder at the entrance of the town, which was one of the great cotton machines.

Yours, &c.

Letter XVI.

Huntsville, December 25th, 1817.

Dear Matt,

A MERRY Christmas to you, in the first place. I was saluted by a few guns, last evening, which reminded me of old times.

The face of the country has changed five times in my tour! From Big Sandy River (the boundary of Kentucky and Virginia) to Mount Sterling, the soil is black, firm, uneven, and covered with heavy timber, beach and oak principally.

From Mount Sterling to Danville, called first rate land, it is generally black as your hat, but in many places, for instance on the margin of creeks, it has a grayish color, and resembles calcined stone, and has a light crumbling appearance; the growth is locust, cherry, and walnut; very low, as I remarked before. I do not think it produces better than Kenhawa bottom. It is well watered. Some of the farms are wretchedly managed. I was told these were the School lands.[28]

Upon leaving Danville, a very handsome little town, the

timber gradually diminishes, and you are soon in the barrens, and the soil changes to a redish, or chocolate color, and very little water: but the land is rich and level. I forgot to inform you that I met with Mrs. Madison, the celebrated Patrick Henry's sister. She has removed to the barrens, and has an excellent farm. I dined at her house. She has two sons who live with her, both single; also, a grand daughter. She is quite an active woman, and very little inferior, it is said, to her brother, in mental powers. Seeing a house on the road, some distance ahead, I sent my servant forward to bespeak breakfast, concluding it was a tavern. When I rode up, what was my surprise to find Mrs. Madison, who formerly lived in the same county I did.[29] I was invited in; but my companions, finding it was a private house, rode on. But to return:—these barrens have no timber but black Jack. They continue to Red river, in Tennessee, one hundred miles. They are not a dead, or prairie like level, but rather waving.

Next to this comes on the lofty timbered black rich soil, and large grape vines, and continues to Nashville. Upon leaving Nashville, the red cedar begins, and though the land is still rich, it is much interrupted with swamps and stones. This is well watered. This description continues to Fayetteville, on Elk river, near the southern boundary of the state. There again we have the black loam and heavy timber, till, within eighteen miles of Huntsville, when the chocolate land comes again, like the barrens; though light, it is not destitute of timber; but water is very scarce; many have to haul the water three miles in summer.

All these varieties of land extends from the mountains, on the left, to the Ohio river on the right.

We forded all the rivers in Kentucky and Tennessee, excepting Kentucky river, which is very often forded.

The Kentuckyans are the handsomest people, by far, in the United States. They are not only stout men, but have fine features, and very beautiful complexions.

The Tennesseeans are not so stout as the Kentuckyans, nor so fair, but they are well shaped, and more active. There is a native bold independence in both, with this difference—the Kentuckyans are great brags, whilst the Tennesseeans, equally brave and gallant, are wholly unconscious of those virtues. The Kentuckyan is rash and hot headed—the Tennesseean is cool and steady. The Kentuckyan is froward and assuming—the Tennesseean is modest and retiring. There is an independence, even in the children, which is neither awed by fear nor won by love. But what astonished me was their careless indifference on the subject of their late gallant achievements, particularly at New Orleans. They spoke of it with perfect unconcern, and only mentioned it when applied to, and then with not half the same interest they would on the subject of hunting or killing a deer. Not so the Kentuckyans: they appreciate their bravery in its widest extent. Nor are the Tennesseeans so distinguished as the former for industry, or the art of acquiring wealth; though both are great jockeys.

The Kentucky ladies are very large, but are fair and well featured, and much more polished (excepting the ladies of Nashville) than the ladies of Tennessee: but the latter are better shaped; are very artless; and the young women have a sweet simplicity in their looks and countenance. Both men and women are without disguise, nor have they any of that impertinent curiosity common to other states; I mean that of teazing travellers. But the most distinguishing trait of a Tennesseean is, that he treats all men alike–the Nabob, with his splendid equipage, receives no more, nor as much attention, as the pedestrian. They are extremely jealous of wealthy, or what we call big, men. One of them, as I came on, being asked rather peremptorily, by one of the big bugs to rub down his horse, cursed him, and told him to "do it yourself—I am no man's servant." He then offered money and apoligized; but the brave Tennesseean was not to be hired.

Yours, &c.

Letter XVII.

Huntsville, January 1st, 1818.

Dear Matt,

Now HERE is the twentieth[30a] letter I have written, without receiving an answer to one of them, until to-day—and that is no answer I may say. What are you about? Have you got the blues again, or blacks; or are you in love? I have been thinking that your complaint is altogether a love matter—I am told it has that effect sometimes. Should that be the case, you had better apply to *Dr. Matrimony* at once, as delays are dangerous. Cupid is a cunning rogue—very likely he has given you a sly shot in your *sleep*.

But seriously, I am sorry to hear you mend so slow. I am convinced this climate would restore you. It is summer here, compared to our country: the trees, many of them, are still green.

HUNTSVILLE. You will expect something of this flourishing town.[30b] It takes its name from a man called Captain Hunt, who built the first cabin on the spot, where the Court House now stands, in 1802. In front of this cabin, which was built on a high bluff, there was a large pond, which is now nearly filled up by the citizens. Captain Hunt cleared a small field west of his cabin, the same year. This was between his cabin and the Huntsville Spring. He spent much of his time in wageing war with the rattlesnakes, who were very numerous in his day, and had entire possession of the Bluff at the Spring. Thousands of them, it appears, were lodged amongst the rocks, and the Captain would shoot hundreds of a day, by thrusting long canes filled with powder, into the scissures of the rocks.[31]

Whether Hunt, or the snakes acquired the victory, I have not heard, as he was compelled to abandon his settlement to a more successful rival, who purchased the land. This was

Colonel L. Pope, who, in company with Dr. Maning, and others, purchased the land at a Land Office opened in Nashville; and though this sale did not stand, these gentlemen at this time own vast bodies of land around Huntsville, and are the wealthiest men in the Territory. Colonel Pope, it is said, tried hard to have the name changed, to *Twickenham*, after the residence of his namesake (and from whom it is said he is descended) in England.[32] But, places, somehow or other, will retain their first names. The land around Huntsville, and the whole of Madison county,[33] of which it is the capital, is rich and beautiful as you can imagine; and the appearance of wealth would baffle belief. The town stands on elevated ground, and enjoys a beautiful prospect. It contains about 260 houses, principally built of brick; has a bank, a court house, and market house. There is a large square in the centre of the town, like the towns in Ohio, and facing this are the stores, twelve in number. These buildings form a solid wall, though divided into apartments.[34] The workmanship is the best I have seen in all the states; and several of the houses are three stories high, and very large. There is no church. The people assemble in the Court House to worship. Huntsville is settled by people mostly from Georgia and the Carolinas—though there are a few from almost every part of the world;—and the town displays much activity. The citizens are gay, polite, and hospitable, and live in great splendor. Nothing like it in our country.

Yours, &c.

Letter XVIII.

Same date.

Dear Matt,

To go on. The Huntsville Spring, is a great natural curiosity. This you, as well as myself, heard before. But I had no conception of it. It flows from under the Bluff mentioned, and forms a stream large enough for the purposes of navigation, and empties into Indian Creek, also navigable. The head of the spring is about sixty yards wide, but spreads out to a much greater length, covering about three acres of ground!!! The Bluff, at its head, forms a perpendicular of 60 or 70 feet in height, perhaps more, and is conical.

Huntsville is situated in latitude 34° 45″, 18 miles from the line of Tennessee, 100 South from Nashville, and 10 miles north of Ditto's Landing, on Tennessee river.

GENERAL COFFEE.[35] Last evening I had the pleasure of seeing this renowned soldier and companion of General Jackson. This hero, of whom you have heard so much, is upwards of six feet in height, and proportionally made. Nor did I ever see so fine a figure. He is 35 or 36 years of age. His face is round and full, and features handsome. His complexion is ruddy, though sunburnt. His hair and eyes black, and a soft serenity diffuses his countenance. His hair is carelessly thrown one side, in front, and displays one of the finest foreheads in nature—high, smoothe, and retreating. His countenance has much animation, while speaking, and his eyes sparkle; but the moment he ceases to speak, it resumes its wonted placidness, which is a characteristic of the Tennesseeans.

In General Coffee, I expected to see a stern, haughty, fierce, warrior. No such thing. You look in vain for that rapidity with which he marched and defeated the Indians at Tallashatches: nor could I trace in his countenance the swiftness of pursuit, and sudden defeat of the Indians again at Emuckfau; much less his severe conflicts at the head of his gallant men at New Orleans. He is as mild as the dew drops; but deep in his soul you see very plain that deliberate, firm, cool, and manly courage, which has covered him with glory. He must be a host when he is roused. All these Tennesseeans are mild and gentle, except they are excited, which is hard to do; but when they are once raised, it is victory or death.—General

Coffee speakes very slow, and may weigh about 200 weight. *Major Rose*, another of the heroes, is a Scotch gentleman, but a Tennessee soldier.[36] You have not to look very deep for the qualities of his mind. It is plainly depicted in his fine open countenance, and soft blue eye. He is a middle aged man, of portly size, and acted in the quartermaster's Department in the late war. This man, from the land of Wallace and Bruce, was in high favor with General Jackson; and his labors in procuring supplies for the army were unequalled by any thing in history. He rode from the seat of war to Huntsville, very often, without sleep or rest! proceeding night and day express: when one horse would give out he would press another. I am called to dinner.

Yours, &c.

Letter XIX.

Same date.

Dear Matt,

I LEFT off with Major Rose, the merriest soul in the world. He is nothing but frolic and fun. He and Mrs. Rose have often called, and nothing pleases me better than his broad Scotch face. He is a merchant, and generally drops in in the evening, to take a game of backgammon, with Talbot, the landlord. It is ludicrous enough to hear their mock quarrels, cursing each other at every word. "Tell the d——d old b——r to come in—I'll be at him, by the Lard will I. Mariah, [Miss Talbot] set away the chairs, and stir up the fire, and draw up tables, and hop round—be brisk—you will never get married while you squeeze yourself up in them d——d *coarse* setts, and stuff them pan handles down your b——."[37] This beats us all hollow, Matt. They are, however, the most generous of the human race.[38]

General Brahan, Benjamin Patterson, Esq. (the cousin of our friend,) Messrs. Reed and Cox, the latter Cashier of the Bank, and Dr. Bradford, are all the citizens I have been introduced to. General Brahan, of the late war, is a prince, in whatever light he may be viewed. He is polite and affable; of great size; handsome person; of middle age, and a man of great wealth. Mr. Reed, a merchant, is also a stout gentlemanly man, and said to be wealthy. Patterson is quite young, and one of the finest men in the world. Cox is a crusty old man, and a bachelor—but the dogs may take him for me.

I tried to see Colonel Pope, one of the first men in Madison county; but he was absent. He lives at the edge of the town.[39]

Mr. Patton, formerly of Monroe county, whom you knew well, and who set out poor, is now one of the richest men in the territory. This fortune he has acquired solely by his own industry and enterprize. Mr. Patton is much respected in Huntsville, and is the proprietor of large plantations, stock, &c.[40] Madison county alone contains more wealth than half west Virginia! But more of it when I have been longer in the country.

Yours, &c.

Letter XX.

January 3d, 1818.

Dear Matt,

NOT WILLING to break in on the thread of my journey, I send you a few particulars of Tennessee, of which you anxiously expressed a wish to be informed. I only stopped one day at Nashville, to rest, and had no opportunity to learn much of the state, though I have picked up a few anecdotes of it in this place.

I learn that, next to General Jackson, General Carroll is the idol of the people.[41] As I travelled through the state, I asked the people "what they would do when they lost General Jackson—that I supposed they would hardly fight under any other man?" They replied, "that they would almost as soon fight under General Carroll, or General Coffee." Astonishing how these men doat on their officers. It would be a serious matter to say any thing against them in this country. General Carroll, as well as General Jackson, are worshipped as Deities.

When General Carroll was descending the Mississippi with his troops, to join General Jackson at New Orleans, he used to exercise his men by moonlight on the decks of the boats, as they floated down the river, to fit them for the conflict with the British, which awaited them on their arrival. General Carroll is said to be a mild good natured man, and contributed no little to the brilliant victory of New Orleans. He commanded the centre of the American line.[42]

I understand a work is now in press, written by one of Jacksons aids, Major Eaton, in which we are to have the principal incidents of the battles, and a sketch of the principal officers.[43] For the rest, Judge Kelly,[44] Judge Haywood,[45] Felix Grundy,[46] and Counsellor Whiteside[47] are reckoned the first men in Tennessee, and rank high at the bench and the bar. Mr. Hayze,[48] whom we knew in Virginia, is tolerable hazy you know, but is much respected. He lives in Nashville, and called to see me at the inn. Grundy is said to be the first orator in Tennessee. He is a pupil of the celebrated Doctor Priestly, once President of Columbia College at Nashville.[49]

Of General Jackson, I shall say nothing till I see him, which pleasure I expect at Melton's Bluff, head of the Muscle Shoals, where I shall be in a few days.

Yours, &c.

N. B.—Do not be afraid, I will notice all the big things, and you may guess at the little ones.

Letter XXI.

Huntsville, January 4th, 1818.

Dear Matt,

AFTER PACKING UP last evening for the Bluff, I sat musing in my parlour, when all at once my ear was saluted with the sound of mirth and jollity below. Eager to learn what was going on, I descended to the parlour, and there I found the sweet girl, the grave matron, the sparkling belle, the conceited fop, the modest young gentleman, vetran soldier, and a sociable old planter. They were all talking and laughing about the gas, (all the rage,) planting cotton, courting, philosophy, biography, &c. Every one expressed themselves with freedom and good humour; but I perceived great deference was paid to the old planter, a Virginian by birth, immensely rich, and a *widower*.

I had scarcely seated myself when my landlady, a sprightly black-eyed woman, and no fool either, joked the old planter about the girls. "Poh, poh," said the planter, "I don't care a cent for the girls: why, they won't let such an old fellow come within a squirrel's jump of 'em." "But you must persevere—don't give up the ship—I'll engage you will succeed—many a girl would jump at you." "Faith, that's the greatest fault I find with them; but instead of jumping at me, they jump away; and if I offer to lay my hand on one, she runs and squalls, as though I were a robber, and were tempting her life." "But," says the sprightly Mrs. Mosely, "there you are wrong: no one offers to touch a lady in these days. I am surprised at you. When you court a girl, you must set off at a distance and talk to her; and write verses in her praise, and send them to her; the old time's fashion, when you and my mother were young people, will not do now-a-days." "The d——l it won't; then they may all die old maids for me. I tell you what,

Mrs. M., I think the *gals* was as virtuous in my young days, and may be, a little more so, than they are now—and many an arm have I laid round 'em, see." "Oh, fie! don't talk so—you will make the ladies faint. These were old times, the fashions have changed." "Faith, I believe so; but it is from good to bad. I am opposed to all these new kick-ups. Whenever I see a gal so very coy and prudish, and won't let a man come near her, it gives me a bad opinion of her; and I'll tell you why—when I was a young man, I happened to be at a ball—your mother was there too. So, there was one gal there; a m-i-g-h-t-y precise creature, and would not let me touch the tip of her finger. 'No, Sir. I d-o-n-'t d-a-n-c-e t-o-n-i-g-h-t;' and primped up and tossed her head, and cried out to a friend, sitting by her, 'how odious it was, for men to be taking hold of ladies' hands—she was surprised at my presumption;' and not long after this, this same nice lady met with a misfortune ladies, which I leave you to guess. Ever since that I marks 'em—I has my own opinion of 'em." "La, what nonsense," said the belle; "such talk *ar* quite ridiculous."

While the old planter and the ladies were conversing, Mr. Fop, and the young gentleman were engaged in an analasys of the gases. "And what is gas?" inquired Mrs. Mosely: "I hear nothing but *gas, gas, gas,* where I go—and I know no more about it than a monkey. I have asked hundreds, and either they, or I, must be fools: Not a soul that I meet can explain it in terms I can comprehend. They stuff it with such a number of outrageous hard words, that I could understand Greek sooner. Now, gentlemen, do if you please, tell me in plain words what is this gas." She looked at Mr. Fop as she spoke, who being appealed to, cocked his head, spit, and hemmed; and edging his chair towards the ladies, said: "Have you never read *Accam's* theoretical, practical, chymistry, Madam?" "No I have not," said Mrs. M. in a pet, "and I should not understand a word of it if I had. I despise your theoreticals and practicals. I understand none of your hard names. If you cannot tell me, in plain English, what gas is; where it comes from; and what it is made of; or whether made at all, or not, you need say no more. I am sick of the gases." Now thought I, I shall hear what these gases are at last. She will certainly get it out of him. "There are several sorts of gases"—"Oh, if you have more than one gas, I am sure I will never understand it, so you may stop at once—just tell me what is gas?" "Gas, Madam, is a combination of certain substances, reduced to a gaseous state, formed by adding a solvent substance, and by their joint formation." "Thank you, Sir, I have heard enough of it," said the lady, very short and illnatured. She must be one of the Honorables, as he took it all in good humour.

The old planter, who had listened attentively, said, "faith Mrs. M. this is more of your new fangled fashions, I suppose. What the d——l it means I don't know. It is like your new fashion of wooing. I mean no disparagement to you, ladies and gentlemen; but I thing the good old times were the best; and I never herd a word about *Gashes*, or what you may call it. Landlord, times are dry, hand round some wine." I was pleased to hear the order, though I could not join them, as I wished to hear the old man talk another talk.

A littl bustle succeeded, but in a short time all were seated again; when I asked Mrs. M. if she gave up the gases?—The other young gentleman blushing deeply, and regarding Mrs. M. earnestly, at first, faultering, but growing firm as he proceeded, (being very young) addressing himself to the ladies expressed himself nearly as follows: "Gas is a fluid substance, and is similar to air. It is transparent like water; and like water, elastic, forcing itself to its level. It is heavy, but invisible. It cannot be affected by cold, but can by heat. Gas exists throughout nature. There is gas, more or less, in all substances; and all gases (for as my friend said, there are several kinds of gas) are a combination of substances, such as common salt and water; to these add half their weight of sulphuric acid; heat applied to these, gas is produced, and may be collected by an instrument suited to the purpose; but to retain it, it must be placed over mercury. There is gas in all substances, and of *three* distinct kinds, viz: Oxygen, hydrogen, and nitrogen, gas. These are produced by different processes, and their properties differ: Oxygen gas, for instance, is indispensable to the respiration of animals—it is the cause of animal heat. In its artificial state, it will, when brought into contact with any combustion, burn, and emit a flame. Hydrogen gas, is what was formerly called inflammable air. Animals will die in it instantly, as they cannot breathe in it, though vegetables will grow in it. When brought in contact with atmospheric air, or what is the same thing, oxygen gas, it will burn fiercely. Nitrogen gas, in its primitive state, will *not* burn on touching combustion. In chymistry it has various uses. It is a component part of all animal substances, and communicates to them their most distinctive characters." He concluded by adding, that he "had a very limited knowledge of the gases, having but just commenced the study of chymistry, and that it was a science the most difficult of all others to explain to those who have not a practical knowledge of the same." Loud were the plaudits of the ladies; and the old planter said, "the young man must take a glass of wine with him: he spoke like a man of sense, though he (the planter) did not understand his *argufication.*" The party ended with a dance, and I retired shortly after they commenced, as I had to rise betimes.[50]

Yours, &c.[51]

Letter XXII.

Melton's Bluff, January 8th, 1818.

Dear Matt,

I WAS three days on the road to this place. Melton's Bluff[52] is at the head of Mussel Shoals. But to see more of the lands shortly to be sold, I went direct to the foot of the Shoals, 70 miles from Huntsville, crossed the river, and came up on the south side of Tennessee river. We had a soaking rain the first day, but the road was fine, the country being a level plain, and the land as rich as any in the world, doubtless, and well watered. Many houses are already built on the road side, and good entertainment. The lady, however, where we staid the first night, said it was very sickly.

The second day, towards evening, as Mr. Beech (my fellow traveller) and I were at our ease, chatting on different subjects, my servant, behind us, cried out "Looky! looky! what a great river!" We had heard a roaring sometime, and Mr. B. who was acquainted with the country, observed we could not be far from the foot of the Shoals. Upon turning our horses out of the road a few steps, we saw the river—a most sublime picture it was! That part which first burst on our view, was three miles in width! the largest body of water I ever saw. It was at this time very high and muddy; and the noise produced by the water washing over the rocks was tremendous.

We saw a boat hung on a rock, about the middle of the stream, and many persons around it on the rocks, endeavoring to get it off; the waves and white caps were dashing furiously around them; and unable even to hail them, we proceeded, being near our destination.

The sun was verging upon the horizon, while I was musing upon the fall in the river (which was evident.) Having travelled over level ground from Huntsville, we began to descend rapidly, almost a precipice, the road making a sudden bend to the left; and shortly the house, at which we were to spend the night, stood before us, on the bank of the river. But it here flowed in a smoothe current; yet, upon looking up the river, the wide spreading Shoals were seen. The grandeur of the scene engrossed my attention, until night-fall compelled me to retire into the house.

Upon entering the tavern, I had the pleasure of meeting with the Reverend Gideon Blackburn, the same who civilized the Cherokee Indians.[53] I had heard of Mr. Blackburn often. He is represented as a man of superior talents, both as a divine and a politician, and rendered his country many signal benefits in co-operating with General Jackson last war, in raising the necessary requisites for the army. He is a stout coarse-featured man, of middle age, and very distant in his manners; but has great expression of countenance, and every mark of a sensible man. He did not seem pleased with the house, and crossed the river, late as it was to seek a lodging elsewhere. It was a great disappointment to me, as I promised myself much pleasure in his society. The landlord, and a number of boatmen had been drinking freely, which, I suspect, displeased the Parson.—The lady of the house, a very beautiful and accomplished woman, was no less sorry, adding, she had known him from her infancy.

Mr. Beech going no farther, I took a guide, one of the pilots, and crossed the river next morning, in a ferry boat. I should have found it difficult, on account of several creeks which were backed up by the river, without a guide. The Tennessee river is wider at the foot of the Shoals than the Ohio, at any part I have seen, and equally beautiful, perhaps superior. It has not those high banks which confine the Ohio, if we except what the people, in this country call Bluffs. These are steep ledges of rocks which appear at very considerable intervals, sometimes on one side of the river, and sometimes on the other—and from appearances I would suppose it often inundates the bottom lands. These are covered with cane, as thick as the hairs on your head, and look like so many fields of green wheat. These, contrasted with the leafless forest, are singularly beautiful. Not only the islands, but the bottoms are so thickly covered with cane, that you could not see a man on horseback five steps from you.

Yours, &c.

Letter XXIII.

Melton's Bluff, January 12th, 1818.

Dear Matt,

UPON LEAVING the ferry, I was pensive and melancholy; for, being told by my guide I was to pass by several Indian farms, it struck a damp on my spirits, of which he was unconscious. He speaks of the Indians and their departure with perfect indifference.

On leaving the river the beauties of this deservedly extolled country broke on my view by degrees. To compare it with the Elysian fields of the ancients, would give but a feeble idea of it. The diminutive vale of Tempe and their thousand sylvan shades, vanish into nothing, compared with this. As you are partial to any thing I say or do, I shall throw my thoughts together for your amusement, and you may arrange them at your leisure.

It is unnecessary to state what you have learned from the newspapers, that this land was abandoned last fall by the Indians.[54] The fires were still smoking, when the white people took possession. Although I had travelled through a beautiful country, the two preceding days, and my mind had been raised to the highest pitch of expectation by repeated descriptions of this land; yet, it far exceeded all I anticipated. On quitting the impervious river-bottom, I emerged into an open country, high and dry. The exuberance of cane and timber subsides. This enables the eye to see to a great distance—no hill nor dale—neither is it a perfect level; but the surface is gently undulating, or alternately elevated or depressed like waves. The eye can range without controul in all directions. This is what charms; and this I was not prepared for.

But what struck me with most wonder was, that I always appeared to occupy the highest ground; and, all from that point, seemed to descend; and when I gained the extreme boundary of view from a given point, it was the same thing as before—this appeared the highest; that which I had left, the lowest. A warm hospitality seemed to breathe among the trees: they have something cheering in their aspect. They do not terrify by their gigantic looks—they open on all sides, as if to let you pass, and welcome your approach. The sun throws a shining lustre over them. How unlike the cold, dreary, hard frozen hills of Monroe, or in fact any thing in our country.

About ten o'clock we came in sight of the first Indian farm —but Indian farm no longer! The smoke was issuing slowly through the chimney. Why, these Indians have been like us!—could not be savage—cornfields—apple trees, and peach-trees. Fences like ours, but not so high—trusted to their neighbor's honesty—perhaps these being more civilized had more reason to fear their neighbor. Provoked with my guide because he could not tell me the original cause of these enclosures among the Indians—from four to five rails high—this would not do among us—'twould breed a civil war.—There were the lusty corn-stalks—looked grayish—some were standing erect, some were broken off at the middle and hung together still, some were prostrate. The house looked tight and comfortable; the fruit-trees are large, and show age—there the Indian sat under their shade, or stood up and plucked the apples—wonder he did not plant more—suppose he did not know how to make cider. Blockhead!—better than whiskey.

My guide says peaches are delightful in this country.

Poor Gourd! That was the Indian's name; had he still been there, I would have called to see him: but I felt no desire to see his successor. Guide says Gourd was very kind; he knew him for fifteen years. He helped to subdue the Creeks, and made an excellent soldier. There was a portico over the door—there Gourd used to sit in the warm summer days. We rode close to the fence, built by his hands, or perhaps his wife's; no matter which it was, it was no less dear!—It was his home! The sun, at this moment, overcast with clouds, threw a solemn gloom upon the Indian farm. Nothing moved but the smoke from the chimney—all was silent and hushed as death!—Poor Gourd had to leave his home, his cornfield, and his apple trees.

There could not exist a greater evidence of unbounded avarice and ambition which distinguished the Christian world, than the one that lay before me. There was a time when the owners of this beauteous country flattered themselves that *distance* alone would screen them from the intrusion of the whites. Vain hope!

Absorbed in pensiveness, I heeded not the loquacity of my servant and guide, who cared for none of these things. My guide tripped lightly along—a tall keen man. I proposed that my servant should walk and let him ride; but he refused; said he would rather walk. "But you will have to swim presently," said he. "How so? I would rather not." "Your horses, I mean; you cross Town Creek, in a canoe, and swim your horses; this will cost you one dollar." "One dollar!" These white people I thought are greedy. Shortly after this we came to the house where the man lived who was to have the dollar—another Indian house, and I hastened to view the interior. It was a roomy tight built cabbin, similar to many you have seen. The logs are round, very light, and lie close upon each other. The door was the only singularity:—It was as high as common doors, but not more than half as wide.

As I sat musing upon the ups and downs of this life, I was roused by the man who was to put us over, observing, "I can't tell what's to be done about putting you over Town Creek. Some of my good neighbours, on the other side, has cut down four or five trees into the crossing; and it is almost impossible to cut them away, as the Creek is high, and they have to be cut in such a manner, (the ends of them lying on the land,) as the water may float them off." "But can we not find another place by going higher up the Creek?" "No! Impossible! and it will be a hard job, if it can be done at all. There is no possible way but to stand in the canoe, to the danger of our lives." "Then," said I, "we will return, and await the falling of the river." I saw through the matter at once; he wished to have something extra; and had he not been a sharper, I would have given him something extra. Now see these white people! These Christians! His Christian neighbours felled the trees in the stream, and he wanted to filch the damage out of me! So would not the Indians! "Oh, we will go and see what can be done. Shall I help you on your horse? The Creek is a good step off."

A few minutes brought us to Town Creek; and there were the trees, sure enough—cut near the margin—four of them; and all their tops lying piled on each other, precisely where our horses were to land. None but a fiend would have thought of such hellish malice, and such an ingenious piece of mischief too. I should never have dreamed of it.

Leaving the horses on this side, the ferryman and Rhea, (my guide's name,) and my servant, crossed over, and commenced chopping the trees, at the surface of the stream, some alternately holding the canoe to the place.

I sat down on a log, and taking a newspaper to pass the time; behold! a long holding forth upon converting the Indians, was the first thing that struck my eye! I would have a much better opinion of robbers and pirates, than such men: *they* do not belie their trade.

In a quarter of an hour the trees were removed, and I, with my horses, were safely on the other side; and do you think the fellow had not the impudence to ask seventy-five cents extra, after drinking between them a bottle of whiskey, which I gave them as a treat, and Rhea and my servant also assisting them!! "No, Sir," said I, "I will advertise you as a sharper besides!" Give him seventy-five cents extra! I was on the rong side of the river for that. Rhea said I had two more creeks to pass! "Big Nance," (called after a woman by that name, who lived there.) These, however, were easily forded—and chatting with Rhea, I learned he was from Rockbridge county, Virginia; had piloted boats through the Muscle Shoals, fifteen years; sometimes four at a time, at *ten* dollars each. He sails down one day, and walks back the next. He never met, in all that time, with an accident! There are several of these pilots.

You cannot imagine a sight so beautiful as this country exhibits to this place. But the sight of the Bluff at a mile's distance, fairly entranced me. It is an even high plain, and resembles a hanging garden. The sun favored us with his rays as we drew in sight, and shed a beautiful lustre on the Bluff.—This land is so clear of undergrowth that you may drive a wagon any where through the woods; and this body extends, I am told, twenty miles in width. We passed many Indian houses in the day, and some beautiful springs.

Yours, &c.

Letter XXIV.

Melton's Bluff,[55] January 14th, 1818.

Dear Matt,

MELTON'S BLUFF is a town, and takes its name from a person by the name of John Melton, a white man, deceased two years since, at an advanced age.[56] Various stories are related of this man; but all agree in this: that he was an Irishman by birth; became displeased with the white people; attached himself to the Cherokee Indians; married a squaw, and settled at this place many years ago; that, with the assistance of the Indians, he used to rob the boats which passed down the river, and murder the crews. By these means he became immensely rich; owned a great number of slaves; most of whom he robbed from these boats. Thus it is said he continued his piracies until the treaty between the United States and the Cherokees.[57]

He had several children by his Indian wife, one of whom married Rhea, the pilot. After peace was signed with the Indians, Melton lived quietly at home, and cultivated his farm; but towards the latter part of his life he became alarmed from the threats of the Creeks, and removed over the river, where he also had a large farm, and built a fine house, (which I have seen,) and died rich in a good old age. Most of his children married white people.

He used to keep a house of entertainment at Melton's Bluff, after his piracies ceased; and kept an excellent house. His table was furnished with the best of liquors, meat, coffee, and tea, and all prepared in the best manner. I met with a gentleman who spent a week at Melton's house, in company with six others. He said he never fared better in any part of the United States: but their bill was excessively high.

I saw and conversed with many of Melton's slaves; amongst whom was a cook whom he purchased in Baltimore, at a very high price, as a first rate cook. She said that Mrs. Melton would sometimes take it into her head to go into the kitchen, (particularly when she took a dram,) and kick up a dust with her about the dinner. Mrs. M. wanted to model the cooking to her own mind, that is, Indian fashion. She, the cook, being responsible to her master for the forthcoming of the dinner would go to her master; upon which the old man would sally forth, with whip in hand, and if fair words failed, the horsewhip always restored order.

You recollect Rhea whom I have mentioned: he married one of Melton's daughters—a most amiable woman, and very lame. When the Cherokee Indians abandoned this territory last fall, some of them went up the river to the Cherokee nation, there to remain, till boats were provided for their removal to the west, by the government; others went directly down the river to Arkansas—of whom Rhea's wife was one. The order for their departure was sudden and unexpected.[58] Rhea, at that time was absent from home, but returned on the same day, and learning what had happened, was almost frantic —jumped into a canoe, and soon overtook the boats. He flew to his wife, and clasped her in his arms. Neither spoke a word, but both wept bitterly. In a few moments he resumed his canoe and returned to the Bluff, and she went on. They had no children.

Whether Rhea was prohibited by the treaty from accompanying his wife, or whether he was under a prior engagement, none here are able to inform me—but certain it is, he is now married to a white woman.

You have heard that this country consists of table and bottom land, also, of the Bluffs. These Bluffs happen where there is no bottom land, but the table land running up to the river forms a high precipice, called a Bluff. This is the case at Melton's Bluff, the highest I have seen. Here is a very large plantation of cotton and maize, worked by about sixty slaves, and owned by General Jackson, who bought the interest of old Melton.[59]

No language can convey an idea of the beauties of Melton's Bluff. It is said to be the handsomest spot in the world, off the seabord; and rich as it is beautiful. I can sit in my room and see the whole plantation; the boats gliding down the river, and the opposite shore, one mile distant. The ducks, geese, and swans, playing at the same time on the bosom of the stream, with a full view of the many islands. It is, after all, the great height of the site that pleases.

I took a walk with some ladies to-day over the plantation, as we wished to have a nearer view of those snowy fields, which so sedulously present themselves to our view, together with orchards, gin houses, gardens, Melton's mansion, and a considerable negro town.

We approached the mansion, by a broad street, running up the river bank east of the town. This street seems suspended between heaven and earth, as the whole premises for two miles, all in sight, appears to be elevated above the horizon, and none above the rest. We entered the court yard, fronting the house, by a stile; and the first thing we met was a large scaffold overspread with cotton: as it was in the seed, their must have been many thousands of pounds. Being damp from dew, and often rain, it must be dried in this manner. The mansion was large, built with logs, shingled roof, and may have been built 25 or 30 years since. I recoiled at the sight of a place once the habitation of such a monster. Some of our party went in: I did not. General Jackson's overseer, who joined us here, said he lived in the lower story, the upper being filled with cotton. The scaffold was about four feet from the ground. From this we crossed another fence, and found ourselves in a cotton field of about one hundred acres, white with cotton and alive with negroes. The centre of this field is said to be the rallying point of viewing the scenery; as it doubtless is. You can see up to Brown's Ferry, eight miles distant, with the naked eye—and the same distance down.—The term *beauty* is applied to any thing which excites pleasant feelings. Beauty is said to be a uniformity amidst variety; a proportion of parts adapted to a whole; fitness of things to an end; quantity and simplicity. All this is realised on the scenery of Melton's Bluff. Here is a noble river which combines in itself all you can conceive of grandeur and utility, adorned with islands spangled with boats, and enlivened with wild fowl. Lift your eye from the river, and lo! magnificent fields, white as snow, orchards, farms, and houses, all in view, without moving out of the spot. You may thus form some idea of this farfamed Bluff. Here the green islands look like floating meadows. Here the boatman wields his massy oar, and guides his freighted boat along. Here the wild fowl arrayed in glossy plumes, wantons as she lists. Here the distant billows breaking o'er the Shoals, echo back in murmuring sounds, and mingling sweetly with the music of the boatman's viol, swells upon the ear and softly dies away upon the breeze. To crown the whole, here the majestic swan, robed in dazzling white, moves in all her graceful attitudes.

These are beauties which may be felt but cannot be described. This combination of objects, each beautiful in itself, and so materially useful, constitutes the beauty of Melton's Bluff. All the trade of East Tennessee passes by the Bluff, and halt here to take in their pilots.

Yours, &c.

Letter XXV.

Same date.

Dear Matt,

Now comes the cotton field again. As you complain of long letters, I will please you if it can be done. This is the first cotton field I have ever been in. It appears an endless business when we cast our eye over so vast a plain of white with a production, the gathering of which is to be effected by the application of the fingers to every individual pod; and these pods as thick as they can stand one by the side of the other. It is discouraging indeed. But these negroes have great patience, and seem to be cut out for the business. Here are from 40 to 50, who scarcely seem to move out of one place; nor can you tell which way they are going. They face about to every point. Some are erect, and others stooping, and all their hands move very fast. It is very light work; and the climate is so mild, they work out the whole winter.

It requires practice to be a good picker; an expert hand will pick about 100 weight per day. It is planted in drills from three to four feet asunder. The stem sends out branches from the bottom to the top, so dense, that you think it is sown like wheat. The branches extend from one row to the other, and so intermingle. It is worked in the same manner you do Indian corn until it blooms, and the first frost that comes, and even before some of the pods open, whilst others are only in bloom. As soon as it opens, the picking begins; but this requires double the hands it took in the cultivation. These go regularly over the field, and by that time, a number of pods which were not open on the first picking, are now ready, and they return to where they first began, and go over the same ground, and so on the whole winter. Large quantities are burnt for want of hands to get it out of the way of the plow, for the plowing must commence at the usual time; and they set fire to it to rid it out of the way. I asked why they did not give it gratis to the poor? without reflecting that every man, woman, and child, able to work, were engaged till the last moment. Children of twelve years of age, and often under, make 75 cents per day. The land is amazingly fertile on the Bluff. We measured one of the stalks and found it 6 feet 6 inches high. From the field we sauntered along to the cotton-gin. Every one who raises cotton, must have a gin. As we walked along, thousands of paroquets flew over us in flocks. They are very handsome, green and yellow. The squirrels were likewise chattering in the trees, shelling their nuts, whilst the friendly jay was sporting in the boughs, and the red bird, in his brilliant scarlet plumage, hopping familiarly before us, and his kindred songsters, were serenading us in the adjoining forest. It is like our springs, music and beauty greet you whichever way you move; and yet I am told foreigners say we have no scenery in America. I do not envy them their barren heaths and tottering castles. We have one here, *Melton's* castle; but like their own it only serves to remain us of the rapine and bloodshed of its former owner.

We found a number of boys and horses at the the cotton gin, which gave variety to our amusement, particularly a considerable tree pulled round and round by a horse; this turned a screw which pressed the bales of cotton—the world and all the boys seem to be made of cotton here—that is all the description I can give of the thing. The pressing part of it is something like pressing cyder; but as to the ginning part of it, with its thousand wheels and saws

"It would puzzle Apollo
"Its whimses to follow."

On our return home, we passed two lines of negro cabins. There were very few but children in them. We found the cabins warm and comfortable, and well stored with provisions: General Jackson, to whom they belong, being one of the best of masters.

As I lingered behind the party, thinking of my own negro children, the little things flocked round me, and as they were looking up in my face, eager to be carressed, I discovered the traces of tears on some of their cheeks. The sight pierced me to the heart. Oh, slavery, slavery! nothing can soften thee! thou art slavery still! Is there no hope high heaven?

Yours, &c.

Letter XXVI.

Melton's Bluff, January 16th, 1818.

Dear Matt,

I AM HERE for the winter, doubtless, and shall while away the time between writing to you, viewing the country, and "chatting with the beaux." As you are desirous to hear a particular account of this beautiful region, I shall finish what I began sometime back.

I said the land was divided into bottom, table land, and Bluffs. It also contains Bayous[60] and mountains. The bottom land is held in little estimation; for, though more fertile than the table land, it is hard to clear, being thickly covered with heavy timber, and often not only by these bayous, but often overflowed; this renders it too wet for cotton, which delights in dry soil. These bayous are formed by the water of the river forsaking the channel, and, running off in various directions, returns to the river and unites with it again. The cotton, or table land, is separated from the bottom land, by the Bluffs, and though they are only called Bluffs where they meet the river, they are evidently the same elivation which divides the bottom from the table land. The table land is not a dead level, but waving, and varies from 20 to 25 miles wide; then comes the mountain, a narrow strip of pine land, very little higher than the table land *generally*, and, though stony, might be tilled. Then comes the table land again; next mountain. These varities run parallel with the Tennessee river.[61]

Then comes the long moss, sixty miles on this side of Cahawba, running in the same direction; and beyond it the table land appears again. In the region of this moss it is sickly, as it also is, on the rivers; but keep off the rivers and it is as healthy as any climate, or perhaps more so, than any part of the Union.[62] There is no such thing as consumptions. Those families subject to it perfectly recover from it in this climate. Of this I have been an eye witness.

I saw some of the moss just mentioned. It looks like hay when cured in the sun, though much finer. It has joints like timothy grass. A gentleman who brought some of it in his saddle bags to this place, informed me that it hangs loosely upon the trees, as though it were thrown on by the hand, and has no connection whatever with the branch upon which it hangs. This is most singular. He said that trees of all descriptions were enveloped with it, from the top to the bottom, hanging down to the ground; and that cattle lived on it. I ought to have said that a narrow blade branches out from the joints of the moss. When it is soaked in water, it discharges a thin coat with which the stem is enveloped; it is then black, and resembles horse hair, and matrasses are made out of it.

But to return. This land produces upon an average 1000 pounds of cotton in the seed. Sweet potatoes grow very fine, and are an article of food for the negroes. Corn grows well, and, also, wheat; though the weavel destroys it almost instantly; consequently, as they can buy it cheaper, and turn their labor and land to better account, by raising cotton, wheat is not raised. Tobacco, also, grows well, but they prefer the cotton as more profitable.

I have seen no meadows since I left Tennessee; and though clover grows well in Madison county, north of the river, the soil is said to be unfavorable to grass. Vast numbers of cattle are raised here upon the cane.

Yours, &c.

Letter XXVII.

Melton's Bluff, same date.

Dear Matt,

It is now high time to introduce you to the ladies and gentlemen of this town, city, or what you please to denominate it. It would be a million of pities not to do so; particularly a young lady, called the beauty of the Territory. There are so many pleasing objects here—the climate so mild—and such a wide and handsome prospect, that I am all delight—like a bird let out of a cage. But I shall take care not to mount my hobby, lest I might gallop off to Cahawba, or some other place.

To begin with my landlord, Colonel Pettis.[63] He is a young man of handsome appearance, and very good natured—weighs about 200 weight, though not corpulent. He is a native of Virginia; lived sometime in Madison, and moved here about the time I arrived. I was introduced to him in Huntsville, and knowing he was about to remove here, I was warmly recommended to him. He is a man of considerable property, and keeps a house of entertainment for the accommodation of the innumerable travellers, who, like locusts, cover the land. He amuses himself in this way, till the land sales approach, when he designs to purchase and settle himself. His wife, young, active, genteel, and sprightly, with a sparkling black eye, is a beautiful woman, and the life and soul of the Bluff, two children, boys, all they have, and two of his wife's sisters, a gay young widow and her child, with the bar-keeper, and myself, compose the family. But the beauty, Matt, the flower of the country, is here. She is only fourteen, but her fame extends and will, doubtless, cause many an aching heart. She is one of the sisters just mentioned, the handsomest piece of mortality I ever met with. Her features are without fault; her eyes are unmatched in expression, as black as sloes; and her cheeks are like roses. But my pen fails me—her name is Martha Patrick. Another tavern is kept here, by Major Wyatt, one of the heroes of New Orleans. The Major, his wife, and his wife's sister, with his mother, compose this other family. Besides these, there are several tipling shops, three stores, an apothecary shop, two doctors, a hatter's shop, a ware house, and several mechanics.

Major Wyatt is by far the most interesting man in the town, as poor as Job, but brave and generous as a prince. At the battle of New Orleans, he held a captain's commission, and was taken prisoner on the night of the 23d December. After forcing the British from one position to another, and dealing death wherever he appeared, deceived by the darkness of the night, he mistook the British for our own men, and was taken prisoner. The officer into whose hands he fell, immediately disarmed him; put him under guard, and treated him very harshly. Next morning he was exchanged. The next engagement, Wyatt had the good fortune to take the same officer prisoner. The officer immediately surrendered his sword, which Wyatt received, but instantly returned it; shook him by the hand very friendly, led him to his tent, ordered refreshments, and setting a bottle of wine before him, after taking a glass, desired him to make himself happy, and that *he* should take the first opportunity of effecting his exchange; saying this, he hastened to take his station at the head of his men, leaving the Englishman overwhelmed with shame and astonishment. Would you believe it, the hero of this Godlike act was master of nothing at the time but his sword and his honor, and at this moment is an humble boatman, and pilots boats through the Shoals! His wife is young, handsome, and industrious, and attends to the tavern. But Mrs. Wyatt, his mother, one of the nobility of the Ancient Dominion, poor and proud, is extremely mortified that her son should have married "so much beneath him."[64] Shocking! She has condenscended to come and spend the winter with *Neddy*, however, but she lowers upon her sweet daughter-in-law like a thunder cloud. This widow of 70, is laced and starched stiff up to the chin; homely face, but a fine figure, ignorant and proud as Lucifer, and if I am not much mistaken, would have no objection to enter into the holy bands of matrimony again. The young widow of our family, is a daughter of the wealthy *Mr. Foaly*, of Natchez.[65] She fell in love and married a Major Chandler against her father's consent, who not only refused to give her a dollar, but forbid her his house.

Chandler was a handsome, accomplished, man, but poor; and about one year after his marriage, died, and left his wife with an infant amongst strangers. Mrs. Chandler was found in this situation by Colonel Pettis, and taken to his house, where she is treated with kindness and respect. Her father, who owns about ninety slaves, has sent for her to return to him, and upon this condition he promises to divide his fortune with her, General Castleton, his son-in-law, and a son, his remaining child. But she, as yet, refuses to return to her parent. She is a very small woman, but handsome and kind hearted.

To go on with the rest. One of the Doctors, Crab, of Botetourt, Virginia, I knew, as well as the whole family. They were respectable, and were formerly of Maryland. The Doctor is a young widower, tall and slender; and pursues his profession.

The other Doctor, Rousseau, descended from the famous writer of that name, is also from Virginia, and near Alexandria. He is a man of genteel manners, young and handsome, and very sociable. One of the merchants, Mitchell, with his wife, is from Nashville, Tennessee, the first people on the Bluff, and are also very pleasant.[66] If we except a little envy on the part of Mrs. Widow W. we have a very pleasant society of our own, independent of the flood of travellers which delight the country, making choice of such lands as they design to purchase at the sales. The whole country exhibits fair roads, produced by the people allured from all the States to settle in this beauteous country. Our house is full every night. In short, there are ten families, which, with the comers and goers, and the arrival of the boats from East Tennessee, we have a merry time of it.

Yours, &c.

N. B. Here is another Jay's Treaty.

Letter XXVIII.

Melton's Bluff, January 18th, 1818.

Dear Matt,

GOOD NEWS awaits you: read on! Having collected a few books, I was devouring Phillips' Speeches (first sight of the book) in a corner, when a loud cry, "General Jackson, General Jackson comes!" and, running to my window, I saw him walking slowly up the hill, between two gentlemen, his aids. He was dressed in a blue frock coat, with epaulettes, a common hat with a black cockade, and a sword by his side. He is very tall and slender. He walked on by our door to Major

Wyatt's, his companion in arms, where he put up for the night, though he called on us that evening and the next morning. His person is finely shaped, and his features not handsome, but strikingly bold and determined. He is very easy and affable in his manners, and loves a jest. He told one of our party, he was "one of the blue hen's chickens." He appears to be about 50 years of age. There is a great deal of dignity about him. He related many hardships endured by his men, in the army, but never breathed a word of his own. His language is pure and fluent, and he has the appearance of having kept the best company.

You will recollect he was ordered by the government against the Seminole Indians. His army is on its march considerably ahead of him, having crossed at Ditto's Landing,[67] up the river, while he came round by this place to see his plantation an slaves.

The hero of the south, as he is called, left us this morning, at 10 o'clock, and our best wishes went with him. Upon seeing him, I called to mind the night I was roused from my sleep in Charlestown, about midnight, by William Quarrier, who knocked at my door and proclaimed aloud, "General Jackson has defeated the British at New Orleans; get up, we are going to illuminate." This was the night of fire-works and rejoicing upon the news of the victory, which you no doubt well remember. Many other anecdotes, particularly of his humanity to the destressed, occured to my mind.

Upon my return once from Ohio, I put up at a Mr. Jones's, on Kentucky river. In the course of the conversation, I observed, "that a new county had been established in Ohio, and was called Jackson; and not satisfied with this mark of respect, they had called the seat of justice Jackson." Mrs. Jones observed they could not have him too much; and it gave her great pleasure to hear of his hapiness and success; that he had been the means once of saving herself and her children from perishing in the wilderness. Mrs. Jones, was the daughter of Captain Arbuckle, of Greenbrier City, Va. with whom you must be acquainted, though you may not be with the history of his daughter, as you are too young.—Her history contains a most surprising train of incidents, and superior to any novel. The story is this: Mr. Arbuckle had several handsome and sensible daughters. One of these was addressed by a Mr. Jones, and a mutual and deep rooted affection grew up between them: but Captain A. opposed their union, and forbid Jones his house; and finally through persuasion and force compelled his daughter to marry the son of Captain Robertson, a near neighbour of mine. Upon this, Jones abandoned the country, and I never heard of him from that day till the night of which I an now speaking. As soon as Robertson married the girl, he removed with her to Natchez, and I heard no more of them. I did see a publication in the newspapers, of a female travelling through the Indian nation, without protection, and that she, and six children, entered the state of Kentucky, nearly famished. Mrs. Jones was the woman! Her own narrative follows: "I was forced to marry Mr. Robertson and be miserable, or marry Mr. Jones, and render my father miserable; I preferred the former. All places being alike to me, after this sacrifice, I accompanied my husband to Natchez. We had received a handsome beginning from both our fathers, and were, for some time prosperous. But my husband, at length, fell in with bad company, and took to gambling and drinking, and spent the whole of his property.—Meantime we had seven children, which I partly maintained by my own labour. Finally, my husband took sick, and after lingering some time, died, and every thing I had was seized and sold by his creditors, with the exception of four horses, which I concealed, with a view of conveying my children and myself to my father in Virginia. I hired a man to go with me, and departed early one night, and never stopped till I got over the boundary line between the white people and the Indians. I had but 8 dollars and a bushel of meal for myself and children; but I was so anxious to get out of the reach of the white people, whom I expected would pursue me, that I travelled without ceasing, or rest, till the second day about 10 o'clock, when I turned out my horses to feed on the pea vine, and began to prepare bread for my children. Several of them being sick when I left Natchez, were stretched upon the ground, while I was preparing food, when, behold, three white men, whom I knew, appeared in sight, having pursued me. They rode towards the horses, as if to surround and take them by force, when I flew between them and the horses, and told them they should not lay hands on them. I acknowledged I owed money in Natchez, which I honestly intended to pay when I reached my fathers. You have deprived me of all but the horses, and without them I cannot reach my fathers. I am out of your jurisdiction. I am on Indian ground, and if you levy your process on my property, you do it at your peril. You know the penalty, and so do I, and I will prosecute you at every hazard. I had been particular enough to learn by certain signs on the line, and I knew I was out of their power. They endeavored to frighten me out of the horses, but finding it vain they returned.

"I pursued my journey all that night, and next day, until evening, when coming to a deep hollow, over which there was a bridge, I drove the horses over, and after taking a slight supper, I lay down on the bridge, with a view of guarding the horses. The man who was with me, an old silly sort of man, had disappeared sometime before I lay down. I lay awake, suspecting some treachery. The moon shone quite bright. The old man had doubtless betrayed me to the same men whom, as I expected, pursued me. When I missed the man I concluded I was undone, and gave way to despair; for, though I saw no possibility of the horses crossing the gully, except by the bridge, I was apprehensive some place was known to my guide, or to the men. As I lay watching, with an aching heart, about midnight I perceived the horses moving slowly towards the bridge, and the same men, with the traitor, pursuing them silently. When the horses drew near the bridge, I jumped up and frightened them back, and the men disappeared. They, doubtless, expected I was asleep, and never dreamed of my securing the bridge. I never saw my men afterwards. I continued my journey, now and then buying a scanty supply of provisions for ourselves and horses, from the Indians. These were the Choctaws, and were very friendly. But it was at a season of the year when provisions were scarce.

"I travelled but slow, as my children were all sick, except one.—One of the children was so ill that I had to carry it in my lap; and though I expected to lose some of them, I strove to get to the white settlements if possible.

"The ninth day, as I was riding slow along, I met a gentleman and his servant. He stopped and spoke very kindly to me, and inquired very particularly into the cause of my travelling in the wilderness; and asked me how much money I had? I informed him I had but two dollars, and at the same time repeating the cause of my journey. He approved my undertakking, and pulling out his purse, gave me *forty dollars!* He told me to keep a good heart, and I would surmount my difficulties. Said he was sorry he was going the opposite way. He spoke kind to all the children, and went on. *It was General Jackson!*[68]

"The day after I left him, as I stopped at an Indian house, I discovered a gentleman, who appeard to be sick. He had been resting awhile, and finding I was going the same way, he had his horse prepared, and went on with me. He was very feeble, and was followed by a mule, which was heavily laden with *specie.* He had been taken sick on the road. We travelled together, very slow, til the third day, when he informed me he could go no further. As I had some knowledge of medicine, and not wishing to travel without his company, I placed him in an Indian cabin, and having medicine with me, left by the physicians when my husband died, I administered it to him—in three days, during which I constantly attended him, he found himself well enough to venture on; and my children, too, being better, we proceeded with greater celerity than before. We did not make as much progress as we could have wished, owing to the want of grain for our horses. He was well armed, but was, nevertheless, timorous—nor was I less so; and the following will prove that our fears were not groundless: As we were lying down one night, all asleep but myself, (I never slept at night,) my eyes being fixed upon the road, watching both ways, I saw a person walking up the road. I turned to the tent where the gentleman slept, (I always stretched a blanket over him at night,) and wakened him; but as I crawled to him, I saw two more men in the other end of the road, also, walking towards us. Their coming in this manner, evidently showed their design, which was to rob the gentleman. He seized a pistol, and called out to the men to stand—upon this, all three ran, and he fired after them. They never appeared after this, although we watched for them the whole of that night.[69]

"In the course of our conversations, I mentioned the money given me by General Jackson; and as we were now drawing near Kentucky, and were soon to part, he said he must give me something before we separated. Taking a fancy to one of my horses, he inquired of me if I would dispose of him—that if I would he would give me the full value, and I could send him the horse when I arrived home. I agreed to this, and he paid me the money, and we parted next morning.

"I struggled with sickness and hardships for the sake of my children, until I arrived in Kentucky, when, having less cause to exert my fortitude, I sunk upon a sick bed, where I lay, until writing to my father, he sent for me, and four months after leaving Natchez, we arrived, all safe, in Greenbrier!"

Yours, &c.

Letter XXIX.

Same date.

Dear Matt,

THE REMAINDER of Mrs. Jones' story is so interesting that I must finish it. It amounts to the following:—When she arrived at home, her father gave her, by way of compensation, one of those fine tracts of land on Kenhawa river, below the "Washington Lands."[70] Meantime Jones, who was still unmarried, wandered about the Western frontier, furing, &c. and by sundry speculations, had collected a considerable sum of money; and the British, on their invasion of New Orleans, sending word to the citizens of Louisville, that they would *dine* with them the next day! many of the inhabitants became panic struck, and sold their possessions for a mere trifle.—Jones became one of the purchasers, and grew, suddenly, rich. He was offered, I think, and received, one hundred per cent. for a part of the property, next day, reserving the best for himself.

When Jones heard of Mrs. Robinson's return, and death of her husband, he hastened to seek her; and, still retaining his partiality for her, and she for him, they were married.—She had been married about two years when I was at her house, and was in the act of packing up to remove to Louisville, where a splendid house and every thing that heart could wish was ready to receive her. I should have been much pleased to have seen Jones, but he was absent from home. I however saw a very handsome child, better than a year old, the fruits of their union. Let any of your novel writers beat this! Mrs. Jones' children were very stout, and the oldest was nearly a woman grown.

Many similar acts of kindness, as related above, are told of General Jackson. He is represented as being particularly good and kind to his soldiers. One of his men informed me he would walk through the mud for miles, and let his sick men ride his horse. He would distribute his biscuit, tea, and whatever his private stores consisted of, amongst the sick, and go to the slaughter pen, and he and his suite would broil and eat the tripe, and other offal, without bread and without salt. This man, also, stated to me, he was present at the battle of the Horse Shoe, and a squaw being killed by accident, her child was found alive, and at the breast of its dead mother.—The General was pierced to the heart, and taking the child in his arms, had it immediately fed and clothed, and hired a person to take it to Huntsville, to be nursed. He has adopted the child since, and calls it *Lencour Jackson*, and both himself and Mrs. Jackson treats it with the utmost tendernes.[71]

Last fall General Jackson came to the Bluff, when every family was down with a fever, it being exceedingly sickly. Many of these were unable to give the others a drink of water. He had heard of the sickness of which his overseer had died, and of several of his slaves being confined at the same time. —Mrs. Mitchell, and her husband, (the merchant before mentioned) were lying, not able to rise, one in one bed, and the other opposite in another. She related to me, that the General and his suite would take the water buckets and go to the river for water; heat it over the fire, and take the sick in their arms, and placing their feet in the warm water, would thus support them, until they were sufficiently bathed, and then bear them back to their bed again. After this the General would administer medicine with his own hands. Thus he went the whole night, and never ceased till he had administered the necessary wants to all, both black and white, and consoling them with the most soothing language. Mrs. M. said, the General had handled her as tenderly as though she were a babe; and when he left the place, he ordered a negro woman of his own to wait on all those who were without servants. You scarcely hear his name mentioned without the repetition of some generous act. Well may the people adore him as they do.

Yours, &c.

Letter XXX.

Melton's Bluff, January 20th, 1818.

Dear Matt,

If I were not the best tempered person in the world, I should get into a pet and quit this correspondence. If it were not for some way to pass off the time, I would do so. I have not received a word from you these three weeks. What are you about? Are you sick, or sullen; or bemiring yourself and your horse by riding up and down the river through the mud; or, taking the opportunity of my absence, gone to your old tricks again? I shall be likely to hear no good of you, I suspect. When I return, I mean to make very particular inquiries about you; and there are not wanting those that will tell me the truth; and a great deal more!

But I will give you only a piece of a letter now, and the residue of it when I get over the fatigue I experienced in a late party of pleasure, or rather expedition, not against, but amongst, the Indians. But such a job, or rather such "a voyage of discovery," as was made by our party on the river, under a commander or leader, who was called a good waterman, but who was more like a land-lubber, unless the character of a good waterman consists in roundly wetting and worrying all his passengers, you never witnessed, perhaps never "read of." The particulars of it, however, would not be at all interesting, because, they would be much like ordinary frights, screams, and "hair-breadth 'scapes" of most large parties, composed chiefly of females crammed into one poor little canoe to navigate a great river. A more ill-looking, frightened, chagrined, fatigued, be-drabbled, and be-drowned set of miserables, than our party exhibited after being rocked and tossed about, not in "the Bay of Biscay, O," but in the broad Tennessee for a considerable time without making a progress of 300 yards, you never beheld in decent people, who started in high spirits and holy-day dresses. All the curls, crimps, and flourishing of gay gowns, new shoes, silk stockings, pantaloons and petticoats, shawls and other flaunting finery *humbled*—not "to the dust," but—to the water! But I will now only give you the "subject of my story," and the object of this "grand expedition," and proceed to the result of it in my next.

To the Same—*in continuation.*

Hearing eleven boats had arrived about two miles from hence, and had haulted up the river, we set off, as I said before, in a little canoe, to see the Indians, which are on their way to their destination beyond the Mississippi. Government, agreeably to their contract, having completed the boats, the news of the arrival of the Indians had been received with much interest; but being unable to proceed by water, we quit the canoe, and proceeded by land in our wet shoes and hose.

We arrived at the Indian camps about eleven o'clock. There were several encampments at the distance of three hundred yards from each other, containing three hundred Indians. The camps were nothing but some forks of wood driven into the ground, and a stick laid across them, on which hung a pot in which they were boiling meat; I took it to be venison. Around these fires were seated, some on the ground, some on logs, and some on chairs, females of all ages; and all employed, except the old women. There were some very old gray-haired women, and several children at each camp. The children were very pretty; but the grown females were not. I saw but few men. I asked the interpreter where they were: he said they had gone to hunt; some of them had returned, and were skinning and others preparing their game for their journey. But none of them were near the womens' department; they kept at a very respectful distance.

I have heard much of the elegant figures of the Indians; true, some nations of Indians are elegantly formed, but such is not the case with the Cherokees. They are low in stature, and there is nothing majestic or dignified about them. They have no expression of countenance. They have a dead eye; but their feet and hands are exceedingly small and beautiful. This is all the beauty I could distinguish about them. No lady that ever I saw has a hand so small or so well turned as these Indian women; and the same may be said of their feet. But, after all, they are ugly lumps of things. They are thick and short. Their hair is jet black, and very coarse. It parts from the crown of the head to its termination on the forehead, as the Dutch women wear theirs, and clubbed up behind with a blue or red ferret. Their colour is that of dark mulattoes. They were all well dressed; at least as well as most white women are, when engaged in their ordinary employment. Some were engaged in sewing, some in cooking, and some in nursing their babies, which were the prettiest little creatures I ever beheld.

Their manner of nursing is singular. They do not hold their infants in their arms, or on their laps, as our women do; but on their backs, confined in such a manner that they are in no danger of falling, or moving in any direction. This is done by means of a blanket, or a part of one, drawn tight round the infant, leaving its head and arms out. This blanket is fastened round the waist of the mother, and the top I do not know exactly how; but the utmost confidence seems to be reposed in its tenacity, as the mother never touches the child with her hands, or is at any more trouble with it whatever. The little things clasp their arms round the necks of their mothers, which they never move: no crying, nor fretting, nor any apprehension of danger disturbed the serenity of these little philosophers, on our approaching them. I have been told that the mothers suckle them, where they are, by raising the breast up to the child's mouth, which is very probable.

The Indian women appear to sustain no inconvenience from the incumbrance of their children. They went through the different vocations of pounding their corn into meal, carrying wood and water, with the same apparent ease as those that had no children. Seeing several little girls of from ten to twelve years old, I asked the women why they did not make those little girls nurse their little ones. They answered no other way than by shaking their heads, and smiling at my ignorance, no doubt. I went up to one of them, who was pounding corn, took the pestle out of her hand and helped her to pound: she laughed at my awkwardness, and took it out of my hand. She had, sitting by her on a washing-tub, a large tray full of parched corn. This it was that she was pounding into meal; and as she finished each portion, she emptied it into another tray. Every thing about her was neat and clean. The Indian corn was parched to a nice light brown, and looked "very interesting." The meal manufactured from this corn, is not fine, nor do they make it into bread at all, but mix it with common water and drink it. 'Tis rarely that they drink water in any other way. No one, who has never tasted it, would believe what a delicious drink it is.

Having walked about and made a number of inquiries, I sat myself down and made signs to an old Indian woman that I wanted to smoke: she very courteously handed me her pipe. The seat I had chosen was near one of those women, whom I had observed for some time, sedulously engaged with her needle. She was engaged making a family dress, in which she discovered all the skill and industry necessary to accomplish it. Their dresses were made like our ladies, and were put on. They had fine cotton shawls on their shoulders, and many of them had men's hats on their heads; but no bonnets were seen amongst them. They all had good shoes or mockasins on their feet, and some hundreds of beads round their necks; but their broad faces and coarse hair (as coarse as a horses mane) were quite disgusting. There is one elegance, however, which they possess in a superior degree to any civilized people that I am acquainted with; and this is not their beautiful hands and feet, already mentioned, but their walk. No lady, however skilled in the art of dancing, can walk with so much grace and dignity as these Indians, both men and women: and this, I am told, is peculiar to almost all Indians.

Although there were such a number of them, so near together as to be seen from one camp to the other, yet there was the greatest arder imaginable: not the least noise to be heard. How would so many whites have managed to maintain the good order evinced by these Indians? Even their dogs were not permitted to bark at us. The poor dogs! I felt for them: they were nothing but skin and bone! The same word that we use to encourage our dogs to seize on any thing, or to bark, the Indians use to control theirs, which is *hiss!* One of our party told me that it was *hiska!* which means "be still." The dress of the men was equally as decent and fashionable as that of the women. Many of them had on very neat half-boots, broad cloth coats, and good hats; though some prefer tying their heads up with a handkerchief, as being more convenient to hunt in.

By all that I have said in regard to these Cherokees, you may perceive they are far advanced in civilized arts and manners. This great work was accomplished by the indefatigable labors of the Reverend Gideon Blackburn! And yet, what an aversion they manifest toward our language! I was told that nearly all those that I saw, both understood and could talk good English; but not one word could I get out of them, of any sort. Their inter-communications were carried on by signs. I saw many of the half-breed, as they are called, here; the off-spring of a white and an Indian—but they were as unsociable as the others. I was thinking that this would be a good plan to promote their civilization, but the result proves that any plan would not succeed. It is very probable, that the most effectual means have been resorted to by our government to overcome their prejudices. I mean our rifles.

Please to give my best respects to Mrs. Wilson and Mrs. Dryden.

Yours, &c.

Letter XXXI.

January 30th, 1818.

Dear Matt,

YOU WANT every-day things, common-life, living-manners, evening-chat, and have I not done so? Not every thing to be sure, for I see and hear many things, that, oh heavens! I would not—what was I going to say?—why, that I hear and see such things that would not look very seemingly on paper. But if I live to see you, I shall let you into the knowledge of *some* things you would not dream of.

But as you are fond of stories, here follows one, which I am pretty certain you never saw. It is the first time I saw it, and is said to be written by Dr. Franklin himself: "The Doctor left Boston when a boy, and came to Philadelphia, where he lived till his death. Upon the death of his father, he went to Boston to comfort and console his mother. He had not seen her since he left Boston, many years, and was sure she would not know him. When he drew near her dwelling, as he was fond of philosophical experiments, it came into his head to pass himself for a stranger, and by this, ascertain whether there was such a thing as natural affection. On a cold, chilly day, in the month of January, in the afternoon, the Doctor knocked at the door, and asked to see Mrs. Franklin. He found the old lady knitting, before the parlour fire, and introduced himself, by observing, that he had been informed she entertained travellers, and requested a night's lodging. She eyed him with that cold look of disapprobation, which most people assume, when they imagine themselves insulted. She assured him, that he had been misinformed, that she did not keep tavern, but that it was true, to oblige some members of the Legislature, she took a number of them into her family during the session; that she then had four members of the Council, and six of the House of Representatives boarding with her; and that all her beds were full; and then betook herself to her knitting, with that intense application, which expressed as much and as forceably as actions could do—if you have done your business, the sooner you leave the better. But on the Doctor's wrapping his coat about him and observing that it was very chilly weather, she pointed to a chair and gave him permission to warm himself. The entrance of the boarders precluded all further conversation. Coffee was soon served, and the Doctor partook with the rest of the family. To the coffee succeeded pipes and a paper of McIntire's best, when the whole family formed a cheerful smoking semi-circle round the fire.

"Perhaps no man ever possessed colloquial powers in a more facinating degree than Doctor Franklin, and never was there an occasion when he displayed those powers to a greater advantage than at this time. He drew the attention of the company by the solidity of his judgment, and the modesty of his deportment; instructed them by the new and varied lights in which he placed his subject, and delighted them with apt and amusing anecdotes. Thus employed, the hours passed merrily along, until eight o'clock, when, punctual to a moment, Mrs. Franklin announced supper. Busied with her household affairs, she fancied the intruding stranger had quitted the house immediately after coffee, and it was with difficulty she restrained resentment when she saw him without invitation seat himself at the table with the freedom of a member of the family. Immediately after supper, she called an elderly gentleman, a member of the Council in whom she was accustomed to confide, to another room, complained bitterly of the rudeness of the stranger, told the manner of his introduction to the house, observed that he appeared like an outlandish man, and she thought he had something very suspicious in his appearance; concluding by soliciting her friend's advice with respect to the way in which she could most easily rid herself of his presence. The old gentleman assured her that the stranger was a man of education, and to all appearances a gentleman; that being in agreeable company, he had paid no attention to the lateness of the hour, and advised her to call him aside, and repeat to him her inability to lodge him. She accordingly sent her maid to him, and then, with as much temper as she could command, recapitulated the situation of her family, observed that it grew late, and mildly intimated, that he would do well to seek himself a lodging. The Doctor said that with her leave he would smoke one more pipe with her boarders, and then retire. He returned to the company, filled his pipe, and with the first whiff his powers of conversation returned with redoubled force. He recounted the hardships, he extolled the piety and policy of our ancestors. A gentleman present mentioned the subject of the day's debate in the House of Representatives—a bill had been introduced to extend the prerogatives of the crown. The Doctor immediately entered upon the subject, separated the Colonial rights with new and forcible arguments, was familiar with the names of the influential members of the house, when Dudly was Governor, recited their speeches, and applauded the noble defence of the Chamber rights.

"During a discourse so appropriately interesting to the company, no wonder the clock struck eleven unperceived by the delighted circle. Nor was it wonderful, that Mrs. Franklin, by this time, grew exhausted: she now entered the room, and, before the whole company, with much warmth, addressed the

Doctor, told him plainly she thought herself imposed on, observed it was true she was a lone woman, but that she had friends, who would protect her, and concluded by insisting on his leaving the house. The Doctor made a slight apology and very deliberately put on his great coat and hat, took a polite leave of the company, and approached the street door, lighted by the maid and attended by the mistress. While the Doctor and his companions had enjoyed themselves within, a most tremendous snow had fallen without, which had filled the streets knee-deep; and when the maid lifted the latch, a roaring northwester forced open the door, extinguished the light, and almost filled the entry with drifted snow and hail. As soon as the candle was relighted, the Doctor cast a woful look towards the door, and thus addressed his mother: "My dear Madam, can you turn me out of doors in this dreadful storm? I am a stranger in this town, and shall certainly perish in the street. You look like a charitable old lady: I don't think you could turn a dog from your door on this tempestuous night." Don't tell me about charity, said the offended matron; charity begins at home. It was your own fault, that you staid so long: to be plain with you, sir, I don't like your conduct; and I fear you have some bad design in thus intruding yourself on my family. The warmth of the parley had drawn the company from the parlour, and by their united interferance the stranger was permitted to lodge in the house; and as no bed could be had, he consented to repose on an easy chair before the parlour fire. Although the boarders entertained no doubt of the stranger's honesty, it was not so with Mrs. Franklin. With suspicious caution she collected all her silver spoons, pepper-box, and porringer, and from the closet, and after securing the parlour-door by sticking a fork over the latch, carried the plate to her chamber, charged the negro-man to sleep with his clothes on, to take the clever to bed with him, and wake and seize the vagrant at the first noise he made in attempting to rob the house.

"Having thus taken every precaution, she retired to bed

with her maid, whom she compelled to sleep in her room.—Mrs. Franklin rose before the sun, roused her domestics, unfastened the parlour door, with timid caution, and was greatly surprised to find her guest quietly sleeping in the chair. A sudden transition from mistrust to perfect confidence was natural. She awakened him with a cheerful good morning, inquiring how he had rested, and invited him to partake of her breakfast, which was always served before that of the boarders. "And pray sir," said the old lady, as she sipped her chocolate, "as you say you are a stranger here, to what distant country do you belong?" "I, Madam, belong to the city of Philadelphia." The Doctor declared he, for the first time, perceived any emotion in her. "Philadelphia!" said she, and all the mother suffused her eyes. "If you live in Philadelphia, perhaps you know our Ben." "Who, Madam!"—"Why, Ben Franklin, my Ben; Oh, he is the best child that ever blest a mother!" "What—is Ben Franklin, the printer, your son? Why he is my most intimate friend." "Oh! God forgive me; and have I suffered a friend of my Benny to sleep on that hard chair, and I in a good bed?"

How the Doctor made himself known to his mother, he has not informed us. But he always said, after that, that there was no such thing as "natural affection." How much like her are all old women! I never found one drop of the milk of human kindness in one of them.[72]

Yours, &c.

Letter XXXII.

Melton's Bluff, same date.

Dear Matt,

THE ANECDOTE of Doctor Franklin, in my last, reminds me of a similar one of my mother.

When I was a child, my parents removed from Maryland to the frontier of Pennsylvania, and settled in the woods at the mouth of Loyalhanah, now in Westmoreland County.[73] I can just remember passing through Tanny Town, and seeing a sign over a tavern door, which represented a boy sitting on a keg with a bunch of grapes in his hand. I thought they were actually grapes, and asked for some to eat. This, and seeing the trees covered with snow, as we rode along, and Isaac Fanosedelle, who travelled with us, is all I recollect of the journey. But, to the anecdote.

A vast number of sugar trees grew in that region, and my mother employed herself in the spring of the year in making sugar. I was about four or five years old, when my father being on a journey, and my mother, as usual, employed at the sugar camp, had left my sister (younger than I) and myself in the house by ourselves. The spring was far advanced, and as my sister and myself were amusing ourselves catching butterflies before the cabin door, on a warm sunshine evening, we were on a sudden surprised by a gentleman on horseback, who rode up to us, and inquired "if he could stay all night." We stood still, staring at the gentleman, not knowing what answer to make, till he inquired where our parents were, and what were there names. I was always the first to speak, and said, "my mama is at the sugar camp, and her name is Mary; and my papa's name is William." "I shall stop," said he, and alighted from his horse, and taking off the saddle, laid it down by the door, and asked me "if we had a stable to put horses in?" I told him I did not know what that was—but we put old Bonny in the pen there, pointing it out to him. "Have you any corn?" said the gentleman. "Yes, sir, we have corn in the crib." "You are a fine girl; come and show me the crib," said he, smiling: and after turning his horse in the pen, I ran to show him the crib, communicating every incident within my memory to him, without reserve, at which he laughed heartily, and chatted with me in turn.—But a violent dispute succeeded to this. I told him he took too much corn for his horse; he must not take more than twelve *ears*, that was all we gave to Bonny. He gave the best of reasons why his horse should have more than Bonny; but he argued to the wind. Our parents had laid down certain rules for us to go by, and these were as firm and steadfast as the laws of the Medes and Persians. I did not grudge him the corn, but thought he was a novice in the art of feeding a horse; and, finally, he was forced to let me have my own way.

Our cabin, or camp rather, was very small—not more than 8 or 10 feet. This contained one bed, four wooden stools, with legs stuck in them through augur holes, half a dozen tin cups, and the like number of pewter plates, knives, forks, and spoons, though my sister (very mischievous) had lost one of the knives, (for which I was chastised,) broke one of the spoons, and seriously damaged one of the plates. Besides these we had a tray and a frying pan, a camp-kettle, and a pot; and our cabin was considered the best furnished on the frontier. Besides this, we had a table made of a puncheon, (a tree split in half,) and like the other furniture, was graced with four substantial legs of rough hewed white oak. I think we had a towel, but as for table-cloth, I had never seen one to my knowledge; and neither trunk nor box incommoded us. There was a few skins upon which those reposed who thought proper to share them. Sometimes we had bread, and always a plenty of meal.[74]

The gentleman upon entering the hut, asked "if we had any thing to eat? I am very hungry; I have eat nothing since morning." "We have plenty of jerk (dried venison) in the chimney," I replied. He soon had a piece in his hand; and hearing a hen at the door, he asked if we had any eggs? My sister upon the inquiry ran out to a nest, hard by, and brought four eggs in, and gave them to him. He made a hole in the ashes, and covered up the eggs, and having salt and biscuit with him, he made a hearty meal. He gave us a cake each.

It was now near night, and after taking a walk to look at his horse, the gentleman being weary, said he would lie down. He had travelled that day from Pittsburg. I offered him the only bed in the house, saying *we* could sleep on the floor; we had done so many a time. He declined the offer, and throw a bear skin, said, "that would do very well. I am used to camping out; this will be delightful," and threw himself on the floor. I ran and brought two or three more, and seeing I was hardly able to drag them along, he laughed and took them from me. He put his saddle under his head, and I took a spare quilt and threw it over him. In a very few minutes he was fast asleep, and still my mother came not, though it was quite dark; I put my sister to bed, as she grew sleepy, and sat up alone.

My mother having a fine day for her business, did not arrive till, perhaps, an hour after dark, and one of the next neighbors, a female (the only one we had, except the Peery's) came with her, as she frequently did, when my mother was alone: and, in turn, my mother would take us children, when their husbands were absent, and spend the night with her. I had heard their approach, and opening the door, ran to meet them with the news I had to impart. I expected to receive the applause of the two; but what was my astonishment to find they were not only displeased, but alarmed. It was just at the commencement of hostilities with the Indians, and several white men were recently detected as spies. "He is a spy, I'll wager," said aunt Molly, (as we called her.) "I'll be bound!" said my mother, "or some robber come to murder us. You ought not to have let him in the house," said she sharply; "never do the like again." Finding I had done wrong in my mother's estimation, I sneaked into the house, and set myself down, leaving the matrons holding a counsel in the yard. At length they entered, on tiptoe, and lighting a lamp, took a peep at the stranger, who was snoring aloud. They drew near the fire, after this, and aunt Molly Carrahan said, "I don't like his looks." "Nor I neither," said my mother. "He looks for all the world," said the former, "like Paddy Dunahan, that was hung in Limerick, for killing of Dennis O'Shaan." My mother said she had a great mind to take her children, and go to Mr. Blane's to-night. "Not a foot will ye stir," said aunt Molly. "I'll tell you what we'll do, Mary. I'll just put on the camp-kettle and have it a boiling in a giffey, and if he offers to stir, I'll scald his eyes out the first thing. He's just one of them English, I'll warrant, come to spy out the land; but if he offers for to go to molest us, I'll put him past spying."

The camp-kettle was put on, and a brisk fire made under it; and for my part, in no apprehension from the stranger, I laid myself down, and soon fell asleep. The first thing I saw in the morning, was the gentleman pulling on his boots, and my mother, (who doubtless sat up the whole night,) with a smile, bid him good morning; and aunt Molly, an Irish woman, "hoped he had had pleasant dreams." The gentleman apologized, said he had been very fortunate in lighting upon a house; that he had travelled the preceding day through the wilderness without meeting with one, and praised me no little for a fine girl; and told the story to my mother about the horse feed. The two ladies were highly delighted, and breakfast was prepared for him before he set out; his horse fed; and, at his departure he gave me a silver dollar, the first I ever saw. And whom do you think was the gentleman? No less than the amiable Mr. Findley, long a member of Congress from Pennsylvania, distinguished for his republican principles, and one of the ablest men in the state. He used to be called "the walking library," from his knowledge of books; and one of the finest *looking* men in the world.[75]

Yours, &c.

Letter XXXIII.

Melton's Bluff, February 6th, 1818.

Dear Matt,

SPRING has commenced—the trees on the river are green and the people are beginning to plough. They plant cotton here the first week in March, and, I think, corn too—the plowing commences the first week in February.

You ask if I have books? Yes; I have read Salmagundi, Phillips' Speeches, and Lady Morgan's France; all new to me.[76] I never saw them before. They are very interesting. Standing in a store one day, I saw a book lying amongst some rubbish, and requesting the clerk to hand it to me, after brushing the dust from it, I found it to be "Salmagundi," a humorous and well written work, by Paulding and Irving, of New York, so it is said. "Oh," said the boy, "that is not a *good* book. If you want a book to read, here is a *good* book," and handed Russell's Seven Sermons. He put me in mind of old Mrs. W____, whom you must have known. She came to our house one Sunday; (she hardly missed a Sunday;) I was reading Buffon, and laying the book on a chair to attend to something about the house, the woman picked it up, and turning the leaves over, exclaimed, "La, do you read such books to-day?" "Why! what is the matter with it?" "Why it an't a *good* book. I would not read such a book on the Sabbath." Now, this woman would pick whortleberries, and even wash her clothes on Sunday. The young man was, doubtless, of the same stamp.

Have you seen Lady Morgan's France? You will be pleased with it. For a woman she is a fine writer. This work will long remain a standing evidence of that towering genius which knows no sex. Her delineation of men and manners are well drawn. Her style is classical, nervous, glowing, and pure, and discovers a perfect knowledge of mankind. She is the best portrayer I have met with, except Voltaire. She descends to the bottom, and searches the lowest depths of society. She re-ascends amongst the nobility and gentry, and unlocks the cabinets of kings and ministers. She examines for herself. She bursts the chains of prejudice, and comes forth arrayed in honors all her own. This female, an honor to her sex, and the brightest ornament of literature, was once, it seems, an actress, and on the stage.

I have seen severeal *new* novels, which, with the exception of Walter Scott's, I do not read. Insipid, frothy, nauseous stuff, I cannot endure them,—they are so stuffed with unmeaning words. Now what do you say to "playfulness, fastidious, witchery;" how silly in sound and signification; it makes one sick, and serves no purpose but to entangle the subject and obscure the sense. And, by the way, these silly novel writers must show their learning. Profound philosophers! deeply read in history! abundance of things irrelevant to the subject. Simpletons, we suppose every one know these things. But, as some one has said, "let blockheads read what blockheads write." But I find these novels corrupt the morals of our females, and engender hardness of heart to real distress. Those most pleased with fictitious distress, have hearts as hard as iron. If they are pleased with one who relieves fictitious distress, the reality ought to please much more, and every one may be a *real* hero, or heroine, with less trouble than writing or reading a romance. Let them just step into the streets, the highways, or the hovel of the widow or orphan, heaven knows they may find enough there; they need not look in books for distress. I have seen pictures of real distress, which greatly exceeded the pen of any novel writers; and yet none heeds it. Relieving these would be Godlike, and would impart a heaven upon earth. But you like short letters.

Adieu!

Letter XXXIV.

Melton's Bluff, February 7th, 1818.

Dear Matt,

I AM never better pleased, than when seated alone by a bright fire, a clean swept hearth, a lighted candle, and a pair of snuffers. I have a snuffer-tray too, but one who was raised in the woods, you know, can easily dispense with a snuffer-tray; but I confess, I abominate that practice of snuffing the candle with your fingers. I was going on, however, to say, that gives me more pleasure than to seize my pen at night, sitting comfortably, as I just observed, and talking to you on paper; and here follows another catalogue of every day incidents, appalling ones indeed, but you *will* have them.

It is on one hand asserted, that human nature is the same in all ages, and in all countries, on our globe. This is denied by others, who say "as the twig is bent, the tree's inclined." That there is a difference in mankind, is certain, and I am forced to believe this difference is the effect of education.—Mankind, say some, are all alike. Alike, in what? This vague conclusion is a violation of justice and truth. If it be meant that mankind are alike in shape—true; but that they are alike in actions, I deny! Else how comes it, that one man will cooly, wantonly, and deliberately spill the blood of his fellow man; whilst another affectionately relieves his sufferings? Whether the cause of this difference lies in nature, or education, I am unable, or rather unwilling, to say. But I am inclined to think it the effect of education. We have a conclusive evidence in the two *puppies* of Lycurgus. One of these was purposely trained to the chase, and the other left to pursue the dictates of nature. Lycurgus, you will recollect, to convince the Spartans of the power and influence of education on children, brought the two dogs, both of the same litter, into the school room, and setting a dish of victuals in the centre of the room, also a live hare, let loose the two dogs; and what was the consequence? the dog trained to the chase took after the hare, and the other ran to the dish of victuals.

It is, however, well known, that the brute, in a state of nature, is superior to the human race; for instance, dog will not eat dog; cat will not eat cat; nor will any of the brute creation feed on its own species. But man will eat man! This fact cannot be denied; and though we have line upon line, and precept upon precept; and teachers from A, B, C, to the mathematics for these 1818 years, yet we have cannibals still.—This proves that something is wrong in our system of education; or while it evidently improves our nature in one place, why does it not improve the whole—and while it has been able to cure one vice, why has it not cured all? It is clear, education improves mankind, and makes them happier, why then does it progress so slow? The system must be wrong. But what I was going to remark, we have great encouragement to press forward in the arts of improvement, and since we have been able to overcome the shocking practice of feeding upon the flesh of our fellow man, we may in time, perchance 1818 years hence, be able to arrive to such a height of refinement, as to cease from the practice of killing him; which I think is a much worse crime than eating him after he is dead. It does the dead no harm to eat him; and yet what an outcry against cannibals. It is not the eating a man after he is dead, that constitutes crime; it is the taking away his life. A lady told me once she would kill an hundred men before she would eat one. She was a christian and not a cannibal. I hope, however, to see the day that we may cease to kill men, since we have ceased to eat them. In the one case we have so far overcome nature, and I hope we will not stop till murder is rooted out from amongst mankind.

I was led into these reflections, by various incidents of recent occurrence, in this region; but no matter, wherever I go, wherever I turn, I see ignorance the most besetting crime, of the blackest die, and vice the most glaring. Amusing myself this evening with a spy-glass, viewing the gambols of a large flock of swans, whilst I had the glass up to my eye, I saw a boat gliding swiftly down the river. It drew near to the shore, on the opposite side, and a solitary man leaped out, and fastening the boat, hastily disappeared in the woods. I sat musing upon the strange appearance of seeing but one man in the boat, when I was called to supper, where I found several strangers, who had just arrived. In the course of the conversation I mentioned the circumstance; when one of the strangers, who was from East Tennessee, inquired the dress, and height of the man, and observed, "that is the man we are in pursuit of." He then added, "that this man had committed two murders in East Tennessee, one in the summer, and one in the fall; and that he was so desperate, people were afraid to risk their lives in apprehending him; and he went at large." He has a sister over the river, three miles from here, where I suspect he has gone to night. His sister lives at Fort Hampton,[77] and is a very fine looking woman. I breakfasted at her house on my way from Huntsville. The gentleman endeavored to collect men to go and take him that night; but no one was willing to join in the enterprize, and we heard no more of him. But the following circumstance would seem to confound the the idea advanced in the commencement of this letter, and seems to decide in favor of man, in a state of nature; so you may see, that by giving both sides of the question, I am free from prejudice at least. About a year since, a widow lady, who lived in East Tennessee, having received several invitations to go to reside with a brother who lived in the lower part of this territory, accordingly, disposing of her property, excepting two beds, a negro girl, a favorite white cow, and three horses upon which she and a daughter, (who was a woman grown,) her beds, &c. were to be conveyed. She took passage by water, in East Tennessee, with other persons, (who were removing,) to this place, intending to pursue the residue of her journey by land. She remained here at the Bluffs, a few days, endeavoring to procure a man to accompany her, both as guide and protector, her way lying through the Choctaw Indian nation. A man, with whom she had been formerly acquainted, and who had followed the business of navigating the Tennessee, (or boating down the river, as it is called,) happened to come to the Bluff; she hired this man, and set forward on her journey. The first day after leaving the Bluff, they overtook two Indians who were travelling the same way. They all proceeded together, until the next night. Some hours, however, before night, the young lady complained of being sick, and wanted water. The Indians informed her, that there was a fine spring, a few miles before them, at which they would arrive about camp time. The young woman being very thirsty, asked if there was no water nearer. They replied that there was a little creek about half way. They travelled on to this creek, when the white man said he would stop for the night. The Indians tried to dissuade him from his purpose, but in vain—he would stay there—the Indians would go on to the spring.

In the night the negro girl was awakened by the screams of her young mistress, and beheld her old mistress weltering in blood, and in the last struggles of death; and the wretch, their guide, in the act of raising an axe to split out the brains of the young lady, which he instantly did, although she begged her life of him on her knees! He then ran to the negro girl, and commanded her to *hush* instantly, or he would split out her brains also; but that, if she would be a good girl, and report (if any inquiries were ever made for the women) that they were killed by the Indians, she should not be hurt. He then took the two dead bodies, one at a time, and dragged them by the heels, as the girl states, and threw them on an island in the aforesaid creek. The next morning he set out with all the property, changing his course a little from that which the Indians had taken. To the first white inhabitant, whose house he reached, he sold the murdered woman's beds, her wearing apparel, and the cow. When questioned about the blood on the beds, he said his wife was travelling with him; that she took sick and died; that she had been bled, and in that way accounted for the blood on the bed. He then proceeded towards the Spanish dominions, taking the negro girl and horses with him. In the course of two months, the same two Indians returned, and happened to call at the same house where the white man sold the clothing and white cow. Seeing the cow in the yard, they knew her instantly, and asked what was become of the two women who owned that cow. The man replied, that he had bought the cow of a travelling *man*, not a woman. To repeated inquiries made by the Indians, they discovered it must be the same man. The horses, the negro girl, &c. corroborated so exactly, that the Indians immediately suspected the man of murdering the women. They stated every circumstance of the young lady's wanting water, the creek, and the spring; and proposed that this man should go with them and they would, probably, find the dead bodies. Accordingly, the man went with the Indians, and found *their* camp by the spring, as they had stated, and the other by the creek, exactly as the Indians had reported; and upon searching the spot sometime, they found the dead bodies in the creek, and round the waist of the young women, they found specie and bank notes to a large amount!!!

The man who purchased the property, said he would have the murderer at the hazard of his life and fortune.—He pursued him, and in the lower country found him, and, securing him in jail, returned home. The murderer broke jail and returned to East Tennessee. The man who first took him, hearing this, proceed to Tennessee, retook him, and placed him in jail, which he again broke, and has not been heard of since. The gentleman who had so often interfered, in endeavoring to bring this murderer to punishment, was heard to say "he would pursue the murderer to the end of the world, but he would find him."[78]

Yours, &c.

Letter XXXV.

Melton's Bluff, February 8th, 1818.

Dear Matt,

I LAID over the other part of my subject (ignorance) for another letter. You may remember the little Natchez widow, our guest; also the proud, haughty, next neighbor. Since that, *another* widow has arrived, different from both these. She is learned, sensible, and gay, though rather satirical. The little widow is very captious, and pronounces "dis, dat, and torra," the common dialect I am told of the country she came from. She does not want sense, however, but is little skilled in the affairs of the world. Old Mrs. Starchy and her can never agree, and the other widow amuses herself at their expense, and often has them almost by the ears. But I am rambling again. Several gentlemen, on a visit to this country to purchase land, spent a few days at the Bluff. They were gentlemen of intelligence, learning, and politeness. While here, they had frequent opportunities of conversing with the ladies, of which they availed themselves with that taste and good sense which ever distinguish well bred people. But, alas! then it was I discovered the disadvantage a female labors under, when destitute of education; and this is still more apparent when contrasted by one of their own sex. It is well for them their ignorance effectually screens them from all knowledge of the ridiculous figure they made. If they were sensible of the pain they inflict upon those who are so unfortunate as to hear them blundering from one thing to another; miscalling some words, and misapplying others; and the no small pains they take to expose their ignorance, shame and mortification would drive them mad.

One evening, when all our females were present, (I have always heard widows were jealous of each other, but this time I had occular proof of the fact,) our newly arrived widow put her rivals to shame, and gained a complete victory. This she was enabled to do, without violating those rules of politeness, which dispose the well bred modesty to concede their talents, rather than wound the feelings of the company. The conversation, at first, general, soon turned upon the victory of New Orleans, and its consequences to the British government; the accumulation of their national debt; and the expenditures of their navy in times of peace. This last was stated by a friend of the lady; in doing which, he inadvertently committed himself. The lady had paid deep attention to the subject, and seemed to participate in it like one thoroughly acquained with the subject; and the moment the gentleman mistated the amount of the expenditures, she smiled, and set him right. He bowed to her, as much as to say, go on, I yield to you. She took up the subject where he left off, and went into a complete investigation of the British policy; the measures of their ministers; and their effects upon the people at large. She introduced many original remarks of her own, upon their system of finance, with the probable effects that may result, or grow out of the contemplated change. Imagine the surprise of the company, who regarded her with deep attention. The ladies turned their eyes upon her in astonishment, and stared at her for some time; but, at length, they began to whisper, and carry on a corversation amongst themselves, with no friendly aspect. I heard one of them say, "Some folks ar very fond o' talkin with men—I never liked men." "Nor I neither," said another lady, in a negro dialect; "it's a bad sign to see some folks so fond o' men." "I never, for my part," said old Starchy, "liked men so well." When I hear a woman say she does not like men, I have the same opinion of her that I have of a man who praises his honesty; or a parson who boasts of his religion. There is a striking analogy between these three descriptions of people, and one conclusion may apply to the whole of them.

On the next morning our guests departed, and a friend of ours took occasion to call on the lady who expressed such a dislike to *men*. He carelessly observed, that he felt quite lonesome upon the departure of the strangers. She bridled up, and said, "Where is Mrs. ——; she is very good company I 'spose?" "Yes," said the gentleman, "she is very agreeable; she has very few equals." "I 'spose she's a great scholar; and I dare say she's very rich. For my part, I don't know what she is, nur I don't care, that's more. She's a mightly game-making sort of woman, for one thing, I know. If I was Mrs ——, I would tell her a piece of my mind, I know—that I would. She's a mighty *comicle* sort of a somebody anyhow, oh!" she ended, and shook her head.

A lady asked me one day "What state Virginia was in?" Another asked "If Canada was not in Kentucky?" and, another "Supposed Joe Graphy was very hard to learn."

Hence arises all our mistakes in religion, morals, and politics. When our reason is cultivated and our minds enlightened by education, we are enabled to strip off that disguise which knavery, bigotry, and superstition wears. It rectifies our judgments, holds the reins of our passions, in short, enables us to discover whatever tends to promote our present and eternal welfare. I was reading a newspaper to-day in which was something respecting Ireland; a genteel, well-dressed looking man was standing by, and asked me if Ireland was not in South America! He lives in this place; he is worth not less than twenty thousand dollars; is a candidate for the office of sheriff, in this county, which is the next wealthiest in the state; he has eight or nine competitors, and the misfortune is, that the electors, or a majority of them, and his rivals, are equally ignorant! Now, what sort of an administration of public affairs are we to expect when it is wielded by such men as these? This is to be the downfall of our country some day!—All republicans have fallen from the same cause. We learn, when the republics of Rome was overturned, it was done by the ignorant vulgar. We find that all the men of learning and polite manners, rallied on the side of liberty, while Caesar was worshipped by the common people—as a friend of mine once said, "all the common people want rope enough." This ignorance is not confined to any one part of the Union; it is universal. I happened to be in court once in a respectable county in Virginia. The court was just commencing, the judge ordered the sheriff to "command silence until he gave the charge to the Grand Jury." The sheriff replied, that "he would thank him (the judge) to do it himself, as he was a new hand at the business." This was the high sheriff of the county. Why, a person who is reputed to know any thing of geography, philosophy, or astronomy, is looked upon with as much abhorrence by the great mass of the people, as if he were in league with the devil. They are jealous of the rich and great. Why then, do they grovel in the dark? Why don't they seek to have their minds enlightened, which is their only security against the oppression and encroachments of the wealthy? In a country like this, where the freedom of elections bestows public honors and public offices on every man alike, how can he discharge the duties of his office with honor to himself, or benefit to his country, who is ignorant of the principles of the very foundation of his government? or how can he tell when the government is administered correctly by others, when he is destitute of the knowledge by which he is to ascertain the fact? Ever since I can remember, this has been the case: the great mass of the people are just the same; not one step do they advance in knowledge. Is there not something wrong in our system of education? If there be, where does the defect lie? I have seen many evils, much sorrow, much oppression, much wickedness of all descriptions and degrees, indeed I see nothing else. I have taken much pains to trace these evils to their source, and find its origin in ignorance. I have pursued them through all those labyrinths, and they all stop here. But to apply a remedy, or to dictate one, would exceed, herhaps, the powers of any one man or woman. If I were to speak from experience upon this desultory view of the subject, I would say, in the first place, that man is a reasonable being, reason is improved by observation and study, and, as we see, hear, and understand from the cradle to the grave, we are learning from the first dawn of understanding. Man's education, therefore, begins with his life, and ends at his death. But first impressions are the most permanent, because they find the mind empty and prepared to take in a greater share than it is ever able to do thereafter; and because the mind is soft and blank, as a sheet of white paper receives the type, so it receives the impression of images which are never effaced, and although he still is improving by observation, yet the original impressions are the strongest and accompanies us to the end of our lives. How necessary is it then to impress the young mind with justice and humanity. How necessary to enforce them, both by precept and example, since these impressions are to influence them all their lives afterwards. But when parents are ignorant themselves, deplorable indeed must be the state of their offspring. Destitute of learning himself, a man sees not the necessity of cultivating the reason of his child, who, thrown on the world like a vessel on the ocean, without sail or rudder, no wonder he is shipwrecked on the rocks of superstition and credulity.—But here lies the misfortune, and here I fear it is long to rest: most parents not only being ignorant but are highly prejudiced against learning. I shall dismiss the subject by a remark on myself, upon the strength and force of early impressions.

When I was yet a very small child, being a *terrible* great scholar, and a *cruel* good reader, my mother, proud of her first born, procured scores of *little histories* for me to read—such as the "Seven Wise Masters," "Moll Flanders," "Paddy from

Cork," &c. and many a weary hour did I pour over these *little histories*. I knew they were stories, that is, falsehoods; and what was the consequence—when I came to read real history, I had no more idea that it was reality than I had that Aladdin and his Lamp, were true. The very name, *history*, of all others, bore the impression of falsehood, and it was long before I could believe that history was a narrative of facts; and had I not fortunately fell in with a person of learning, I should always have delved at *little histories*.

Every country have their little histories. Since I have been here, numbers have asked me to loan them a *little history:* all have the *little*. From not mixing with the common people, not one in a thousand is aware of this state of society. One would think that it would be the first and only object with men of letters, to set on foot some method to enlighten the great mass of the people, as they must, inevitably, and that before long, have the management of matters in their own hands!—And many a one, at this moment, are in office, by the instrumentality of a vote purchased for half a pint of whiskey! But says one, "there always have been degrees of knowledge, and always will be distinctions in society;—nor was it intended all men should be upon an equality." That there has always existed degrees in knowledge, I admit, but that ignorance is a necessary consequence, is most false. There is another Jay's treaty for you.

Yours, &c.

Letter XXXVI.

Melton's Bluff, February 19th, 1818.

Dear Matt,

Now we have it from real life. If this does not cure you of the *blues*, nothing that I can give you will. You have heard of electioneering, and have seen it too. But your elections bear no comparison to those here.

This country exhibits man in all his varieties, and in all his gradations, from the country boor, to the most polished gentleman.—There is something truly amusing in contemplating the progress of society. To see man slowly emerging from a state of nature, to take his stand in civilized life—to behold him in defiance of rules and maxims thrusting himself forward, his means small, and at most, precarious—his understanding limited—his heart ingenuous, exposing him to the subtleties of his designing neighbor—to consider man in this point of view, is a luxury to a thinking mind.

This morning, while we were sitting at breakfast, a stranger stepped in, who proved to be one of the neighbors. He was rather coarsely dressed, but had a pleasing aspect. "Well, old fellow," said the Colonel, "how goes it;" shaking hands cordially. "How do you do? Come, Sir, sit down, and take some breakfast with us—[Maria bring a plate, and knife and fork]—Come, Sir, take a dram first—[Hand a glass Maria."] The stranger took a dram, and then seated himself at the table; and the Colonel and him carried on a kind of dialogue, for some time. "How is your family, Sir?" "Why I'm 'obliged to you, Colonel, the'r all about, but Mary: She's got her ager yet. How's it wi' yourself?" "We are all well thank you, Sir. Let me help you to another piece of steak. Have some of the gravy, Sir. Well, lets hear the news: who do the people talk of voting for—[take some butter, Sir]—in your part? What do they talk about?" "Why, some on 'em is mighty feard, see, of losin their land; and some on 'em agin is 'mind to stand 'em a pull. I tell you what, Colonel"—[Sam put more wood on the fire]—"its hard upon a poor man, after all, after clearin on himself a smart patch o' ground, and puttin it under a good fence." —[Pour out some more coffee, Maria]—"see, and buildin on him a snug cabin, and then for a rich man like you, Colonel, because he rebounds in most money, to come to buy it from over his head, see t'll 'e what, it's little sort o' hard. But I reviewed it so from the first. I saw how it was a goin and sold out. If they fool me they have but one more to fool." "Well, but tell me, old fellow, who do the people talk of voting for on Flint?" "Why, to tell the truth, Colonel, they'r purty much divided. Some on 'em talks a runnin Doctor Crab—[Maria set that decanter on the table]—and some on 'em agin talk o' votin for Lawyer L." [Take some whiskey, Sir.]—"But tell me, who do you intend to vote for?" "Well, I was jist goin to say, I don't hold with sendin none of these here doctors, and lawyers, and 'losophers.—I look upon it, see, that these here men of larnin jist lay the'r heads together, and cologue, and jist make laws to 'press the poor. I'm for 'sportin a plain farmer, like myself, Colonel, that will act upon nomical principles—an't I right?" "But tell us, old fellow,[79] have you any corn to sell up your way?" "Why, it's purty tol'able sca'ce. I raised a fine chance this year, and my wife had the finest passel of *truck*—I da'e say, she had greens enough to a 'splied the whole neighborhood; but Jim Wilson's critters broke in and most 'stroyed the whole affair: so it is, I shall have to buy. The neighbors told me, if it had abin them, as it was me, they would a shot the critters. But that would abin too sneakin. But an't you comin to the barbacue, next Friday? Doctor Crab is goin to have a great barbacue, and goin to make a stump speech; and there's to be the greatest doins that ever was heard on. He's sent up two barrels of whiskey, and—" "Where is it to be?"—"Why it's to be at Elum's Mill; and old Molly's goin to do her best. I dare say sh'll make her own out on 'em. She's one of your most inactive women folks in all my knowin, and she has plenty to go upon. Come up, Thursday, to my house, and bring your gun, and we'll take the hounds and have a hunt. Thank God, I have plenty to go upon, enough to eat and drink, and plenty to feed your critter. We'll knock up a fat chicken or two, and my wife is first rate at a cup of coffee. Stay all night, and we'll take a hunt in the mornin!"

"Well, Sir, I believe I will." "That's clever: I shall look for you." "So, some of your neighbors are a mind to contest the public sales?" "They say so. Tom Towns says he has a friend that will help him out. But you know how it was the first land sales; every poor fellow as *fout* for his country, was forgotton, see, and kicked off, and thought nothin of—Don't tell me about *premptions;* oh! I seed enough! Colonel Donalson said it was a disabolical business." Though I was unable to discover the Colonel's candidate, I was pleased with the blunt honesty of the countryman, who was now interrupted by the entrance of another countryman.[80a]

The ladies withdrew, but I was spell-bound to the spot. —It is in the rude state of the species, we are to seek for the true characteristics of man. When he becomes polished, his resources enables him to conceal his real character.

The second guest was alike known to the Colonel and the first guest. "How goes it, how goes it, old fellow?" said the Colonel, to the second guest. "Why purty well, I'm 'bliged to you. How's it wi' yourself. How goes it [to the first guest] Mr. Smith?" "Purty well, how's it wi' yourself?—And how is all your consarns?"

First Guest. All well but my oldest darter; she's got her ager yet—How's all your consarns?"

Colonel. Maria, set that decanter back, and get some hot coffee, and set a plate. Come, Sir, [to second guest] help yourself; that is old Kentucky—come, Sir, take some breakfast; the girl will soon have you a hot steak.

First Guest. Well, what's for times your way?

Second Guest. I tell you what, it's purty diggin—[seats himself at table]—Corn's a dollar a bushel, and can't be got at that—and some is runin away, and some talkin o' the 'lection, and some's talkin o' the land sales. This whiskey's prime.

First Guest. Who's runaway.

Second Guest. Bill Cheatum's cleared out. He sarved Tom

Marchant the slickest as every you heard on in all the days o' your life. We was all settin talkin and takin a dram in at Marchant's last Friday, before breakfast, when who should come along, ridin of a critter,[80b] but Bill. I seed he had skins tied behind him; so he hitches his critter, and comes in, and after talkin awhile, and takin a dram, he axed to look at some cloth, and told Marchant to cut off four yards, and takes out a 100 dollar note, and pays for the cloth, and puts the change in his pocket, and axed Marchant if he didn't want to trade for some *coonskins*. Marchant said he didn't care if he did, if they were good. So Bill goes out and brings in the coonskins. Marchant looks at them—very good skins—counted the tails, and axed what for trade he'd make? So, Bill said he'd take same he'd always gave, and would take it in domestic cotton; and the other agreed to it, and the skins lay on the counter. So, after awhile Bill went off, and I went off home, too, and never heard any more of it till yesterday; I was at the store, and Marchant, says to me, says he, "do you think that r——l Cheatum didn't cheat me that day, give me a counterfeit note —and didn't you see how slick he sarved me about the coonskins. Didn't you see the coonskins, and didn't you see the note?" "Yes, says I, I saw the coonskins, and the *note, too*." "Nothing in the world but possom skins, coontails tied to them, and only bare two coonskins in the whole, one at top and one at bottom." With that he showed me the skins; and sure enough nothing but possum skins, and the note not worth one cent. It's as fair cheatin says I, as ever I seed in my life; and you can make him smoke for it. Yes, says Marchant, but catching's before hanging—the villain's cleared out.

Thus the Colonel and his guests talked and laughed at the *coonskins*—drank whiskey, electioneered, and finally settled the affairs of the nation among themselves.

Yours, &c.

N.B. I leave this for Virginia, next week.

Letter XXXVII.

Melton's Bluff, December 25th, 1818.

Dear Matt,

A MERRY Christmas to you; and a merrier one than we have, you need not. I cannot hold the pen for laughing. Such another comic farce was never played on any stage as was played here last night. But first, without meeting or seeing your brother, I arrived, on my way from Virginia, at the Bluff, last night. I met with the Colonel at Limestone Court, and the evening being fine, and our company lively and jovial, we concluded to proceed all the way to the Bluff, where we arrived about 10 o'clock, and found the company still up. For though they had no expectation of seeing me, till I entered the house, they were looking for the Colonel, who, by promise, was to be home that night.

The Colonel has been appointed to marry people since I left the Bluff; and, late as the hour was, he had to marry a couple, who had been waiting for him from an early hour in the day. The clerk of the county, who boards with the Colonel, and who had issued the license, came in to apprise him, and the Colonel forthwith sent for the couple. Imagine our surprise, at seeing an old man of about sixty, and the bride little under. The Colonel, being a man of humour, blends sundry ceremonies with the marriage contract, suited to his fancy and the persons he marries.

In the first place he told the couple to stand forth, asked them several ludicrous questions—made them repeat the Lord's prayer—and when the ceremony was ended, (being put up to it by the young men who boarded with him) directed them to a room of his own house, to spend the night. We then separated, and retired to rest, and this morning we were thrown into convulsions with laughter, at the merry dance the lovers were led after they left us. During my absence from the Bluff, several young doctors and lawyers have arrived, and have their residence here. Being young, wild, and frolicksome, they are always devising some means of amusement, and the old couple were selected as a subject of sport, upon whom it appeared they played sundry mischievous pranks, in the course of the night. For this purpose they laid their plan during the day, selecting a room for the purpose. They went so far, in the first place, to persuade a merry old soul of a bar-keeper to marry the couple during the day; and they were in the act of setting off to their home, when the bar-keeper told them he "was not the Colonel; that he was only an apprentice, and married them by way of getting his hand in." But the party contrived to keep them, knowing the Colonel would certainly be at home.—Meantime they had removed every thing out of the room which might serve as weapons of defence, and carefully disposed some plank in a corner of the room, and was at no small pains to dress up one of the party like a ghost, and esconsed him behind the plank.

The houses at the Bluff are nothing but rude cabins built of logs, with cracks between the logs, so that any one without can see what passes within. These mischievous wags, had fixed the bed upon a lilt, which by pulling a rope fastened to it, would fall down. This rope they drew through, in the outside, between the logs. They had also provided themselves with a number of canes, of different sizes—the cane being hollow, served as bugles, and make a hollow, doleful sound, when blown through with the mouth. Some of the canes were large, and others small, so as to have *treble*, *tenour*, *bass*. Thus, the bride and bridegroom were no sooner beded, and a bright fire in the hearth, than the ghost, upwards of six feet in height, stalked forth with a white sheet round it, and advanced towards the lovers, with a slow grave step. Those without began to blow their bugles, at the same time. The bride shrieked out, and covered her head—not so the bridegroom—being an old soldier, it would have taken more ghosts than one to have frightened him. Finding the ghost continued to advance, he sprang out of bed, and looked about for some weapon for defence; finding nothing but a box of nails, which from its weight he was unable to wield, he flew round the room for something else. Meanwhile the ghost slipped out of doors.—The hero finding he had fled, exclaimed, "Ah, d——n you, if you had only waited a moment longer, I'd a tore your long trappings for you." "Oh, my dear," said the bride, "what was that? Listen—only hear—Oh, mercy, we'll be carried away—we'll be murdered—help me up—I always heard old Melton haunted the Bluff." "Haunt the d——l; its them fellows, I tell you, makin their fun—lie still. Oh, blow away and be d——d," said the old man. "But you don't come in here again," and pushed the door too; but finding neither bolt nor latch, he placed one of the planks against it, and betook himself to bed again. The imps watching him through the cracks all the while, he no sooner drew the clothes over him than down came the bed and all, with a sudden crash! Report says, instead of praying for his enemies, like a good christian, he uttered many hard names; and running out of doors, swore vengence against every *shoe-boot* gentleman on the Bluff. He flew round the cabin with the agility of a youth of fifteen; and the gentlemen took to flight. "Where are you," cried the enraged lover; "I dare you to show your faces; I'll whip the best of you; I'll take you one by one, and whip the whole of you. Pretty gentlemen with your high crowned hats, and shoe-boots, a screaking." It was to no purpose he drove his enemies from one position to another; he would no sooner return to bed, than his tormentors renewed the music of canes—sometimes putting them through the cracks of the house, near to the ear of the bride: the old man losing all patience, left the place, with his bride, before day, and it is supposed without sleep!—This was really cruel! In these, as well as all other cases, we ought to fulfil the golden rule.[81]

This place looks precisely as it did when I arrived last year, and my absence seems only a dream. The ducks and geese, and swans, seem to be playing where I left them. There are great doings going on here. The population has greatly increased, and the whole country round is one scene of activity.

Yours, &c.

Letter XXXVIII.

Moulton, March 2d, 1819.

Dear Matt,

SINCE the weather became mild, I frequently ride out through this beautiful country, and find not little to admire and amuse. This town is in the centre of Lawrence county, and it is supposed will be the county seat of *justice*.[82] It is 20 miles south of the Bluff, in a most enchanting situation. Several very respectable families live here;[83] the town is handsomely laid off, and the country around it is as rich as heart can wish. I have formed an acquaintance here with an elderly Tennessean, the incidents of whose life is a complete novel.

His father was the first white man that made a permanent settlement on the waters of the Holston, now in the bounds of Tennessee. He settled on the *Wataga*, a creek that empties into the Holston. His name was Burlison, a native of New Jersey, and moved from thence to North Carolina, and finally to Wataga. He was allured, in the first place by the prospect of game, and, in the second place, by good land, and was soon followed by others; and by their united efforts successfully disputed the hunting grounds with the Indians. The timid deer, assailed on all sides by deadly foes, fled before the white man for shelter amongst the Indians. The adventurous white man pursued the game, but in doing so, he was fiercely opposed by the Indians, who disputed every inch of ground with him, at the mouths of their rifles, until they were fairly compelled to yield. Thus was Tennessee settled. This settlement was made about the year 1774 or 1775.[84]

Mr. Burlison was so young at this time, that he recollects nothing of the enterprize. He lost his father at twelve years of age, and from that day, to the end of the Creek war, he has been almost constantly with arms in his hands!—He is a stout man, about 50 years of age—is honest, affable, and generous as a prince; has experienced every vicissitude of fortune, and endured every species of suffering! Peace and war, sickness and health, poverty, and plenty, has at different times been his lot.—He is at this time possessed of an independent fortune, and yet this man, with the manners of a courtier, cannot write his own name! though he reads very well.

This gentleman, for such he is, losing his father at the early age he did, with eight more children, the widow had to struggle with the Indians on one side, and the tories on the other. Most of the children were boys, and their father left property sufficient to educate them, and left strict injunctions to that amount; but the revolutionary war coming on, the widow, between the tories and Indians, was stripped of every thing she had, excepting a valuable brood mare! In order to save this last of her property, she was forced to keep it in the house where she slept every night! But those lawless ruffians, the tories, gaining intelligence of the fact, proceeded to the house, and forcing the door, took her off. This was the last thing she had. Her situation was now at the highest pitch of human misery. Without a friend, without provision; the Indians in alliance with the British, killing all that fell in their way, she dared not flee in that direction. The tories, burning and murdering all before them, on the other side, it was but death, and she resolved to meet it in the woods where she was!

Meantime her oldest son, not 14, and Joseph, (of whom I learned the story,) about 12 years old, would sally forth with gun on shoulder, sometimes alone, but often with others of their own age, to watch the motions of the Indians; and whenever they saw them approach, would hasten to apprize their parents. These little heroes would pass whole days in the woods, at all seasons, almost naked, and without tasting food; for though they saw plenty of game, they were afraid to shoot lest the report of the gun might betray them to the Indians. The two oldest brothers would sometimes take their next eldest brother with them. On this occasion they would wander farther into the forest than usual, and once became so bewildered they lost their course, and wandered about till they were quite spent with fatigue and hunger. The youngest was carrying one of his brother's guns, having none of his own, and seeing a deer jump before him, he levelled the piece at the deer, and killed it; saying, "Indians, or no Indians, he would have something to eat—he might as well die one way as another." The eldest one being alarmed, forced him away, and they concealed themselves in the brushwood to await the result, concluding the Indians, if within hearing, would soon appear. As they lay concealed, the little one who had done the mischief, would often arise up to take a peep at his meat. At length he saw a wolf marching up to it, and pointing it out to his brothers, they bid him be still; but finding he could not be restrained, they all ran together and frightened off the wolf. They then skinned the deer, and kindling a fire, broiled a part of it and swallowed it hastily; and taking what they could carry, once more sought their way home, entirely ignorant of the course. At length night overtook them, and, losing heart, they threw away their venison, and still wandered on, without seeing a human face, and without knowing whither they were going. Late in the night they were overtaken by a hunter, who conducted them home to the no small joy of their mother, who concluded they were killed by the Indians. She had been running through the forest, from the time it grew dark, in a state of distraction. Thus Mr. Burlison, and his brothers, spent nine years, guarding the settlements in this perilous manner, suffering every species of misery. He was three years of the time without shoes, and no sort of clothing, but a shirt made of buckskin!

He states that he had become so inured to cold, hunger, danger, and fatigue, that he was a stranger to their opposites. Meantime their settlement advanced by degrees. Those who survived the fire and sword of the British and the tories, sought their brothers in the wilderness. Their highborn souls fired by their wrongs, glowing with resentment, and inspired by the example of their companions in the wilderness, took courage from despair. Having nothing left but their lives, and disdaining alike British gold and British chains, united with their friends for the common safety. Thus they nurtured a germ, which, in time, hurled destruction on their proud oppressors. Many of these lived to overwhelm their imperious foe with a complete vengeance. Little did the impolitic Briton think those outcasts, those little victims of his wanton barbarity, would ever dare to face him, much less that he would teach him such a lesson in the art of war, as he never learned before. If it be asked in time to come, how so potent an army of vetrans came to be slaughtered by an inferior force, it may be answered, these were the men, and the sons of those men, who, thirty-three years back, nobly resolved never to submit to the British yoke. These were the highminded few, who, in the tender years of childhood, indignant at their wrongs, rushed into the woods, destitute of every comfort; but in their youthful breasts they carried a spark which they cherished at the hazard of their lives; this spark it was, that, bursting into a flame, at New Orleans, laid their daring foe at their feet!—The astonished Britons will long remember, too, that it was his ill judged policy, and inhuman cruelty, that paved the way to it.

Mr. Burlison related many anecdotes of those enterprizing men. As they increased in numbers, they extended their settlements, always keeping a party of choice spirits watching the enemy—of these he was one. In one of their excursions they discovered the fertile plains on Cumberland river; now West Tennessee. In one of those exploring expeditions he made two narrow escapes. Coming suddenly upon the Indians one day, he instantly threw himself flat on the ground, in some brush wood, and the Indians passed within a few steps of him. At another time, he and his companions came near perishing with cold. They had travelled several days in a succession of snow and rain; one night, however, when they went to strike their camp, they found their powder wet, and they had to remain in their wet clothes all night, wet to the skin, the snow deep, and the night cold and freezing. Thus was Tennessee settled; and by such men.[85]

It has been said that Tennessee was an asylum for outlaws and horse thieves. That Tennessee should be exempt from an evil, common to the settling of all our States, I should be happy to know. I would recommend to horse thieves in particular to choose some other asylum in future, as there is not a state in the Union in which they receive less hospitality.[86]

Yours, &c.

Letter XXXIX.

Moulton, March 10th, 1819.

Dear Matt,

I SPEND much of my time with the Tennesseean. He has a fund of anecdote, and the most retentive memory of any person I ever conversed with. As I have nothing better to amuse you with, I send you more of his history. I was reading this evening of the treachery of Lord Dunmore. Mr. Burlison (or Captain, as he is,) listened to me some time, but at last exclaimed, "Blast him—don't read any more about him. It makes my blood boil whenever I hear the name of a Briton." See how deep rooted their enmity to the British. They are all so! In the course of the conversation that followed, I asked him "if he ever felt the effects of fear; that is, did he ever know what fear was?" "Never but once," he replied, "and that was during the *shakes;*" meaning the earthquakes on the borders of the Ohio and Mississippi, some years back. You recollect them, though they were nothing with us in comparison to those further west.[87]

Taking offence at the general government, Mr. Burlison quit the country, and removed over the Ohio river, not far from New Madrid, in 1811. The first shock happened in the night, when he and his family were all in bed asleep. All on a sudden, they were alarmed by the shaking of the beds; he sprung out of bed, between sleep and awake, but from the reeling of the house he was unable to keep his feet. The hens croaked, and the dogs barked. He could not conceive what it could be. He never thought of an earthquake; but concluded that either the house was haunted, or the end of the world was at hand. The terror of the family was beyond description. They all gave themselves up for lost. He thought he ought to pray, but could not think of any thing proper to say. After the first shock was over, he determined, if he lived till morning, to go to the nearest neighbor and ascertain whether it was the end of the world, or whether the house was haunted. When the morning came, while he was considering what to do, he was surprised with another shock, worse than the first. As this happened in the day time, he thought, within himself, it could not be spirits, as he never heard of their doing mischief in the day time, therefore it must be the end of the world! He was very wicked himself; his children were wicked, and the neighborhood was very wicked, and he concluded they were about to receive the chastisement of heaven. He had a very fleet horse in the stable, but not wishing to leave his family, and being unwell, he desired his son, a man grown, to gallop over to neighbor______, and see how it was there, and if it were the same, he would leave the place instantly. The young man, John, set off to the stable, while the earth, the trees and stable, were swinging backwards and forwards, to such a degree, that it was with difficulty he reached it. He at length brought out the horse, and mounting him, flew over the rocking plain. But it was just as bad there, said Mr. Burlison, and I now bethought myself it must be an earthquake. But let it be what it might, I saw we were all doomed to destruction; for, upon going to the door, I saw the earth sinking, and the trees falling. The great road passed by my door; this road was alive with men, women, and children, shrieking and crying, and some of them almost without clothes, as they had escaped from their beds, and nearly frozen with cold. Some were without hats or shoes—some running one way, some another, in a state of distraction.

Mr. Burlison had heard of a neighborhood, not far off, where the people were professors of religion. I thought if I could live to get there, they would teach me how to prepare for death. My family, were, many of them, sick. I had a new wagon, and a fine team of horses, and several good saddle horses besides. I harnessed up my team without delay, and put the sick ones in the wagon, and the well ones on horses, and set off for the religious neighborhood.

My wife had been sick a long time, and had eat nothing for some days. As we drew near the neighborhood, we espied a woman sitting in a door, as it were, eating mush and milk. My wife's appetite revived at the moment, and she expressed an eager desire to have some of the mush and milk. We approached the door and stopped the wagon, and made our business known to the woman. She had none to spare. She had but little meal in the house—had a great way to go to mill, and could not tell when she could get more. But my wife is sick, and has eat nothing for several days, and as she fancies she can eat the mush and milk, I will give any price you may ask. I took out a silver dollar, at the same time, and held it out to her. She then handed my wife a tin cup about half full of mush and milk, for which I paid her half a dollar! I now began to think I had made a bad exchange, for the people I had left, though wicked, were kind.

When I arrived at the house I had been directed to, the man informed me I could have a house, but it was very small, without a floor, and full of corn: but if I would be at the trouble of emptying it of the corn, and put it in a crib, I might have the house, or pen rather, for so much—ten times the worth of it. I had no choice, and feeble as myself and family were, we joined too and soon dislodged the corn; and my family, (nine children,) my wife, and myself, crowded in this miserable hole. I was little concerned about worldly affairs, however, as I expected an end of all things; for there was no alteration for the *better* in the *shakes;* indeed they were rather wose; all I wanted, or cared for, was to be amongst Godly people, that they might instruct me how to prepare for my doom. In short, I cared nothing about the things of this world. But such was not the case with my religious friends. Some admired my fine wagon; some admired my horses; and others admired my fine new saddles and bridles; and some one thing, and some another, and they must have this, and they must have that. I cared nothing about property provided they would pray for me, and preach for me! They plied me with enough of both! But I soon discovered there were wicked people here too, and, inured to the *shakes*, they resumed their old practices. Some horse-raced it; some played cards, and some preached, whilst others were cheating their neighbors! I saw some running races, some playing cards, some preaching, and the earth shaking, all at the same instant. No wonder, I thought, these people have called down the judgment of heaven. I thought I had seen all strange sights that were to be seen in the world, but never saw the equal of this.

By degrees I grew familiar to the *shakes* myself; but in the meantime these religious people had cheated me out of all my property, and I thought it high time to quit the country; and, from that day to this, I put no faith in religious people. My fine wagon and team; all my horses and all my money, 1,500 dollars in silver, and a fine drove of cattle, gone. I mustered up enough to buy a couple of little ponies for my wife and the two youngest children, to ride, and returned to Tennessee worse than nothing, and had to begin the world again. I now left my wife and children to shift for themselves, and went into the army, and acting as Commissary under General Jackson, I soon recovered my losses. So much for getting in a pet with the government.[88]

As the German's say, "I suspect" this will please you.

Yours, &c.

Letter XL.

Moulton, March 12th, 1819.

Dear Matt,

I CAN find nothing better to amuse you than the anecdotes and history of the old Tennesseean, particularly as I know you to be partial to them. Mr. Burlison is equal to the best library; and, in fact, no library contains a greater variety of amusement. He can commence at the beginning of his life, and relate every incident, not only of himself, but of the times. But chiefly I love to hear his anecdotes of General Jackson's struggles and difficulties in his various campaigns, and the incidents of those brave men who suffered with him.

There is now, I am told, in press, a well written book,

which gives a detail of the southern army, and the principal incidents of General Jackson's life.[89] Such a book is much wanted, and must be very gratifying to the friends and admirers of this great man. The smallest incident of his companions, and his unequalled courage, is devoured with avidity. The settlers of this new country love him to idolatry; and my Tennessee friend is not amongst the least. He was with the General during the whole of the war—as also two of his sons, and a son-in-law. The hardships and privations endured by the General, and his men, are almost incredible. Mr. Burlison, as well as his brother, and a son of each, held a captain's commission in the Creek war; and he gives the clearest description of it I have ever heard. He says the army suffered almost to starvation for want of provisions; and as they were principally militia, it required all the General's skill and address to keep the army together; sometimes, however, a mutinous spirit would appear, in spite of him, and once in particular, their sufferings were so great, that all the appeals of the General to their patriotism, failed; and though, like a common soldier, he shared all their wants and hardships, it would not do, they determined to leave him. His appeals were so pathetic on this occasion as to draw tears from the bystanders. After he thought they were reconciled, he rode out alone, one day, and was astonished to find the whole brigade in the act of marching to Tennessee. He instantly snatched a gun from one of the men, and his left arm being useless from a wound, he rested the gun between his horses ears, and placing himself in front of the column, swore "the first man that moved one step forward, was a dead man." His gun was cocked, ready to fire, and at this critical moment his friends, having missed him, flew to his side. Thus each party stood some minutes; at length the men turned back to camp. "I thought I had seen courage and boldness before," said Mr. Burlison, "but there is not such a men in the world—for one men with one arm to stop a whole brigade! He is the most undaunted being in creation." Mr. Burlison was one of those who adhered to General Jackson.

That inimitable writer, Voltaire, observes, "that to convey a just idea of the characteristics of men, you must strictly observe the expressions which accompany their actions." This was fully illustrated by the expression of General Jackson as he was steadying the gun between his horses ears. This act, and the expression that accompanied it, conveys a better idea of the man than volumes elaborately written.

At another of those mutinies, he threw himself before them, and told them they should not succeed but by passing over his dead body. "In opposing you I am only doing my duty, and I will die where I stand, before I will dishonor my country. What! will you have it said, you abandoned your General?"

On another occasion, he addressed them in a speech of some length, and thus concluded: "I know you are anxious to see your families—and so am I—yet, *do* stay a little longer!—Go with me—the enemy is near—we will conquer him—and then go to our homes!" Again, he told them, "the heart of your General has been pierced! The first object of his affections, and the first glory of his life, were the volunteers of Tennessee. The very name recalls to my mind a thousand tender recollections. Oh, then, my brothers in arms, do not, do not leave me." You see how much he bore rather than resort to cruel measures towards those he loved dear as his own soul. He humoured and carressed his men to such a degree, Mr. Burlison says, that they were like spoiled children—the camp exhibited nothing but a scene of uproar—singing songs, laughing, and loud talking. This laxity of manners led them to frequent mutinies, till the General was exhausted, and he was compelled to make an example of one of the ringleaders, though it wrung his heart with the bitterest sorrow. After this, he had no trouble with the army. Mr. Burlison, who was present at the execution, said he had seen many fall in battle—he had seen many wounded—and had witnessed distress and death in all its shapes, but never saw any thing so awful, or that shocked him more, than this execution. The army was drawn out on parade—the criminal seated in the centre on a stool—his eyes tied with a handkerchief, and eight men, with never failing rifles, standing round him. Mr. Burlison's brother was one, but neither Mr. Burlison, his brother, nor a single man in the army, least of all, the criminal, expected he would be shot, till the word "fire;" and eight bullets pierced him at once! It was expected he would be pardoned, as many had been before. That night not a word was heard in camp. They were all as silent as death. What an effect! General Jackson had no more plague with mutinies.[90]

The men, for want of roads, were compelled to take the horses from the wagons, and carry them up the mountains themselves. On these occasions, the General would throw off his coat and aid the men.

At one time he overtook the baggage wagons at Tennessee River, and the landing being steep, the men were in the act of pushing the wheels up the bank; the general, as usual threw off his coat, and laid hold of the wheels, but seeing one man idle, "friend," said the General, "why do you not assist your companions?" "I am a *corporall*, Sir." "Ah! and what of that; I am a *Generall*." Some one by this time discovered who the stranger was, and informed the corporal. It is hardly necessary to add that the corporal soon put his shoulder to the wheel.

General Jackson, however true it be, is, nevertheless, charged with partiality to his friends; and who is not? But it is said, by those who would lose their lives for him, that he advances his friends or intimates, in preference to others, equally capable. How did he know this? He preferred his friends, because his long acquaintance with their integrity and honor justified the choice! He is, also, accused of being arbitrary. Whether the charge be just or unjust, the result proves he has few equals in the art of war.

To judge accurately of any subject it requires a thorough knowledge of the thing submitted. War is an art, if it be not a science, which above all others, required genius to conceive, skill to concert, wisdom to conduct, judgment to determine, promptness to execute, ability to command, fortitude to endure; patriotism, energy, firmness, decision, perseverance and courage. That General Jackson, possesses all these, in an eminent degree, his enemies admit. But, independently of these, he possesses magnanimity, candour, humanity—a knowledge of the world—a liberal education. He is just, he is bountiful, and beyond, far beyond example, compassionate. This is his character. Now, where will you find a man, at once competent to judge of all these qualities! Not one in an hundred, to say the least. He must possess a competent knowledge of them in the first place; and, in the next place, he must be divested of prejudice. The first requires a mind highly improved by observation and study—and, as for prejudice, it is without remedy, if it be not in education. It requires men of the first science to judge accurately of a single blade of grass—but for an illiterate man to judge accurately on the qualities of general, is out of the question; because, it would be to know what he does not, which is impossible! And, because, he does not understand the subject submitted, he has no idea within himself to correspond with it, and both are necessary to pass sentence of judgment. A man *may* be competent to decide upon the qualities in question; yet, he may err from prejudice, and all reasoning, founded on error, is false. Of prejudice there are several—Prejudices arising from *things*, from *words*, from *ourselves*, from *others;* but none of these are so apt to lead us astray, as self. This is beautifully illustrated by the judge who reversed his own judgment, in the case of the ox; and envy in a few individuals has, doubtless, led them to instil it into the minds of others, who are unable to judge for themselves. In all countries there are not wanting something to keep envy and malice alive. It is prone in the human species. General Jackson has fewer enemies, perhaps, than any man of his notoriety. Yet he has some.[91]

With respect to General Jackson's conduct at New Orleans, it reminds one of Columbus and the egg. He had undertaken to defend his country against fearful odds. It was an enterprize deep with hazard. It was a desperate case, and required a desperate remedy. His mind was equal to the enterprize, and every act of the man's life proves, that love of country is his ruling passion. What a curse this passion of envy is. One would think that an American did not exist who did not admire General Jackson.

It would seem that the God of Nature has annexed to this unnatural passion of envy, its own punishment, whilst the objects of it sustain no injury. Wherever envy prevails, all is misery. It not only destroys all relish for those things we actually possess, but sinks us into contemptible wretches.

Wealth is another great cause of envy in the human family; and while I am on the subject, I will give you an anecdote of yesterday: Tom Envy came into my parlor, while he was under the influence of an affront put upon him by his rich neighbor. "D——n him," said Tom; "I remember the time when he had to borrow twenty-five cents from me to pay for his breakfast; and do you think he had not like to have drove over me, just now! I saw him, driving along in his carriage. I was on foot. I knew his waiter. I stood still till he came up to me, and I bowed to him: "drive on." said he, and went by me like fury." "Well, friend," said I, "let him do so.—He only degrades himself, while you are just as you were before. When he treats you ungratefully, he is guilty of the blackest crime, while you sustain no injury, except in your own imagination. But are you sure, friend, you would not act as he did, were you to change places with him? Wealth, you say, has had this effect upon him, and the same cause always produces the same effect. In that case you would act the part you now condemn." Tom was struck by the force of the argument, and after rolling up a fresh quid of tobacco, and thrusting it in his mouth, he said I was right, he believed; "but, for all that, I would like to be rich, if it were only to mortify that upstart neighbor." "There, now, you are wrong again. If you wish to punish him, only be more wise and virtuous, and the fame of your good name will mortify him much more than wealth. But if this does not satisfy you, you have only to go to work. If you wish to be a rich man, industry and economy will soon do the business. You have the example of your rich neighbor before you; tread in his steps." Tom scratches his head, and said, he believed it was dinner time, and departed.

"Some pray for riches—riches they obtain,
"And, watched by villains, for their wealth are slain!"

Yours, &c.

[Here the Correspondence breaks off for better than a year.][92]

Letter XLI.

Moulton, April 30th, 1821.

Dear Matt,

You say you are pleased with the countryman in my last. Here is a score of them. Perhaps this may bring another reply. I am much pleased, in the meantime, to hear your health is restored, and hope to wish you much joy, on a certain occasion, ere long.

I strolled out with a friend to see a neighbor yesterday, who lives on the skirts of the town, merely for the sake of amusement. If you wish to ascertain the dialect of a country, you must seek for it amongst the common, or in other words, the lower order of the people, as all well bred people speak alike. But the children of both classes are good specimens of dialect, as the better sort, in this country, particularly, consign their children to the care of negroes. You see I am for another dish of philosophy. But to go on. Those who have black nurses, and those who have illiterate white nurses to attend children, are at much pains and cost for teachers to unlearn them what they need never have learned, had they kept illiterate people from them at first. This is not the case with the poorer class of people, as their children are nursed by themselves, and speak *their* language.

While we were chatting with our neighbor, a number of people rode up to the door, and we went out to see what was the matter. It appeared they were on their return from a barbacue, and had heard a stump speech. Some of these were mere children, and some were grown persons. Our neighbor, who was aware of their business, asked "What news from the barbacue?" "Oh there was a proper sight of people—Oh, my! but there was—You never seed the like! And a heap of 'em had on ruffled shirts, and shoeboots, and was so proud, stepin about; and there was some monstrous purty gals there, and some dinged ugly ones, too; and such a powerful chance of apples and cyder, and ginger cakes. I tell ye what, they were prime; and they made such a fuss, and *covaulted*, and was going to fight; you never saw the like in all the days of your life. Then these fellows that lives on Flint,[93] had liked to abin whipped, steppin about. I tell you what, them fellows is monstrous proud; and old F——, was there, too, and got the maddest, he fairly snorted. Oh, he was rearin. And them fellows from Elum's Mill, turned in with old F——, and snorted and covaulted, and dared them ruffle-shirt fellows to turn out. Oh, they got the maddest! And Mr. E—— made a stump speech. He said if we voted for that there 'tother man, I forgot his name, that government would come and take away our land,

and we would have to pay taxes and all that." These were mostly Tennesseeans and North Carolinians.

I saw a piece in the papers not long since, which went to satirize the Tennessee dialect. I would advise such people to look at home. Those who live in glass houses, ought not to throw stones. Let us compare this with the dialect of Virginia. You remember the bear hunting party from Bedford. I will stake them against the whole United States. One of them called at our house on his return, and entertained us with the following account of his adventures: "You know da is heap of baw (bear) on da Kenhawa; so I and Bill Prout, Jess Passin, and Zack Miller, are all goin to Kenhawa to hunt baw—Kenhawa mighty far—so we walk—we walk—last we come to da Kenhawa—Kenhawa b—i—g river, for true—Tell you what, it skears me—well, I goes out into de woods—I hear noise—I look up tree, and see a baw!—I went to da root o' da tree—I bark like any dog—presently da baw come husslin down—Ah, boy!—I took to my keels, and did hook it."—Now for the Pennsylvania dialect: "Jim, where are you and Sam; why but ye's pit (put) you cow in the pester, (pasture;) 'am sure a towled ye's the mornin.—Ye's cruel bad children—and there a fine job ye's done to leave you gears out by." The Yankee: "Flora you want (ought) to wash them clothes right away. You hadn't ought to left 'em so." "What say?"[94]

Covault is of Tennessee birth, and not unaptly applied in the sense they use it. It signifies an unruly or ungovernable man; also an untame horse, or any thing that cannot be controuled. It is quite a classical word, and I hope to see it admitted into the English language. It appears to be a compound of co and vault, which are both very significant. For the rest I find the Tennesseeans are a very plain people, and have a very high sense of honor. Their houses and equipage are void of ostentation: The North Carolinians next; the South Carolians and Georgians, next; and the Virginians the the most ostentatious of any. But the preaching; you must hear that. This country is run mad after preaching.—Here is a new sect called Cumberland presbyterians; and between these, the baptists, and methodists, the woods resound.[95] As they have no churches they preach out of doors mostly. I have just returned from preaching, where I remained about two hours, and the parson, when I left him appeared to be only about midway through his sermon. He ought to have a patent-right, for he certainly has the strongest voice in the state.

I have met with several excellent orators since I have been in the country; the best I ever heard. Parson Burress, formerly of Virginia, is, doubtless, the finest public speaker in the Union.[96] I have seen no parallel for him. The Reverend Mr. Butler and McMahon, the latter of Nashville, Tennessee, are, also, men of handsome delivery.[97] These are methodists. I was truly astonished at this, as I never saw one of the sect, before, hardly worth hearing. The baptists, and the Cumberland presbyterians, are continually preaching and *covaulting*. Mr. Porter, a most amiable man; also a Mr. Madden, preached in Mr. B's house since I was here, and that busybody, Mr. *They say*, reported Mr. B. was to preach here to day, that is, out at the stand in the woods. I observed, "I will go and hear Mr. Porter." "Oh," said a bystander, "it is another preacher than Mr. Porter that preaches today—there is not such another preacher it the known world—he's a monstrous fine preacher." As I had heard some fine preaching, for the oratory I went to hear this none such. But never was I so disappointed. I placed myself in front of the preacher, (a great rough looking man,) and the congregation sat some on fallen timber, some on benches carried there for the purpose—some sat flat on the ground, and many stood up—about 500 in all. His text was, "He that hath ears to hear, let him hear." The people must have been deaf indeed that could not have heard him. He neither made division nor subdivision. He is one of the Cumberland presbyterians. They are Calvinists, it is said, but do not deem education a necessary qualification to preach the

Gospel. But to the sermon: He began low but soon bawled to deafening. He spit in his hands, rubbed them against each other, and then would smite them together, till he made the woods ring. The people now began to covault, and dance, and shout, till they fairly drowned the speaker. Many of the people, however, burst out into a laugh. Seeing this, the preacher cried out, pointing to them with his finger, "Now look at them sinners there—You'll see how they will come tumbling down presently—I'll bring them down." He now redoubled his strength; spit in his hands and smote them together, till he made the forest resound, and took a fresh start; and sure enough the sinners came tumbling down. The scene that succeeded baffles description. Principally confined to women and children, the young women had carefully taken out their combs, from their hair, and laid them and their bonnets in a place of safety, as though they were going to set in for a fight; and it was much like a battle. After tumbling on the ground, and kicking sometime, the old women were employed in keeping their clothes civil, and the young men (never saw an old man go near them) would help them up, and taking them by each hand, by *their* assistance, and their own agility, they would spring nearly a yard from the ground at every jump, one jump after another, crying out, glory, glory, as loud as their strength would admit; others would be singing a lively tune to which they kept time—hundreds might be seen and heard going on in this manner at once. Others, again, exhausted by this jumping, would fall down, and here they lay cross and pile, heads and points, yelling and screaming like wild beasts of the forest, rolling on the ground, like hogs in a mire,—very much like they do at camp meetings in our country, but more shameless; their clothes were the color of the dirt; and like those who attend the camp meetings, they were all of the lower class of the people. I saw no genteel person among them. Are not people of education answerable for this degradation of society? It appears to me, since I have had opportunities of mixing with the world, that there are a certain class of citizens, whose interest it is to keep their fellow men in ignorance. I am very sure, half a dozen words of common sense, well applied, would convince those infatuated young women that they were acting like fools. In fact a fool is more rational. Not one of those but would think it a crying sin to dance.

The noise of the preacher was effectually drowned at length, and a universal uproar succeeded louder than ever.—Whilst this was going on, I observed an old woman near me, snivelling and turning up the whites of her eyes, (she was a widow—all the windows, old and young, covaulted,) and often applying her handkerchief to her eyes, and throwing herself into contortions, but it would not do, she could not raise the steam.

I pointed to one young woman, with a red scarf, who had tired down several young men, and was still covaulting, and seeing she jumped higher than the rest, I asked "who she might be?" One of the gentlemen, a Mr. Gallagher, who was standing near, gave such an account of her (men know these things) as would shock a modest ear. "D——n her, she gets converted every meeting she goes to." How much better had she been at a ball, (if they must dance,) where they would be obliged to behave decent, and where vile characters dare not appear.

Shortly after they began to rear and covault, a daughter of Mr. B's began too. He walked up to her, and led her off some distance, and sat her down at the root of a tree. When he returned, I inquired "if she was sick?" "No," he answered, "but she was beginning to go on as the rest, and I told her if she wished to worship God, to do it there, and not to expose herself before faces."[98]

The preacher having spent all his ammunition, made a pause, and then called upon all the sinners to approach and be prayed for. Numbers went forward, all women and children,

(children of ten years old get religion!) and the priest began to pray; when a decent looking man approached the stand, and took a female by the arm, and led her away. As he walked along, the preacher pointed to him, and said, "God, strike that sinner down!" The man turned around and in an angry tone said, "God has more sense than to mind such a d____d fool as you are!" and resumed his course. He was one of the brave Tennesseeans; and the lady was his wife.

Being tired of such an abominable scene, I proposed returning home, and, taking a near cut through a slip of woodland, we surprized the red scarf lady in a manner that gave us no favorable opinion of her piety.

Meeting has broke up, and several are coming to our house to dine. I wish to have some conversation with them, and shall finish my letter afterwards.

I took my seat at the table, by a stout, jolly looking lady, who, in replying to some of the party, observed "a great many had got religion that day." Now was my time—"Any pray, Madam," said I, "what religion did they get?" "Why that is a queer question—there is but one religion, every body knows." "There you are a little mistaken, Madam; there are various religions. There is the Christian religion; the Jewish religion; the Mahometan religion, &c. &c.; which of those religions was it you spoke of?" "I never heard of them before;" and stared at me in astonishment. "And what religion are you of?" said the lady. I told her my religion was piety. "Never heard of it before;" and doubtless she told the truth. And what sort of a religion is piety? "Why, Madam, it is simply to love God and my neighbor." "It is a queer name, and it's the first I ever heard of it. Is there many of the pieties where you come from?" "Not many." Mr. G. and several at the table could scarcely suppress a laugh. "And pray, Madam, since we have made up our acquaintance, may I take the liberty of asking which of these religions you profess?" "Ne're one," said the lady; "I'm a Cumberland presbyterian." The company could no longer retain themselves; they roared; whilst the subject of it had not the least idea of the cause.

Now, this woman, take her on any other subject, was a reasonable and intelligent woman. Thoroughly acquainted with the ordinary business of life. She was from the interior of Kentucky; and had attended preaching for twenty years! and yet is ignorant, not only of the duties, but of the very name of a christian! Whose fault if this? The fault of the priest! So they can draw the women (they do not seem partial to men) after them, they care for nothing else. If there is a hell, there will be more priests in it than any other description of people.[99]

Yours, &c.

Letter XLII.

Same date.

Dear Matt,

IN ANSWER to yours—This place is growing. The county seat of justice is fixed here, ever since the state was admitted in the Union. It contains several genteel families, mostly merchants, lawyers, and doctor. When I first came here there were but four cabins: It is now a considerable town. I dare say you will be pleased with it. It has no navigation, but it is healthy. This is the richest county, in land, in the state, and contains many planters of great wealth. But the society is the best this side of Huntsville, and the flower of it boards at our house.[100]

In the first place we have two Irish *gentlemen*, Mr. Gallegher, and Mr. Maden, and Doctor Baker, the latter of North Carolina. Mr. Gallegher is a man of highly accomplished manners, very sprightly and gay, and tells a good story. Mr. Maden is also good company, and sings, and plays well on the flute.

The Doctor is the best singer I ever heard. He sings the "Turban'd Turk," "Blithe Sandy," and "Poll, and my partner Joe," with much taste. These are all young men, and full of mirth and fun. Mr. B. himself, is not a bad hand at a story; and Mrs. Burlison is one of the most amiable of her sex. These, and Miss Burlison, a great beauty, form the society at Mr. B's, besides a great number of travellers; of course I spend my time pleasant enough.[101]

We had had a shower of rain after dinner, and being late, Mr. G. (who is a merchant) declined going to the store; the strangers had proceeded to their respective homes, and the air being cooled by the rain, rendered it necessary to have a fire. A fire has something cheering and social in its aspect, and always inspires pleasure and converse.

We all drew our chairs round the hearth, which was neatly swept, and amused ourselves on the incidents of the day; and I gained no small credit for my ingenuity in taking the lady in at dinner. Mr. B. said it was the best preaching he ever heard—that the woman insisted she was "not a christian." Mrs. B. who would do honor to any church, is a baptist, and dislikes this tumbling about, and said she "did not think there was any good in it." All had something to say, and the whole of it was very justly turned into ridicule. Now, what astonished me was, that when Mr. Porter preached here, he did not excite the least noise—but to-day, when this babbler preached, you could not hear your neighbors speak. You may judge of his qualifications to teach the ignorant—In speaking of the children of Israel, he said, "they were conveyed captive to the Babylon by the Romans!" With such leaders, no wonder they both fall into the ditch. But I am going to apprise you of a singular occurrence which has excited much interest in the country round. The house being thronged a few evenings since, on account of the court which is sitting, I arose from the table when I had supped, to make roon for those who were waiting, and walked to the door. While I was standing at the door with a glas of water in my hand, it being now quite dark, a ragged old looking man, with a heavy pack on his back, followed by a little boy, approached, and asked me "if he could stay all night," supposing me to be the woman of the house. I spoke to Mr. B. who went to the door and told the man to come in. He came in, and taking his pack from his back, (which was a skin with the hair on,) laid it down on the floor, and, seeming weary, sat down. He was all in tatters; a small man, and about 60 years of age. The son, for it was his son, was about 12 years, and something better dressed. When the rest had supped, he and the boy, also sat down to supper; and while he was eating, some of the party asked him how far he had travelled, and what course he came. He said "from toward Tuscaloosy;" and made no other reply. When he went to bed, which was in another house, he left his pack where he first laid it down. Next morning he walked about the town, and was out most of the day: sometimes his boy was with him, and sometimes he loitered about the door—the pack still lying in the same place. But when Mrs. B. went to sweep the dining room, she gave the pack a kick with her foot, to move it out of her way, thinking it was nothing but clothing. "Hump!" said she, "you are heavy;" and applying her hands to it, was not able to lift it, but with difficulty rolled it over out of her way; and no more was said about it. Towards evening, the man came in, and said he would be going, and asked Mrs. B. what was to pay? She told him, nothing; supposing him to be very poor, from his appearance; though she said she saw him with money in his hand, when he asked "what was to pay."

Sometime after dark he returned, and to our astonishment, said he had been robbed of 1500 dollars in silver! Every one was amazed, that a man with so much money, should dress as he did, and walk on foot; he was in his shirt sleeves, and they were hanging in ribbands. Mrs. B. now repeated the weight of the pack; and various were the opinions on the subject. Some thought his story correct, and that he dressed in that manner to avoid suspicion; and others gave him no credit, as he was so careless about the pack.

He stated, that drawing near a house about three miles distant from the town, where he intended to stay all night, he saw several men standing in the yard drinking. When he came up to them he did not like their looks, and laying his pack on the fence, to rest himself, made some inquiry about the distance to the next house. The men cursed and swore, and turned him into ridicule, instead of giving him satisfaction; pressed him to drink with them; which he refused. But while he was considering what to do, one of the men went to the pack, and felt it. Finally, he resolved to return; and putting on his pack, said he would go back to town. As he said this, one of the men sat off from the house, nearly in the same direction, but did not keep the road. He left the house and proceeded back the same road he came; and another man, he said, followed. When he had proceeded some distance from the house, the first man jumped out of the bushes, with a large club, and threatened his life, if he did not immediately stop and deliver his pack. By this time the other man appeared and by them he was robbed of every dollar!

The men he spoke of, were immediately taken, and proved to be men of bad character, one in particular; but no money was found with them. As court was sitting, they were immediately brought to trial, before his Honor, C. C. Clay,[102] and Mrs. B. and myself were called on by both parties successively. The Commonwealth summoned us the first day, and the prisoners the next, when and where we stated the substance which has been related. A number of witnesses were summoned, and the boy was examined apart from his father, and agreed nearly with him; and always told the same story, which was not a very probable one; but neither would tell how they obtained the money, except that they made it by trading in furs, towards the Rocky Mountains, and were absent seven years; and were amoungst the Pawnee Indians, and at the lead mines.[103] But his appearance, and his coming such a circuitous route, induced the most people to think he did not tell truth; and though a few of the witnesses seemed to corroborate, with his testimony, as to the weight of the bundle, not one ever saw the money. The men accused were acquitted. I never was more staggered in my opinion, as was also the judge, and almost every one, so much so, that the smallest particle would have turned the scale one way or the other. Some said it must have been lead; others said it might have been silver oar, For the honor of Judge Clay, he gave the old man every opportunity to establish the fact; sending off, to a great distance, for witnesses; protracting the trial, and seemed anxious to do the old man justice.

The Judge did not put up at our house, but very politely called several times. Judge Clay is a very young man, of pleasing manners, handsome person, and said to be a man of the first talents in the state. Though this is a new country, I have witnessed very few judges who might rank with Judge Clay in elegance of manners.

Thus ended the mighty matter, which excited much interest, and is still a cause of wonder in the neighborhood. The old man seems quite chop-fallen, and still hangs about the house.[104]

Another strange occurrence has, for some time, thrown the whole neighborhood into confusion and surprize. A woman, a few miles hence, was taken strangely ill, and said she was bewitched! She threw up knots of pins, and other things equally unaccountable; was racked with excruciating pains, so that she had no rest night or day. She laid this upon one of the neighboring women, whom she pointed out by name! Her neighbors attended her, and was often present when she threw up the pins, knots of hair, and other unaccountable substances. The matter ran on for several weeks, during which she contrived to inspire a large portion of the neighbors with the belief that she was actually bewitched. Even respectable physicians were imposed upon, and were ready, and actually did testify that she was afflicted with some supernatural disease, over which medicine had no controul. Finally, they carried on the farce so far, as to have the supposed witch apprehended and brought before the magistrate, and hundreds (likewise bewitched) attended to hear the trial. But the magistrate happened not to be bewitched, and the woman, producing proof of a fair character, was acquitted. The patient now became worse than ever, and the neighbors said it was a shame that the witch should have been acquitted; and the whole neighborhood seemed to combine in a dangerous conspiracy, and the phrenzy of witchcraft at length alarmed the thinking part of the community, and three or four gentlemen took horses and rode to the house of the bewitched, with a view of putting an end to the cheat. It appeared that the husband of the bewitched woman, had traded for a barrel of brandy, to speculate on, and this barrel was in the house where the woman lay. The gentlemen having made this discovery, together with certain symptoms of the afflicted woman, kept a close watch, and at length discovered the real witch, which was the brandy barrel, having detected the lady drawing the brandy. They immediately made this known, and told the husband (who was deeply concerned for his wife) to send the barrel of brandy away, and his wife would soon be well. The neighbors now turned against the woman, and the husband of the lady who was persecuted, brought an action for slander, and finally, the bewitched lady, and her worse bewitched husband, became so obnoxious, they were compelled to leave the country. So much for ignorance.

Yours, &c.

Letter XLIII.

Moulton, May 3d, 1821.

Dear Matt,

I AM fertile in anecdotes, and I send you the following, not quite three days old: Three evenings since, as I stood in our door, a genteel looking man rode up, and dismounting, asked "if he could be entertained?" I replied in the affirmative: he passed by me into the house, as though he felt little concern for my reply. I still remained in the door, and Mr. Burlison, who had been at his plantation, appeared, walking slowly towards the door, with his eyes fixed on the stranger's horse; and when he came up, slapped his hands on it and said, "this is my horse; who rode it?" I replied, a stranger. He stepped in the house, and I turned from the door at the same time to look at the gentleman, who had taken a seat, and found him smiling at Mr. Burlison, as he heard him claim the horse. This was a mere joke, it appeared, got up for amusement, between the stranger and a nephew of the Captain's, who had also arrived from East Tennessee. Mr. Burlison had loaned the horse to his nephew some time back, to ride home to Tennessee; and when they arrived in Moulton, the young man stopped up in town, with the stranger's horse, and sent the stranger forward with the borrowed horse. As it turned out, however, it was quite a flat joke, and is merely referred to as a preface to something more interesting.

The gentleman, like all those who visit the country, was endless in his praises, and entertained us until a late hour with his travels, and the incidents of the journey, which was several hundred miles, namely, from Salem, Virginia—though he was now, he said, near the end of his journey—but never dropped a hint of his business. Thus the evening passed away, and every one was pleased with the stranger, and all seemed anxious to know his business in this part of the country; and no one, for a wonder, asked his name. He was well dressed; by no means foppish; rather spare, and rode a first rate horse, followed by another equally valuable. Some of us thought, most of us, indeed, were certain, he came to purchase land, as nothing else brings people to this country. Not a syllable of purchasing, or a word, on the object of his journey escaped him. This was provoking, particularly to us females.

The stranger retired to his bed, and next morning chatted till after breakfast, and seemed in no hurry to leave the house, and we concluded he was going to spend the day with us. We retired to dress and was absent some time; when returning to the parlor, we found the gentleman still sitting there, familiarly engaged in conversation, and seemed to win much upon the respect and esteem of the company. At length, about 10 o'clock, he took out his pocket book, and taking a paper from thence, asked Mr. Burlison how far it was to a Mr. King's? As there are several of that name, the question remained unanswered, until he, the stranger, named the distance he lived from a particular Mill, which was down, as the river runs, about seven miles distant from Moulton. This being ascertained, the stranger sat musing sometime with the paper in his hand, and his eyes bent on the floor, absorbed in thought. —At length, he said, "I have a sister at this Mr. King's, if she still be living!" We women held our breath, and a painful silence reigned throughout the company. The stranger, after a pause, during which he labored under strong emotions, proceeded: "I am full of hopes and fears, respecting my sister.— She wrote to us six months since, but her letter never reached us until about a few hours before I sat out on this journey, and I have not seen her for nearly four years." As I lived in the same county some years, from which he was, though unacquainted with the family, I became rather more interested than the company, and inquired, "by what means his sister happened to be so far from her friends?" He replied, "it was a long and rather a melancholy story, but he would relate it as briefly as possible. About four years ago, a French Doctor, as he called himself, came to our town, and spent several months. During the time, he called often at my father's, and before we were aware, he succeeded in gaining the affections of one of my sisters, and made proposals of marriage. This was opposed by all the family, as the man was a total stranger, and was forbid the house, and my sister forbid his company—here we thought the matter at an end. Meanwhile my younger brother and him meeting by accident, quarrelled and fought a duel. During the time, however, he procured letters from New York, and Philadelphia, from various persons, whether genuine or forged, I do not know; but these letters represented him to be a man of the highest respectability, and a man of fortune, which lay principally in the Spanish dominions, near Pnsacola. He contrived to have these letters shown to my father; but it had no effect; and the matter seemed (as we thought) to have died away. But my sister, whom it appears, kept up a correspondence with him, declared she would never be happy if she did not marry Doctor Gennee, and that she would have him if she were forced to run away with him. Thus she teased us all, night and day, and finally prevailed, though against the wishes of every friend she had. The Doctor, after his marriage, was anxious to go on to his possessions in Florida; and to induce him to treat my sister well, my father gave him 1000 dollars in cash, and bought a first rate wagon, entirely new, filled it with every species of best furniture, for house keeping, put a fine team of horses in it, with a slave to drive it, and with a saddle horse for my sister. They took leave, and we heard no more of them, till we received a letter from my sister dated about six months since, which filled us with astonishment and distress. I have the letter here now," he added, "and will read it." It was a long letter, and the young man was so overpowered by his feelings, that he was forced to pause several times, often the tear stealing down his cheek. The amount of the letter was:

—That they arrived in safety in Florida; but her husband had no property there, and left her often without money to help herself, and went off she could not tell where, a long time; that he was very cross and ill natured to her from the time she left her father's, and at last he sold every thing they had, and went off no one knew wither, leaving her without one cent in the world, or a particle of property. She was ashamed to apprize her father and brothers, as they had opposed her marriage; that she struggled to sustain life, though at the same time she prayed for death: At length, growing calm, she thought of returning to her friends, if she had to beg her way, which she would certainly have to do.—Finally, her wrongs and her sufferings excited the compassion of some humane individuals, who furnished her with a pony, and a few dollars. She set forward alone, steering towards Nashville, pursuing Coffee's Trace.[105] This was an appaling undertaking for a female, through an uninhabited country of swamps and cane-breaks. She often lost her way, and wandered about for days and for nights without food, and often without water. At length she gave out, and could travel no farther. She had been for some time aiming to reach a settlement, she had had in view from the first, and intended to stop there and write to her friends. This is the settlement (principally religious people) where she now is. The first house she called at, the people refused even to let her come in, much less would they give her food to eat. What are you travelling alone for? It is a bad sign—you must be a bad woman. She went to another, and another house, but was turned away from all, with more than brutal cruelty. She now lost all hope, and sat down on the road side! While she was sitting there, this Mr. King was passing by, and telling him her story, he took her to his house and treated her with great kindness. In a few days she wrote the letter mentioned, but by some means it did not reach its destination for six months.

The letter contained a pathetic appeal to her father and

brothers for forgiveness, and if they thought her worthy to be received into the family again, to send for her; if not, she would remain with her kind friend.

Shortly after the letter arrived, this young man, who kept a Latin School in the neighborhood, came home, and his father requested him to get ready to go for her as quick as possible.

After relating the story, he ordered his horses, and set out; and this day (the 2d) he passed by here, about one o'clock, P.M., with his sister, a very fine looking woman; but they were in a great hurry, and we only saw her on horseback.—While they were yet in sight, some of the neighbors of Mr. King, who were at the house when the brother called, and who had rode up with them part of the way, stopped at our house, and related a most pathetic scene between the brother and sister. They flew into each others arms, and were for many minutes unable to speak. The sister at length burst into a flood of tears, and the brother likewise wept. But this was a trifle to the scene that followed. This lady had never been taught to work, and by way of amusement, she had induced Mrs. King to teach her how to work, such as spinning, carding, &c. She soon became very expert, and by way of remunerating her friends for their kindness in saving her life, worked late and early, thinking she could never do enough for them. But when the people who had turned her out of doors found she was a decent woman, and was industrious, they had the effrontry to come to King's to seduce her away. "His house, (being a poor man) was not fit for her to stay at; come to our house," was their language. The lady refused their invitation with disdain, and remained with her friends; and so strong was her attachment to Mrs. King, and Mrs. King for her, that when they came to take leave, it was difficult to tear them asunder. Thus ends the story.[106]

What think you, Matt, of the christian religion? Between you and I, and the bed post, I begin to think it is all a plot of the priests.[107] I have ever marked those professors, whenever humanity demanded their attention, the veriest savages under the sun. Now, this King made no pretensions to religion, and though this is, as you say, a Jay's treaty, I must add another instance of their brutality—it happened when I was very young, and made an impression on me which I shall never forget. A presbyterian Elder, (and to this day I do not know the meaning of the word,) who prayed a long prayer, night and morning, owned a ferry. A poor woman, as I supposed then, (as she was on foot,) stopped at his door, and inquired what the ferryage was, saying she wanted to cross. She looked tired, hungry, miserable. The wretch asked her how much money she had? She showed him some in an old rag, and taking up a *bit*, I think it was, asked him "if that was enough?" "No." She took a half bit[108] up, and holding them in her hand, asked "if that would do?" He shook his head. She had but one more *bit*, which she said was all she had. He would not touch it. She said, "I must cross; for God's sake take all, and put me over." No; he turned off and was going into the house. The woman wiped the tears from her eyes with her sleeve, and pulling off a blue and white checked handkerchief, which she wore round her neck, called him back, and told him "she must cross the river if she had to go without a handkerchief;" and the wretch took it and the money too!!! One of these hypocrites told me once "I ought not to judge *all* by *one*." No! But I judge *all* by *all*, for they are all the same.

This man lived on North river, Virginia.

Yours, &c.

Letter XLIV.

Courtland,[109] June 2d, 1821.

Dear Matt,

My old acquaintance, the Colonel, has moved from the Bluff (or Marathon) to this place, which, though now a considerable town, consisting of fine brick houses, was a cornfield 18 months ago, and the corn furrows are still visible in many parts of the town. The Colonel, and all the citizens, however, are much disappointed that they did not obtain the seat of justice here; and the Colonel particularly takes it much to heart, as he purchased lots under that view. But he is forced to submit. *Courtland,* (you see they counted their chickens before they were hatched) being eight miles from the river, the boundary of the county, Courtland was too far from the centre.

And the great beauty is married! At a few months over 14 years of age! She married a South Carolinian, by the name of Daniel Wright, Esq. a very genteel, amiable man, and clerk of the court. He was a member of the convention that framed the Constitution for the state, and is a man of princely manners. The lady had a considerable fortune, and they will doubtless do well. So you have missed it again.

This is the region of the Carolina pink and Colomba root. Wagon loads of the latter may be gathered any where in the woods; it, and the pink, cover the ground. The pink grows much like the garden pink, and the flower is similar in size and figure, but is of a scarlet. I am sure I have seen it in some part of the Union before, but cannot tell where. The woods are alive with it here, and a profusion of other beautiful flowers. It is quite a treat to ride through the woods. The Colomba root has several broad leaves near the ground, in the shape like the hound's tongue, of a yellowish green—the leaf thick and fuzzy—and a stem runs up from these from one to two feet in height, without leaves, and has a flower near the top—but it is not now in bloom.

The greatest curiosity here, is the sensitive brier.[110] It is in its nature, (but not in shape,) like the sensitive plant, though with this difference, only *that* part of the plant shrinks which you touch. For instance, if you touch *one* leaf, it draws up instantly, but this does not affect the other leaves—not so the brier: It grows like the raspberry brier, long, and still more slender, with narrow leaves; if you touch the stem at one end, the leaves instantly pucker themselves up from one end of the brier to the other, the most astonishing phenomenon I have witnessed in the vegetable kingdom. The brier grows spontaneously. Those I saw were from one to five feet high, and about the thickness of a wheat straw. The leaves are very small, narrow, and notched, not larger than the smallest pink leaf. I amused myself sometime in tormenting these little whimsical rogues.

Since I have began with the curious, we have another great curiosity here, viz: the jointed snake, which, if struck with a stick flies to pieces with a jingling noise. No blood is emitted from the broken parts, and it is said the pieces unite again. This I was told was a fact, though I did not see the snake.[111] The Camelion is also a native of this place. They are found every where; but the prairies abound with them.—They are called the "Green Lizard," by the inhabitants.—Mrs. Burlison informed me, that its general color was green, but if provoked, it changed to a grayish color, and the throat, which swells to a great size, when it is made angry, changes to a pale crimson.[112] I did not happen to see one, as you may ride for days through the prairies without being able to distinguish them from the grass, of which color they are. Speaking of prairies—these *prairies* are too damp for cotton, but corn grows well on them, and in the season for strawberries, you may gather wagon loads of them; and these are of a superior flavor to any in our part of the country. You cannot *walk* through a prairie in strawberry time, they take you up to the ankle.

Another curiosity—Tobacco grows spontaneously in this state! It grows in Madison county in the forest, and attains the same height as when cultivated—but the leaves are thin, and unfit for use. It is also found in West Tennessee. It was found in Madison, by the first white people who visited the country, nor can the oldest Indian account for its origin.—Some think it is a native, and others, again, suppose it possible the seed might have been scattered by some adventurous traveller.

This, and the adjoining states, on the Mississippi, is beyond doubt to become the wealthiest part of the United States. In fact, it is so now. The inhabitants of this state, however, not contented with the overflowing productions of their thrice happy soil, have vainly attempted to introduce the sugar cane—but, doubtless, it will fail.[113] By covering the roots it lives through the winter, and grows to a considerable height. Though it is now in perfection of two year's growth, the winters are evidently too cold for the plant.

Upland rice grows here with success. It looks like oats, is sown in drills, and plowed and hoed like corn. It is of a reddish color when cooked. Every planter rears enough for his own use.

I fell in with a traveller of intelligence, from whom I gathered a few particulars of those new Southern States, and taking the whole together, it is beyond doubt the most desirable country on earth. The gentleman is from the Red River last: His information amounts to the following:

He has been several years in that country, and assisted in surveying and running the boundary lines, both of Mississippi and Louisiana. "The lands (he says) on the Mississippi, on both sides, far exceeds this in fertility, and producing two thousand weight of cotton to the acre: whereas fifteen hundred is the most that is calculated on here. Indigo, tobacco, and rice grow there in great abundance. Indian corn grows with such rapidity, that two crops can be raised in one year, below thirty two or thirty one degrees of North latitude. From one to two hundred bushels of Indian corn are produced to the acre. Sugar and oranges grow in the same latitude, but neither will grow to any degree of perfection above thirty-two. Cotton and sugar are the staples of Louisiana and Mississippi; and people amass great wealth there in a short time, from the culture of those articles. Even poor men, that go there, and attend to large stocks of cattle that run on the great natural meadows, which abound in Louisiana, for which they get a certain part, soon become rich. Sugar is cultivated by laying the stalks in furrows once in three years, and from the joints new stems arise.

"The best cotton grows on Red River. All, who have visited that country, agree on this point. The stalks grow to such thickness and strength there, that they are strong enough to bear a man's weight. [I have heard this asserted by many.] Red River falls into the Mississippi from the West side below Natchez, in about the thirty-first degree of latitude. Beyond Louisiana, that is, west of it, there is another vast region equally as productive, and almost without inhabitants: I mean Texas—though it belongs to the Spanish government.—The Spaniard offer a considerable bounty in land to all persons, who will go and settle it.[114] The Southern part of Louisiana extends from the East side of the Mississippi river, which bounds it East, to the Saline river, which bounds it on the West, and divides it from Texas. There is no difference in the soil or productions of the states of Louisiana and Mississippi; but the former is more liable to be everflowed by the rivers that flow through the former, and much more of it is covered with swamps—but there is enough to reward industry and enterprise, exclusive of the swamps.

"The Mississippi state extends from the river of the same name, which bounds it on the West, but I give the boundary. The boundary commences on the Mississippi river, at the point where the Southern boundary line of the state of Tennessee strikes the said river; thence East along the said boundary line to the Tennessee river; thence up the same to the mouth of Bear creek; thence, by a direct line to the Northwest corner of the county of Washington, in Alabama; thence due South to the Gulf of Mexico; thence Westwardly, including all the Islands within six leagues of the shore, to the most Eastern junction of Pearl river with Lake Borgne; thence up said river to the thirty-first degree of North latitude; thence west along the said degree of latitude to the Mississippi river; and thence up the same to the beginning. Mississippi is watered by the Pascagula, Mississippi, Tennessee, Pearl, Yazoo, and Big Black rivers. Although the bottoms are not so wide and extensive on the east side of Mississippi river, yet they are equally as fertile, producing cotton, &c. in abundance. There are three distinct species of land, both in this state and Alabama: The bottom, the bluff, (or high, dry, rich cotton land,) and pine land. Take it all in all, it is not exceeded in fertility by any in the world: Neither is it so sickly as is represented.—Consumptions, which sweep so many of our Northern people to the grave, are unknown here. I have seen a gentleman, that was far gone with that complaint, who tells me that he has entirely recovered. The moschitoes, however, are troublesome; but the small expense they are at, to secure themselves from them, is amply remunerated by the soil's overflowing productiveness."

There is a country for you, Matt: and am I not a good old lady to send you so much amusement. I *have* some notion of turning author some of these days, for though I know you are only indulging your irony, (you saucy rogue, is that the way to treat your betters,) let me tell you I would not make the worst in the world. You, and Joe Fry, may laugh again; I was never blind to your winks and nods; and if ever I do take up my pen, I mean to write a book, and I will flay you two saucy rogues.

I have this moment received your letter of March! If you are as slow a traveller as your letters, you may find it necessary to bring a summer-house with you.

The people have elected C. C. Was there ever such fools? They must have been intoxicated. Can America stand? Can she preserve her liberty thus? She cannot; she ought not! They are prodigal of their sovereignty, indeed. It appears to be painful to them. To elect the greatest *fool*, by odds the greatest fool in the country.[115] You know he always has Lord Hale in his mouth. In my husband's lifetime, this Lord Hale came to our house and spent a day. You knew my husband's hospitality. He entertained all alike. Court was sitting at this time, at the Sweet Springs, and this booby, (how he came to be licensed a lawyer, is strange,) while at the dinner table, began to repeat part of a defence, it appeared he made for a criminal; in doing which, he referred to "Lord Hale's Pleas of the Crown." Finding we were all silent, he took it for granted, we were delighted, and launched out in the praise of *Demosthenes* and *Cicero.* My husband, who had remained silent, and weary of the fool, at length, asked who this Demosthenes was, "as I an very ignorant in these things." "You don't know who Demosthenes was? Why he was a great Roman Emperor; and Cicero was another great Emperor; and Cato was another. There are very few things come amiss to me." Thus he went on till he swept away all the great men of antiquity; whilst I suffered the ordeal, as being at my own table, I dare not laugh. My husband never laughed at any thing; but he did something much better this day. He always sat sometime after the cloth was removed, and had a fashion of leaning forward, when displeased, upon his arms, which were usually crossed, and at the same time biting his thumb. I always trembled when I saw this; nor dare I rise from the table till he made a signal; and though our house was usually full, we happened to have no one this day, but Lord Hale. At length, my husband, addressing his Lordship, said, "Now, what a d——d fool you are; this is the way you expose yourself; do you know you are a laughing stock for the whole country? My dog, *Citizen*, (a favorite pointer,) has more sense. Just go home, and go to plow, for if my dog could speak, he would make a better lawyer." He took it in good part, and said it was the best lesson he ever had heard. It was lost upon such a fool. Strange, that whatever side he took at the bar, was sure to be victorious; as, true to their nature, the people, or rabble, rather always think the greatest fool the wisest man. They have proved it in this instance, by their selecting him to make laws for them. Alas, for my country! all your citizens want is rope.

Good bye; I am going to Florence, foot of the Muscle Shoals; I give Kenhawa joy of her representative.[116]

Yours, &c.

N. B. What a pity this fellow had not chosen the profession of a preacher. He would have made a *Lady Hale* of all the women in the country round. He would have left the Cumberland preacher, (I mentioned some time back,) for behind, in causing them "to come tumbling down!" Handsome language, I confess, for a preacher of the gospel to use. They ought, at least, to go halves.

Letter XLV.

Florence,[117] July 10th, 1821.

AND HERE I AM, my Dear Matt—foot of the Shoals, once more. I have been here ten days; and what do you think I came here for? Of all people you, *you*, I say, are the most extraordinary and neglectful of men? Where are my trunks? What has become of them? Were they not to have been sent long since? I have just seen Major S. and he tells me a fine tale of Gardner, and a few more, of whom I was going to say you must be one. But I would as soon expect to see the sun start from its centre, as that you would countenance such an infamous transaction. But what were you about, that you suffered this infamous Yankee tin pedlar, Whitiker, to surrender my furniture into the hands of the wretch, Gardner? S. lest he might be charged with what he is innocent of, did not, and would not tell me, but the gentleman who came with him, did. It is enough that I know it; I saw by S____'s countenance that all was not right. But that Mr. Fry would pay over money of mine, to Gardner, without an order from me, I cannot believe, until I have better evidence! He doubtless sets a high value upon his character; but it would seem that honesty cannot breathe in Kenhawa. It is fatal to the principle. If it be true that Whitiker has delivered my property into the hands of Gardner, a curse will pursue him to his grave, nor will his offspring ever prosper.[118] But I will endeavor not to believe that human nature is so depraved. I give you joy on your marriage, and I hope you may be as happy as I wish.

Florence is one of the new towns of this beautiful and rapid rising state. It is happily situated for commerce at the head of steamboat navigation, on the north side of Tennessee river, in the county of Lauderdale, five miles below the port of the Muscle Shoals, and ten miles from the line of the state of Tennessee.

Florence is to be the great emporium of the northern part of this state.[119] I do not see why it should not; it has a great capital and is patronized by the wealthiest gentlemen in the state. It has a great state at its back; another in front, and a noble river on all sides, the steamboats pouring every necessary and every luxury into its lap. Its citizens, bold, enterprising, and industrious—much more so than any I have seen in the state.

Many large and elegant brick buildings are already built here, (although it was sold out, but two years since,) and frame houses are putting up daily. It is not uncommon to see a framed building begun in the morning and finished by night.

Several respectable mercantile houses are established here, and much business is done on commission also. The site of the town is beautifully situated on an eminence, commanding an extensive view of the surrounding country, and Tennessee river, from which it is three quarters of a mile distant.—It has two springs of excellent and never failing water. Florence has communication by water with *Mississippi, Missouri, Louisiana, Indiana, Illinois, Ohio, Kentucky, West Pennsylvania, West Virginia, and East Tennessee*, and very shortly will communicate with the Eastern States, through the great canal!!![120] The great Military road that leads from Nashville to New Orleans, by way of Lake Ponchartrain, passes through this town, and the number of people who travel through it, and the numerous droves of horses for the lower country, for market, are incredible. Florence contains one printing press, and publishes a paper weekly called the Florence Gazette it is ably patronized, and edited by one of our first men, and said to be the best paper in the state. Florence is inhabited by people from almost all parts of Europe and the United States; here are English, Irish, Welch, Scotch, French, Dutch, Germans, and *Grecians*. The first Greek I ever saw was in this town. I conversed with him on the subject of his country, but found him grossly ignorant. He butchers for the town, and has taken to his arms a mullatto woman for a wife. He very often takes an airing on horseback of a Sunday afternoon, with his wife riding by his side, and both arrayed in shining costume.

The river at Florence is upwards of five-hundred yards wide; it is ferried in a large boat worked by four horses, and crosses in a few minutes.

There are two large and well kept Taverns in Florence, and several *Doggeries*. A Doggery is a place where spirituous liquors are sold; and where men get drunk, quarrel, and fight, as often as they choose, but where there is nothing to eat for man or beast. Did you ever hear any thing better named. "I sware!" said a Yankee pedlar, one day, with both his eyes bunged up, "that are Doggery, be rightly named. Never seed the like on't. If I get to hum agin it 'il be a nice man 'il catch me in these here parts. Awfullest place one could be at." It appeared the inmates of the Doggery enticed him under pretence of buying his wares, and forced him to drink; and then forced him to fight; but the poor little Yankee was sadly beaten. Not content with blacking up his eyes, they overturned his tin-cart, and scattered his tins to the four winds; frightened his horse, and tormented his very soul out about *lasses*, &c. He was a laughable object—but to hear his dialect in laying off the law, was a complete farce, particularly when Pat came to invite him into the same Doggery to drink friends—"I ben't a dog to go into that are dog house."

The people, you see, *know* a *thing* or two, here; they call things by their right names. But to proceed—there may be about one hundred dwelling houses and stores, a court house, and several ware houses in Florence. The latter are however on the river. One of the longest buildings I ever saw, is in Florence. It was built by a company of gentlemen, and is said to have cost $90,000, and is not yet finished. The proprietors, being of this place, are men of immense wealth, and are pushing their capital with great foresight and activity. For industry and activity, Florence outstrips all the northern towns in the state. More people travel this road than all our western roads put together. I was just going to conclude, when an old German passing through my room from that of my landlady's, made me laugh, in reply to something uttered by the lady, he said "poverty was no crime, when we came honestly by it."

Yours, &c.

Letter XLVI.

Florence, July 15, 1821.

Dear Matt,

MORE of Florence. I observed in my last, the surprizing wealth of this place. The principal gentlemen of wealth are General Coffee, James Jackson, Esq., Major McKinley, and Messrs. Simpson and Gaither.[121] Of these J. Jackson is said to be not only wealthy, but the wealthiest man in the state.—There are, however, many others quite easy in their circumstances. General Coffee, and J. Jackson live out of town. Major McKinley lives in Florence, and is reputed to be the first lawyer in the three states. He is a stout, fine looking man; of easy manners, as all gentlemen are; and his dwelling contains more taste and splendor, by one half, than I ever saw in my whole life put together. But this is nothing.—Mrs. McKinley, the elegance of her manners, and the sweetness of her conversation, joined with her interesting children, completely disconcerted me. Every thing in the house had, to me the appearance of enchantment. I never was in such a paradise before. Mrs. McKinley looked as though she had dropped from above. I never was more confounded. And the children! They are truly a pattern! The dear little things were in the nursery, and hearing there was a stranger in the parlour, prevailed on the nurse to open the door a few inches, that they might see who was there—but they were instantly upbraided by their mother. Make these a pattern for your children, if you should have any. I begged admission for the dear creatures, and they were admitted upon condition of good behavior. They were the handsomest children I ever beheld, and I was so completely facinated by their manners, I forgot every thing else. Mrs. McKinley informed me she was from Philadelphia, and was acquainted with Mrs. Doctor Charles Lewis.

All the ladies of Florence excel in the domestic virtues. No gadding abroad. They demean themselves with that modesty and attention to their domestic affairs, beyond any ladies I have seen in the state. Mrs. Coffee (a niece of Mrs. General Jackson,) comes to preaching in a plain bonnet and calico dress.[122] General Coffee was here since I arrived, and appears to be much reduced since I saw him in Huntsville. His constitution was much injured by the hardships he suffered in the army. I was never within speaking of James Jackson. It is said he is a native of Ireland. Mrs. Ward, Mrs. Gibson, and Mrs. Southworth, the printer's wife, and several others, are charming women. Captain Gibson, a son of the brave Colonel Gibson, of Tennessee, is one of the most amiable men on earth.

It is unaccountable why such a number of physicians should flock to this country. Every town is flooded with them. They are strung along the roads like so many blacksmith's shops. You can neither walk nor ride, but you have a physician on each side, one in front, and one in rear. Here are seven in Florence—seven more went away, for want of room. There are also, here, *six* lawyers. I left *thirteen* doctors in *Courtland*, a much smaller place. One hundred passed through the latter, south, unable to get in. You cannot, as I stated before, travel a mile on any great road, without meeting with a Doctor's shop. But this is not all. Almost every practising doctor has three or four students. I have known mechanics quit their trade and commence the study of medicine. This would lead one to think the country was sickly. No such thing. It is a much healthier country than ours. It appears that the first doctors, who came here, made great fortunes, and every young man studied medicine, so that mankind has, indeed, given themselves up to the guidance of folly. They remind one of Erasmus' drunken man attempting to mount his horse; if you help him up on one side, he falls over on the other. Many of these physicians, however, are becoming planters, by which they will doubtless make their bread. They add, however, much to society, and help to pass off the time. They are all life and gaiety, and are constantly playing pranks on each other, for want of other employment. A most laughable scene occurred here the other day, which, for ingenuity of plot, and fertility of humor, might challenge the author of Don Quixotte.

The first we heard of it was the voice of a female entering the town, on foot, in a violent rage, cursing and swearing, (for it appears ladies do swear, or women I mean, as the word lady cannot possibly belong to one who would use such vulgar language.) She smote her fists together violently, and (passing over about ninety-nine oaths, at least) declared vengeance against every young man in Florence. Those who were in the secret, began to laugh; others laughed for company; but the most of the people were astonished. "Twenty-four miles here I've walked, and torn myself to pieces with thorns, and bruises; look at my arms d——n you; look at my clothes; yes, laugh, laugh; see my shoes and stockings, wading all the creeks, you sons of b__________s. Oh, yes, you're the ones." Her face was as red as scarlet, from the heat and rage together.—Briefly —a number of boats are generally lying at the landing, and it appears that the young men in Florence are no better than the young men of other towns, or what I would say, rather, that all young men are alike. This is an undeniable fact, and has been the case since the world began, if history be true, and will doubtless continue to the end of it. Whether this be the effect of preaching, or the want of it, I pretend not to say. All I have to say, is, that the priests have been preaching these 1821 years, and yet young men, and young women, too, are still the same, and may be, a little worse. This may, however, be a part of the religion they preach, as I always find most of it where there is most preaching. The sensible reader will understand me as wishing to check the evil of swearing, and without any desire to wound the delicacy of my fair sisters, though, like myself, they never ceased until they unravelled the mystery; and with no other view than to guard them against temptations and the cunning of young men. It was ascertained, that parties of both sexes, for want of house room, doubtless, had often spent the night in these boats. It is said that people live in boats in China; probably this gave rise to the idea in this country. Let this be as it may, a very decent and respectable young man was seen leading a lady in the dusk of the evening into one of these boats; and sometime in the night, somebody untied the cable of the boat, and down the river she sailed of her own accord. There are shoals in Tennessee river, about 20 or 24 miles below Florence, and the first intelligence the inmates of the boat had of being under way, was the noise of the Shoals, which awakened them from a sound sleep! The woman waked first, and being alarmed at the noise, roused the young man, no other person happening to be on board. Upon looking out, and rubbing his eyes, the truth burst upon him; but there was no remedy, and their fears were no little, lest the boat might hang or break upon a rock. Fortunately the boat lodged against an island, fair and softly—and there the gentleman and his companion had to remain, till fortune might send a boat for their relief, either up or down the river, which, by chance, happened sometime the ensuing day. But it appears the gentleman proved rather ungallant, in the end, as he left the lady to shift for herself, the moment he set foot on shore; and turning back to back, he went down the river, and she came up to Florence. It is supposed he had two reasons for this: First—he did not wish to be seen walking side by side with the lady into Florence, which would have subjected him to the ridicule of his friends. Secondly—within six or seven miles below "Lover's Landing," as it has since been called, there was a small town, where he wished to refresh himself, and procure a horse, to ride back, being clerk of the court, his absence could not well be dispensed with.

These incidents we learned partly from the women, partly from observation, and partly from the contrivers of the plot. The woman said, "It was very unkind," or in words to that amount, to go off, and leave her to come home through the swamps, by herself, without a road. And all the ladies thought so too: but they spoke differently, for they said she deserved it all, and a great deal more. They did not in my hearing cast the smallest reflection upon the young man. He returned the next day, and in a very ill humour; and without adverting to his misfortunes, examined the countenance of every and each of his friends, with a view of detecting the party concerned. Being a man of spirit, he would have certainly walked the man or men out; but this part of the farce will never be known; and he is very silent himself, for obvious reasons. This incident has afforded much amusement.

I ought to have mentioned Mr. Mayers,[123] your old acquaintance. He lives in Franklin county, over the river from hence. I dined at his house on my way to Florence. He is delighted with the country, owns a valuable plantation, and is up to the eyes rearing cotton. But he lacks one very essential comfort, which is water; having to haul it about two miles.—He has been at great expense digging for water on his land, but has failed. Miss Ann, looks as charming as ever, and is often a visiter at the house of my friend, Judge Ellis, one of the most interesting families in Alabama. I never, though long acquainted with Mr. Mayers, and Miss M. saw Mrs. Mayers before. She is one of the finest women I have seen in this or any other country. They are all highly pleased with the change; and Mr. Mayers has a number of very promising children. But he talks of removing to Tuscaloosa, if he can sell out to advantage.

In noting all the fine things of Florence, I overlooked a Mr. Fulton, an eminent lawyer, and a gentleman of first rate talents. He is from Maryland, and one of the ornaments of society.[124] I was just now called on for a toast, and gave an old one which is *said* to have been given extempore by one of my Irish ancestors, and which follows:

"Health to the sick;
Wealth to the brave;
A husband to the widow,
And freedom to the slave!"

I should have no objection to realize one line of the toast. You may readily guess which; but that is between ourselves.

Yours, &c.

N.B. Pray give my respects to Mrs. Dunbar.

Letter XLVII.

Huntsville, January 29th, 1822.

Dear Matt,

HEARING Colonel Biern, of Monroe, was to be here, I came up to learn the news from my old neighborhood. But

Colonel B. looked cold and frowning. I cannot account for this, unless I am to join in the opinion with Tom Envy, mentioned in a former letter, viz: that wealth changes the manners of men.

"Whatever is, is right!" says Pope. So be it. I concur. But I should think, my friends would have sent some message at least. Grant me patience, good heavens!

Huntsville, has greatly increased since my first visit; and notwithstanding the check it has received, in the great number of new towns on the river, it will always be a place of wealth and business. Its capital is considerable, and the proprietors are thoroughgoing business men. It has now a population of 1300 inhabitants. Two churches have been built since I have been here; a theatre, (now burnt,) and a number of dwelling houses. It has now two printing offices—each publish a paper; sixteen stores; several commission merchants; auctioneer; a land office; and various other public offices, which draw numbers of people from the country. They have a very fine fire engine, and a well regulated company. There are two academies for young ladies; one for young gentlemen, and several common schools. Great encouragement is given to the encouragement of learning throughout the state. Every sixteenth section of land is set apart for the benefit of education, and provision is made by law for a university, which is soon to go into operation.[125] There's your chance Mr. Black-Coats! They have a tolerable library; fine taverns; several Doggeries; twenty-one lawyers! and eight practising physicians![126]

I mentioned to you the Huntsville Spring. The citizens of Huntsville are now employed in collecting the water which flows from it into a canal; this canal is to have five locks, and to communicate with Indian Creek, which is navigable to the river.

Few places combine more blessings than Huntsville; and not a town in the world, perhaps, in proportion to its population, except Florence, has more wealth, more talent, more taste, more hospitality, mirth and gaiety, than Huntsville. The ladies of Huntsville, distance every thing in the costliness of their dress; nor do I like their manners so well as I do the manners of the Florence ladies. They are always in the streets. But they are beautiful women, and very familiar. The young gentlemen are rather better informed; are gay and lively; play and sing well. They often go out serenading, and have a Thespian society, who entertain the citizens at stated periods; to these are added balls and cotillion parties.[127] I shall remain here till I hear from Virginia, and shall then pay a visit to Blakely, to see Mrs. Biern, formerly Kitty Davis, whom I partly raised.[128] You recollect her—Mr. Caperton is dead, and she is married to a Mr. Biern, and doing well.

Respecting your last letter, you say, and very plausibly too, "No wonder the ignorant are prejudiced against learning, when they see learned men inflicting every evil, cheating, defrauding, and oppressing the poor." Aware of these objections made, acted and done, to use your law phrases, I am ready to enter my rejoinder. The very reason you adduce to excuse the ignorant, is the reason I would advance against them. If their minds were improved, they would not become the dupes and victims of their learned neighbors. They would then be able to cope with him. If men of the best learning and parts often fall a sacrifice to the artful disguise which hypocracy and knavery put on, how then are the ignorant to escape? If education was better attended to, it would greatly alleviate the evils of fraud and oppression. If a few, now and then, emerge from the night and ignorance, the great mass of the people are still the same. And this ignorance is to be our downfall. It strikes at the vitals of our liberty. It affects morally and politically, and the *few* are soon to rule the *many*, instead of the many ruling the few. I would not, as some one said, have them all philosophers; but I would have them raised a little above the brute creation. I would have them know they were endowed with *reason*. I would have them know, this reason was bestowed on them as a guide to enable them to distinguish right from wrong—truth from falsehood—good from evil. I would have them know, that it is the cultivation of this reason alone that can secure to them its advantages. As a fertile field, without cultivation, produces nothing but noxious weeds, so our reason, without cultivation, is no more advantage to us in transacting the common concerns of life, than if it were destitute of this glory of human nature. But I am sleepy, and must bid you good night. Remember me to Mrs. D.

Yours, &c.

Letter XLVIII.

Huntsville, February 22d, 1822.

Dear Matt,

THIS DAY, the anniversary of our beloved Washington, was ushered in with all manner of rejoicing. The star spangled banner is now waving on the cupola, before my window, and an elegant ball is to conclude the day.

While I sat in my window, with my eye on the flag, my mind was thrown back to the Revolutionary War; and whilst I gazed on this emblem of our liberty, I thought on the day that I first saw the colors of the then conflicting states: the occasion nor the date I do not now remember. But I well remember the brilliant striped flag. I was then a child, and lived in Hannah's Town, not far from Pittsburg. I was standing in the street one morning, with other little children, and happening to turn my eyes in the direction of Pittsburg, I caught a view of soldiers marching into the Town, their colours flying, and drums beating. I remember the order of march—I remember, too, that there were several women: but I am sorry I cannot tell how they came to visit Hannah's Town, or to pass through it, which they did. I never saw the United States' colors since, that it does not recall that day! and the whole repasses again before me, and with it all the sufferings of those trying times. I suffered all that human nature could bear, both with cold and hunger. Oh, ye wealthy of those times, little idea had ye of what the poor frontier settlers suffered. Often running for our lives to the forts, the Indians pursuing and shooting at us. At other times lying concealed in brushwood, exposed to rain and snakes, for days and nights without food, and almost without clothes! We were one half of the time without salt or bread! pinned our scanty clothing with thorns; lived on nuts, bear's meat, and dried venison! All these things revive in my mind, and I love to dwell on them.[129]

The company are now marching before me, under arms, in a handsome uniform; they step light and graceful, and are tall fine looking men. Their captain, Howard, boards with me; I mean at the same house. He is just six feet in height, and one of the finest figures of them all, and has a martial look. He is a great favorite among the ladies, and is, doubtless, to open the ball this evening with some of the fairest of the fair.

I board with Major Rose, the merry old veteran mentioned some time back. He has met with a dreadful reverse of fortune since I first saw him. He was then one of the first merchants in the place, but was overwhelmed in the general wreck, which prostrated so many of our merchants. But the Major is as merry as ever; keeps a tavern and boarding house; amuses himself with a pet crow; and sings "Jerry go Nimble." Mrs. Rose, too, bears her misfortunes like a philosopher. She is a mild, sensible woman, and the most benevolent of her sex. —Captain Luke Howard, just mentioned, Mr. Tharp, and Mr. Wooldridge, and two Italians, are the only new acquaintance I have made. Captain Howard, is an Irish gentleman, highly polished, and breathes the very soul of philanthropy and feeling. Nature has showered her bounties on him liberally, and these are cultivated with great care and taste. He is the soul of music—performs well on the flute—sings a good song—is lively and facetious, which, united with a general knowledge of the world, renders him a most desirable companion. It appears to me, that all the Irish who visit this country, are very different from any I every saw with us. They have none of those habits of drinking, common to all I knew in other states. These are perfect gentlemen and men of business. Mr. Tharp is a neat, pleasant young man, with the sweetest temper in the world; though he conceives he is *mighty* ill sometimes, and it is amusing enough to hear Mr. Howard quizzing, and advising him to make his will. I sometimes advise him to marry, and this seems to agree with his malady, better than Howard's prescription. I think he will take my advice. Mr. Wooldridge is a lawyer, next door, retiring, learned and modest.—He is little known in Huntsville. He is a man of reading, taste and abilities, and one of the most amiable and polite.—But the *Italians*—they are brothers, and seem to belong to a different species of the human race. They have fine full features, round faces, and dark complexions. Their eyes and hair are jet black. But such eyes belong to no other nation—they sparkle like diamonds. Their manners and dispositions, likewise, differ from those of any people, or nation, I have seen. They are men of rich imaginations, very gay and lively in conversation, and philanthropy itself. Their company is courted by all.

Yours, &c.

Letter XLIX.

Huntsville, April, 1822.

Dear Matt,

I HAVE NOT, as you suppose, forgotten you, though you are a sad boy. But I will lay the matter over till we meet.

You have heard and read of tornadoes. We had the most dreadful tornado, last week, that was every known in this country. The ravages of this dreadful calamity was confined to a ridge of high poor land, the nearest part of which, is about three miles from hence, though we had a severe gale here, the hardest by far I ever witnessed. It prostrated everything before it in its career, trees, houses, fences, all raised to the foundation. Trees were said to be carried fifteen miles, twisted and split to atoms, and though strange, no lives were lost; most of the people were bruised and mangled, and lying on the ground, unable to disengage themselves from the fallen trees and houses; some with broken legs, some with broken arms, and all more or less injured, excepting one man and a few children. There they lay, and the rain pouring on them in torrents, and as dark as Egypt. It happened a little before midnight. By daylight, next morning, their situation being discovered, by their nearest neighbors, several expresses on horseback came into Huntsville, for surgeons, doctors, and assistance of every sort, as their clothing, and every atom they had in their houses were blown off, and never seen afterwards. Numbers jumped on their horses, doctors and all, and fled with the utmost speed to the sufferers; and amongst the foremost of these were the Sonano's, the Italian gentlemen. But in their haste they did not forget to take clothes, money, wine, biscuit, coffee, sugar, and tea; and these are Roman Catholics, who have been stigmatized as worse than the d——l. You will expect to hear that the christian went, I mean those professing religion. No such thing. Howard was sick, but he sent them money and food, and he is another Roman Catholic. But you have not heard the worst of it yet. Word was soon brought in, that there were twenty-one persons in all wounded, without food and clothing, and houseless—many of them widows and orphans[130]—a subscription was instantly set on foot, for their relief, and a paper carried round. Now, you would suppose that a Turk would not refuse relief in such a case; and you would suppose right: but do not imagine the professors subscribed—with the exception of one or two. When the paper was handed to them, they said "There were so many, they could not help all; and it was not adviseable to help any unless they gave all some!!!" One of these, a wealthy merchant, was the most abominable iron souled man in the world—a presbyterian elder, by the name, I think, of Hilton,[131] and used to make long prayers. What do you think of this sample of professors, as they are called?

I conversed with one of these sufferers, and inquired what were her sensations during the storm; and how she felt when carried away before it. She replied, that the storm was very sudden, and from the noise of crashing timber, thunder, and the dreadful roaring, she concluded she was to meet instant death. She had three children, and covering the two eldest in the bed, as she thought, for the last time, she took her babe in her arms, and crept under the bed, and resigned herself to the will of her maker. This is the last thing she remembered.—Upon regaining her senses, she was over an hundred yards from the place where the house had stood, with one of the logs of the house lying on her, and her leg broke. Her babe was lying near her, with a log across its neck, but did not touch the child, as it rested on the other timber. Her other two children were within a few steps of her, unhurt. She heard them talking to each other, and could see them very plain by the flashes of lightning. One man, an overseer, was very commodiously carried off in his bed, bedstead, and all, just as he lay, and put down about fifty yards off, and the first he knew of it was the rain pouring on him. He was in an upper story, which alone was blown off. These tornadoes must be more terrible than any storm at sea.

I have been told by those who have witnessed them by daylight, that the sky suddenly becomes black, after a still clear atmosphere—the winds then follow so quick, it is impossible to escape. Their ravages are generally confined to a narrow straight line, of different lengths. The one above described, was about 50 miles long, and not exceeding one quarter or one half a mile in breadth. No one can give a clear description of these sweeping desolations, for the darkness, dust, &c. they occasion, and, above all, the total absence of the senses. I did not go to see the one above, but I saw the effects of one in Kentucky, which must have been moderate, as it was not more than five or six hundred yards wide; but it levelled every tree to the earth. Some of these trees were the largest of the forest, and uniformly lay with their tops one way. I should suppose the noise alone would *stun* any one to death, as it must exceed the united artillery of heaven and earth! And here follows another of the wonders.

In this county (Madison) there is a stone, called the mad-dog stone, which effectually cures the bite of a mad dog, and all poisonous snakes. It is said to be about the size of a walnut, and porus, like a honey comb. This stone is applied to the wound, where it sticks fast, until the pores become full, when it drops off of itself. It is then washed in warm milk and water, and again applied to the wound, when it sticks, as at first, and so on, until the poison is extracted, when it will stick no longer. The man who owns it, lives about twenty miles from hence, and receives no compensation for the use of the stone; nor will he sell it. I have not been able to trace its history, though I saw several who have been cured by it. I am told there is one similar to it in East Virginia. I should think them of more value than the most costly diamonds.[132]

But I have still stranger news for you. I have never heard a word on the subject of politics, or tea parties, since I have been in this country! I mean the two great parties, Federal and Republican—for this good substantial reason—there are no parties here—they are all Republicans.[133] The country people, and very few of the city, know the meaning of the word *Federalist!* Nor have I heard of a tea party, in the whole country. No such thing, as "will you come and spend the evening?" They visit each other without ceremony, morning, noon, and night, and are invited to await breakfast, dinner, and supper; but no such thing as that bane of society, a "Tea party."

As some amends for the terrible, (to make a Jay's treaty of it,) in the first of this letter, I must relate an amusing anecdote, at which I have laughed enough. During the Creek war, (not long since,) some mischievous ill disposed man, reported that there was a large body of Indians within a day's march of Huntsville, coming to take the town. The citizens of Huntsville, and the whole of Madison county, were instantly panic struck, and immediately flew towards Nashville. Some left their calves fastened up in the pens, and some their horses in the stable, some their horses in the plow; most of them taking their flight on foot. Others, again, mounted their horses, without saddles or bridles. Of these were four young ladies on one horse, riding like gentlemen, without saddle or bridle, and making good speed by applying their heels to the horses sides!!! One man took another man's child, and left his own. In one place would be seen ladies on foot, running with their night caps on, and no bonnet; and in another, husbands riding, and wives walking. Some of the women mistook other men for their husbands, and some husbands mistook other men's wives for theirs. One stout fat woman, though she had horses and slaves in abundance, picked up her youngest child, and taking it in her arms, on foot outstripped every man and horse in company! Indeed, it is said a gentleman even left his sweetheart! He could not have been a Kentuckian or a Tennessean, as they never desert the ladies. The fat lady, however, walked twenty-five miles, without halting, when one of her slaves overtook her, having outran his fellow servants.—They were now near Fayetteville. The lady inquired "what news?" "Oh, bad news enough, Missee." "Are the Indians coming?" "Oh, yes, Missee! When I got 'pon top dat big hill you see da, Missee, I look back, and see most hundred comin long, wid da guns." The lady gave him the child, and mended her pace. Not long after this, as she trudged through the mud, with petticoats tucked up, the negro cried out, "Yonder da comes, now, Missee!" Her face which was scarlet red, now became a deadly pale; but she was afraid to take time to look at her foes, as she supposed them to be. At length, five or six of her own *neighbors* hailed her, and told her the whole was a false alarm.

About a thousand people were on the road to Nashville, and were within a day's journey of that place before they were undeceived. Only two families remained in Huntsville.—These barricaded the door of the Court House, which served them for a fort; and old Captain Wyatt, the father of Major Wyatt, of Melton's Bluff, assumed the command. He had but two guns, but being well charged with whiskey and courage, he kept up a constant fire, crying out, "by two's, fire!" Spang, spang went the two guns; and being instantly reloaded, he would raise his voice to the highest pitch again, and give the word, "by two's, fire!" Thus he went on till daylight; and at the same time there was not an hostile Indian within an hundred miles.

Yours, &c.

Letter L.

Huntsville, June 8th, 1822.

WELL, MATT, what shall I give you now? It is so long since I wrote to you, that I forgot what I last said. If I recollect right, I have, upon the whole, entertained you with a little of every thing, except love; and I confess I do not know how to write upon that subject; and yet, how easy it appears to be to most people. But I can give you a little upon hatred.

I have often mentioned the great wealth of this place.—

Here are Colonel Leroy Pope, General Brayhan, Doctor Fern, Doctor Chambers, Doctor Manning, Thomas Bibb, Esq. and a score or two besides, that are rich as princes, and are stigmatized, by a few of the vicious, by the appellation of nobility![134] If by this designation, they mean the performance of noble actions, which is really the origin of the word, they could not better apply the term. But I am inclined to think, in the present instance, it is used by way of contempt. But let envy alone. Only because these people, by their own foresight and industry, laid out their money in the right time, and at the right place, instead of spending it in taverns and gambling houses, they have drawn down upon them the envy of little minds, who never did a generous act in their lives.—But what do you think of Doctor Manning, the greatest planter in the state, but one—and him I know nothing of; he living in Laurence county, over the river. Doctor Manning, this year, has *seven hundred and sixty acres* in cultivation; and Doctor Chambers, and a dozen others, very little behind him!

The merchants, in other states, hold the farmers in vassalage—but, here, the merchant is held in subjection by the planter. The planter does not ship his own cotton: this is done by the merchant, and at his own risk. The planter delivers it at the gin, and has no more to do with it. The merchant is glad to get it at the planter's own price, as he has no other way to pay for his goods, in New York, where the money of this country will not pass.

The merchant goes to market but once a year. The usual mode of transportation for goods is to wagon them to Pittsburg, and thence down the Ohio, and up the Cumberland and Tennessee rivers. Groceries are laid in at New Orleans.

It is in contemplation, I am told, to establish a mercantile house at New Orleans, or some point in these states, to import direct from Liverpool.

Through the politeness of Colonel Pope, I obtained the following intelligence, which I send as I received it in a letter:

"Poplar Grove, 25th January.

"I beg leave to apologize to you for not answering your letter sooner, which I had the pleasure of receiving some days ago. My absence from home was the cause of this neglect. I regret much that it is not in my power to furnish you such information, on all your inquiries, as would be of interest to yourself, or others. On such of your inquiries as I am able to answer with any degree of correctness, I will do with pleasure Your first question—The quantity of cotton raised in Madison, the last three years? From the best information that I have been able to obtain, and which I think is pretty correct, there has been raised about fourteen thousand bales, annually, the last three years, being in the total weight, about fourteen millions two hundred thousand pounds; the average price I conceive may be fairly said to have been twelve and an half cents per pound, making the total sum, annually, in this article shipped from the county of Madison, five hundred and twenty-five thousand dollars. The quantity of land cultivated in this article is about sixteen thousand eight hundred acres, which produces upon the average, one thousand pounds of seed cotton per acre, and from five to six acres cultivated to the hand. —The use made of the cotton seed after it is ginned, is various: some make manure of them, for which they answer a good purpose; some feed horned cattle, and if properly prepared, it is excellent food for stock of that description; and sheep will eat them freely. The carriage from here to Tuscaloosa varies, it is from two to four dollars per hundred weight. With respect to the temperature of the air, and other particulars, I refer you to John Boardman, Esq. of this place, who will furnish you with the information you want.

"Respectfully, yours, &c.

"POPE."

Since this communication, I have received the receipts of shipments of cotton for this year, which amounts to upwards of two millions of dollars, from all the counties bordering on the Tennessee river!!!

There is a country for you. All, except Madison, was in woods two years ago. I have known cotton to bring *twenty five cents;* but Colonel Pope gives the average. Would you believe it? The people are leaving this beautiful country, and going, some to Texas, some to Missouri, and some to Red River, and others, the plague knows where. But if they find a handsomer, or richer country, I am much mistaken.

The rapid growth of vegetables would astonish you. Go into a garden one day, and the next you would scarcely know th same. I have never been more surprized at this rapid growth.

In the common way we had strawberries and peas the last week in April. Irish potatoes and snaps, first week in May. Early York's and cucumbers the last day of May; and on the same day, a summer turnip that measured seven and an half inches round. This being near the northern boundary, I am told they are two weeks earlier to the south. But no country can excel in fruit. You may sit down in one place in the gardens, and gather half a bushel of strawberries. The wild fruit, such as plumbs, &c. are as delicious as our tame fruits. The woods and praries abound with all sorts of fruit, and they have, it is said, the true Muscodine grape: I have seen and eat them. They are larger than our Fox grapes, and of a greenish color. They grow in profusion on all the rivers, upon a large vine, which runs to the top of the tallest trees. Ten bushels at the least might be gathered from one tree; and were it not for the overflowing abundance of other good things, I am certain, though I never heard it mentioned, these grapes would make good wine.

You have often heard said, "Oh, that Alabama, is so hot, I could not live there; and it is so sickly, too." What abominable fools. It is much warmer there (West Virginia) than here, in summer; and why? Because our days here are much shorter—

Even a goose knows this. Again, we have a pleasant breeze through summer here, which sets in a little after sunrise, every fair day, and blows till sundown. Our nights in summer are long, in proportion as the days are short; it is therefore cool and pleasant. It is, however, sultry in cloudy weather, as there is then no breeze. But I have never seen the Thermometer, in summer, here, as high as it is where you live.

You recollect your old school mate, Doctor Erskine: he lives here, and has become wealthy. He married, sometime since, the beautiful Miss Russel, and has one child. The Doctor is highly respected in Huntsville, both as a gentleman and a physician; and has handsome practice. He rides in his carriage, and ranks with the first men in the place.[135] Almost every one rides in carriages here—very few are ever seen on horseback.

With all these blessings, however, we have a few curses; and one of them is slavery! Not that the slaves are treated bad. If we except the total neglect, on the part of their owners, to enlighten their minds, they live as well as their masters; and are by no means hard tasked. But they are the most immoral and cruel brutes in the world. One shrinks with horror at their barbarity to poor innocent brutes. I never have looked into the streets, since I have been here, but I see those brutal negroes torturing and wounding poor innocent cats, dogs, hogs, or oxen, and no one interferes to prevent it. The white people do not see it, as they are seasoned to it by habit, and appear as callous as the brutes themselves. I have (but it is almost too shocking to relate) seen cats lying with their backs broke, for two days at a time, in the street, and when I entreated these ruffians to kill them, to put them out of their misery, they burst into a laugh in my face. A curse must fall on a land so lost to feeling. Those innocent creatures were given to us for our use, and not to glut a worse than savage disposition. And yet, these negroes are very pious. They have two churches, and prayer meetings very night. There were seven fights here, between negroes, near the doors of their churches.

We went to hear a Missionary preach the other night, and he collected a large sum, several hundred dollars, to convert the Heathen.[136] What a burlesque. Where are greater Heathens to be found, than these negroes. There is a great deal of preaching here; and a great many ill natured remarks pass between the presbyterians and methodists; but whether it be to determine which shall save most souls, or receive most money, I am too ignorant to discover. I hope that the one or the other may take those in hand. They need not go far for the Heathen.

From what I have heard, it appears the methodists have braved every danger, and preached to the people gratis, in the settling of the country; and now that there is no danger, and the people have become wealthy, those sly fellows, the presbyterians, are creeping in to reap the harvest. But the methodists have a great advantage, in point of talent, many of them being the best orators in the country. But they all draw too many women after them, in my humble opinion.

Yours, &c.

NOTES

Introduction: Anne Royall—Tireless Traveler and Common Nuisance

[1] For information on these travelers, see Thomas D. Clark, *Travels in the Old South, A Bibliography*, 3 vols. (Norman, Oklahoma, 1956). Volume 2 has material for the period under discussion here.

[2] Adam Hodgson, *Letters from North America, Written during a Tour in the United States and Canada*, 2 vols. (London, 1824). A résumé of this work appears in Clark, *Travels*, vol. 2, pp. 244–245, entry no. 208.

[3] Auguste Levasseur, *Lafayette en Amérique, en 1824 et 1825, ou, Journal d'un voyage aux Etats-Unis* . . . . 2 vols. (Paris, 1829); Clark, *Travels*, vol. 2, pp. 250–252, entry no. 213.

[4] *Reise sr. Hoheit des Herzogs Bernhard zee Sachson-Weimar-Eisenach durch Nord-Amerika in den Jahren 1825 und 1826*, ed. by Heinrich Luden . . . (Weimar, 1828).

[5] *The Rambler, or a tour Through Virginia, Tennessee, Alabama, Mississippi, and Louisiana* . . . . (Annapolis, 1828), cited in Clark, *Travels in the Old South*, vol. 2, p. 63.

[6] Anne Royall, *Letters from Alabama on Various subjects to which is added an appendix containing remarks on sundry members of the 20th and 21st Congress, and other high characters, etc. etc. at the seat of government* (Washington, 1830).

[7] There are two published biographies of Anne Royall: Sarah Harvey Porter, *The Life and Times of Anne Royall* (Cedar Rapids, Ia., 1909), and George Stuyesant Jackson, *Uncommon Scold, The Story of Anne Royall* (Boston, 1937). Mrs. Porter wrote at a time when there were still living people who remembered Mrs. Royall personally, and her biography contains much information not available in print elsewhere. Mr. Jackson's small volume is more an analysis or evaluation than it is a biography, but it has a distinct advantage over Mrs. Porter's work in that it is footnoted, making it possible to verify the accuracy of his statements. There are a few articles about Anne Royall, most of which appeared in newspapers at the time of her death in 1854. The source materials, mostly letters to publishers or booksellers, are widely scattered. Yale University, Duke University, University of Virginia, and New York Public Library each has a small collection. The National Archives, Washington, D.C., has her pension claims and the court record of her trial in 1829. There is little more than business letters in the collections of papers. Most of them are about collecting payments for books sold.

[8] Porter, *Life and Times*, pp. 31–35; George S. Jackson, *The Uncommon Scold*, pp. 26–28.

[9] This rumor, if indeed it is such, is based on a letter to Maryland Governor Sharpe from Lord Baltimore from London, 1767, which says, "an absurd report, *I* am informed, has been spread through the Province that my late uncle, Mr. Calvert's son, was doubted to be legitimate and consequently I had settled the Province on him after my death. Whereas Mr. Calvert has appointed me by his will his guardian and Executor, expressly declares him as *not* Legitimate, and before his death got me to give him an annuity by the name he goes by of Mr. Newport, son of Judith, I forgett her name." Quoted in Porter, *Life and Times*, p. 19.

[10] *Montgomery Advertiser*, Oct. 18, 1854, quoting the *Washington Sentinel; Washington Post*, Oct. 6, 1901; "She was a Holy Terror," *Washington Post*, Feb. 22, 1891.

[11] Anne also had a sister who at maturity married a man named Cowan and lived in the Mount Pisgah settlement in Pennsylvania where the family had formerly resided. The younger half brother

James Butler, was in the War of 1812 and later moved to Indiana. Anne Royall says very little about her family. Porter, *Life and Times*, pp. 29–30.

[12] Baltimore *Sun*, October 18, 1931; Porter, *Life and Times*, pp. 34–35. Anne's mother lived until 1831.

[13] One of the remembered eccentricities of William Royall is the fact that he kept all his cattle and horses "in their natural state; there were neither geldings nor steers to be found in his herds." Porter, *Life and Times*, p. 34, quoting Eva Grant Maloney.

[14] For this phase of Virginia history see Lucille Griffith, *Virginia House of Burgesses 1750–1774* (Northport, Alabama, 1963) pp. 174–189, passim. The story of William Royall is told by his wife in *Sketches of History, Life and Manners in the United States, By a Traveller* (New Haven, 1826), pp. 89–90. Burmuda Hundred is at the place where Appomattox River runs into the James. The exact location of the Royall plantation is not known, and it may have faced either river. Charles E. Hatch, Jr., *The First Seventeen Years, Virginia, 1607–1624*, Jamestown 350th Anniversary Historical Booklet, no. 6, pp. 32, 62; *Virginia, a Guide to the Old Dominion*, American Guide Series (New York, 1940), pp. 576–577.

[15] Porter, *Life and Times*, passim; Jackson, *Uncommon Scold*, passim.

[16] Amelia Will Book #2, p. 340; *Virginia Magazine of History and Biography*, vol. 33, pp. 107, 208.

[17] Porter, *Life and Times*, p. 39.

[18] *The Huntress*, July 14, 1838; Porter, *Life and Times*, 38–39. The latter contains a lengthy unidentified quote from Mrs. Royall's writings. There is an account of the gunpowder raid in William Wirt, *Sketches of the Life and Character of Patrick Henry* (Philadelphia, 1844), pp. 149–165. However, there is no mention of Royall's part in it.

[19] James Whitcomb, Commissioner, General Land Office, to Mrs. Anne Royall, Mar. 3, 1840, National Archives, Washington, D.C.; *The Huntress*, Feb. 4, 1843.

[20] A copy of the marriage certificate is in the Pensions Claims papers in the National Archives. There can be no question that the marriage took place and was legally recorded.

[21] Porter, *Life and Times*, pp. 36, 37.

[22] Royall must have been at least twenty-five years older than his wife.

[23] Thomas D. Clark in *Travels in the Old South*, vol. 3, p. 81, says that Mrs. Royall began her southern tour in 1813, shortly after her husband's death, but there is no evidence to support this assertion.

[24] The will is recorded in the Monroe County Court House, Order Book, 1809–1811, quoted in Jackson, *Uncommon Scold*, p. 49. The land he left to Anne Cowan was at the mouth of Elk River, County of Kennahway, or four hundred acres in lieu thereof if she so desired.

[25] William Archer sat in both the United States House of Representatives and the Senate, serving Virginia at the nation's capital from 1812 to 1835. He was born at "The Lodge" in Amelia County in 1789, and was buried there in 1855. He was a lawyer by profession. *Biographical Directory of the American Congress* (Washington, 1950), p. 788.

[26] *Sketches of History, Life and Manners in the United States, By a Traveller* (New Haven, 1826), p. 2. This was the first travel book that Mrs. Royall deliberately planned.

[27] Monroe County Order Book, 1808–1811, quoted in Jackson, *Uncommon Scold*, p. 49.

[28] Anne Royall, *Mrs. Royall's Southern Tour, or Second Series of the Black Book* (Washington, 1831), vol. 1, p. 110.

[29] Porter, *Life and Times*, p. 44.

[30] All of Mrs. Royall's books were published by 1831. A complete list includes (in chronological order of their publication): *Sketches of History, Life and Manners in the United States*, "By a Traveller" (New Haven, 1826); *The Tennessean* (New Haven, 1827); *The Black Book; or, A Continuation of Travels in the United States*, 3 vols. (Washington, 1828, 1829); *Mrs. Royall's Pennsylvania, or, Travels Continued in the United States*, 2 vols. (Washington, 1829); *Letters from Alabama on various Subjects to which is added an Appendix containing Remarks on Sundry Members of the Twentieth and Twenty First Congress and other High characters*, etc. (Washington, 1830); *Mrs. Royall's Southern Tour, or Second Series of the Black Book*, 3 vols. (Washington, 1831).

[31] *Sketches, By a Traveller*, p. 2.

[32] Porter, *Life and Times*, passim; Jackson, *Uncommon Scold*, passim.

[33] Mrs. Porter has compiled a "Partial Index to Personal Descriptions in Mrs. Royall's Newspapers of Members of Congress and Others, 1831–1854" that probably would be twice as long if it included names in her travel books too.

[34] Porter, *Life and Times*, pp. 254–292.

[35] *Letters from Alabama*, Letter XVIII. This passage apparently comes from *Sketches*, By a Traveller, but is quoted in Porter, *Life and Times*, p. 71.

[36] Mrs. Royall makes many references to this episode, which she describes in full in *The Black Book*, vol. 3, pp. 33 ff. The term "blue skin" seems to be Mrs. Royall's version of "blue nose," an uncomplimentary description of the pious, straight-laced New Englander.

[37] A summary of laws regarding Revolutionary War pensions is in W. T. R. Saffell, *Records of the Revolutionary War: containing the military and Financial correspondence of Distinguished officers* . . . (New York, 1858). Virginia's laws are on pp. 488–511.

[38] Ibid., pp. 511–512, pp. 522–525.

[39] George Jackson to Pension Office, July 16, 1935, Widow of William Royall claims, National Archives, Washington, D.C.

[40] *Paul Pry*, June 2, 1832. See also *The Huntress*, Dec. 2, 1836; July 14, 1838; Feb. 11, 1843.

[41] Report no. 796, House of Representatives, 27th Congress, 2nd Session, May 26, 1842. Several petitions and considerable correspondence are in the William Royall Claims in the National Archives, Washington, D.C.

[42] Royall Claims in Senate Report on House of Representatives Bill 450, Jan. 20, 1843; Porter, *Life and Times*, pp. 215–216.

[43] Porter, *Life and Times*, pp. 215–216.

[44] Ibid., p. 217, evidently quoting *The Huntress*.

[45] Jackson, *The Uncommon Scold*, p. 95. This information is not contained in the official papers and Mr. Jackson does not offer any supporting evidence.

[46] The two sources for this trial are the official court records, *U.S.* vs. *Royall*, Records of Circuit Court, District of Columbia,

3 Cranch (now in National Archives, Record Group no. 21); and Mrs. Royall's own bitter and emotional version which is appended to *Mrs. Royall's Pennsylvania*, vol. 2. The trial was well attended by the curious and reportedly attracted much attention, but there seems to have been little written about it at the time.

[47] Anne Royall to Captain "Yankie" Hall, Harper's Ferry, May 3, 1828. The original of this letter is in the library of the University of Virginia, by whose permission I use it.

[48] Some days later this young woman, who was unmarried, stopped by to see her mistress, displaying a bouncing baby boy who looked to Mrs. Royall for the world like "Holy Willy," the leader of the Engine House Congregation. *Mrs. Royall's Pennsylvania*, vol. 2, appendix, p. 1.

[49] Ibid., pp. 2, 8.

[50] Ibid.; *U.S.* vs. *Anne Royall*, Andrew Way, foreman of the jury. The original is in National Archives. Mrs. Royall's two biographers give extensive coverage to the trial: Porter, *Life and Times*, pp. 131–145; Jackson, *Uncommon Scold*, pp. 113–121.

[51] All of this information is in *Mrs. Royall's Pennsylvania*, vol. 2, appendix.

[52] As Mrs. Royall entered the courtroom, someone placed in her hand a letter containing a caricature of a "ducking car." In it she was chained in "hard fast." The car was pulled by a horse driven by "Tench Ringgold, naked with a tail like a monkey." The gentlemen to whom she showed the picture "were amused at Mr. Ringgold" but by no means relished the joke. Mrs. Royall was quite sure she could not have survived the ducking car or stool itself. A model of it on display at the city hall "consisted of a shaft which was to be from eleven to fifteen feet in length, and at the extremety of this" she was to be fastened. The shaft was to be worked by a windlass by a great number of people and was to go round like a windmill with a circumference of some "thirty-six or perhaps an hundred feet, first in the river and then in the air." The device must have looked like a medieval torture machine or perhaps like something Rube Goldberg might have thought up. *Mrs. Royall's Pennsylvania*, vol. 2, appendix, p. 28.

[53] Porter, *Life and Times*, pp. 131–133.

[54] Jackson, *Uncommon Scold*, pp. 110–112.

[55] *The Huntress*, June 10, 1837.

[56] *Mrs. Royall's Pennsylvania*, vol. 2, appendix.

[57] *Black Book*, vol. 1, p. 41.

[58] This is a review of *Sketches By a Traveller* in 1828, quoted in Porter, *Life and Times*, p. 77.

[59] Porter, *Life and Times*, pp. 219–220.

[60] *Paul Pry*, Mar. 2, 1833; Mar. 16, 1833; Mar. 20, 1833.

[61] *The Huntress*, Mar. 20, 1841.

[62] *Paul Pry*, Mar. 16, 1832.

[63] *Paul Pry*, Apr. 6, 1833.

[64] *Paul Pry*, Apr. 14, 1832.

[65] Ibid., Jackson is of the opinion she was strongly motivated by a desire for revenge after her humiliating trial in 1829. *Uncommon Scold*, p. 121. The files of both *Paul Pry* and *The Huntress*, are in the Rare Books Room, Library of Congress. Interestingly, the library stands on the place where Mrs. Royall lived during much of her residence in Washington.

[66] *Paul Pry*, Feb. 11, 1832.

[67] The first issue of *The Huntress*, Dec. 2, 1836, contained "A Tale of the French Revolution," picked up from the *London Literary Gazette;* "Louise of Lorraine," by Miss Agnes Strickland; "Julian and Leonora," by R. Shelton Mackenzie, L.L.D.; a long article about Santa Anna in addition to essays and news items about domestic abuses. On page 4 of this first issue she explained at length reasons for the change. The name *Huntress* is thought to have come from a song in a ballad-opera *The Archers* (1796), written by Benjamin Carr (1768–1831). The words by William Dunlop are as follows:

Why, Huntress, Why?

Why, Huntress, why, wilt thou thy life expose?
So valued by your friends.
If thou shouldst fall, the death of all our foes,
Can never make amends.
Then, Huntress, why? Wilt thou thy life expose?

Ah! think what pangs thy Father still must feel,
What pangs must Arnold know,
When thou'rt exposed unto the biting steel

Shall rush admidst the foe
Then, Huntress, why wilt thou thy life expose?

The text is in W. Thomas Marracoo and Harold Gleason, *Music in America* (New York, 1964), p. 179. Mrs. Linda McDonald Soest provided me with a copy of the song-poem.

[68] *Paul Pry*, May 19, 1832.

[69] *Paul Pry*, Feb. 18, 1832. She also printed less complimentary comments. The editor of the *Manchester Whig and Yazoo Register* (published in Manchester, Mississippi), for example, accused her of using abusive language. "What does he mean?" she asked. "Does he mean to say we are a black guard?" And then she went on for paragraphs challenging him to put his finger on one word she had written that was not "strictly chaste," no matter how "abandoned" the subject was. *The Huntress*, Feb. 24, 1838.

[70] There are many references to Mrs. Royall's friend Sally. Mrs. Sarah Stack was the widowed daughter of the family of Dorrets that had befriended Anne when she first came to Washington. Sally went to live with Mrs. Royall in 1831, about the time *Paul Pry* began publication, and for the rest of Anne's life was her closest friend, acting as circulation manager and chief assistant. She was considerably younger than Mrs. Royall and was tall and angular in appearance, providing decided contrast to the small older woman. Jackson, *Uncommon Scold*, pp. 121–122.

[71] *The Huntress*, Mar. 12, 1842; Apr. 1, 1843; Mar. 3, 1844; Feb. 21, 1852.

[72] *Paul Pry*, Apr. 7, 1832.

[73] This story appears without documentation in popular publications like *This Week Magazine*.

[74] This story has been copied widely. See Jackson, *Uncommon Scold*, pp. 134–138.

[75] *The Huntress*, Mar. 5, 1842.

[76] *The Huntress*, Nov. 27, 1837.

[77] *Paul Pry*, Dec. 31, 1831; Feb. 24, 1832.

[78] Heber Blankenhorn, "The Grandma of the Muckrakers," *American Mercury*, September, 1927.

[79] Anne Newport Royall Papers, University of Virginia Library.

[80] This phrase is quoted in practically everything that is written about Mrs. Royall. This writer, however, has been unable to find the origin of it. The description gives a wrong impression of the relations between the two of them. Actually, President Adams felt very kindly toward the old woman: he received her in his office many times, he once gave her a shawl that had belonged to his wife (a gift that Anne displayed proudly), and later, when he was again in the House of Representatives, he handled her pension bills (which he introduced regularly).

[81] *Paul Pry*, Feb. 11, 1832.

[82] *The Huntress*, Aug. 12, 1837.

[83] Ibid.

[84] *Paul Pry*, Jan. 14, 1832.

[85] *The Huntress*, July 24, 1852.

[86] Ibid., Aug. 7, 1852.

[87] Ibid., July 24, 1854.

[88] Ibid., Aug. 21, 1841.

[89] Royall, *Southern Tour*, vol. 3, pp. 67, 245.

[90] *Paul Pry*, Feb. 11, 1832.

[91] Royall, *Letters from Alabama*, Letter XLI.

[92] Royall, *Southern Tour*, vol. 2, p. 184.

[93] The Millerites were followers of William Miller, founder of the Adventist movement, who taught that the end of the world and the second coming of Christ would take place in 1843. Thousands of people believed him and hundreds of them assembled to await the end of time on days he had set. See *Dictionary of American Biography* (Chicago, 1933), vol. 12, p. 642; William W. Sweet, *The Story of Religion in America* (New York, 1930), pp. 401–403.

[94] *Mrs. Royall's Pennsylvania*, Vol. 2, appendix.

[95] Quoted in Porter, *Life and Times*, p. 167.

[96] *Southern Tour*, Vol. 1, p. 110.

[97] Porter, *Life and Times*, p. 117.

[98] *Paul Pry*, Feb. 18, 1832.

[99] Ibid., Apr. 20, 1833.

[100] Royall, *Southern Tour*, vol. 3, p. 132. The Bank was the other one.

[101] Porter, *Life and Times*, p. 98, quoting Henry O'Reilley. Porter gives a lengthy account of this episode, pp. 92–113. See also

Charles McCarthy, *The Anti-Masonic Party* (New York, 1903).

[102] This first third party in the United States was the first to hold a presidential nominating convention. William Wirt, a former United States attorney general, was the presidential candidate.

[103] There is much in print about the Bank controversy. Probably the best brief study is *Jackson versus Biddle. The Struggle over the Second United States Bank* (Boston, 1949), in the Amherst "Problems in American Civilization" series.

[104] *Paul Pry*, Feb. 11, 1832.

[105] Ibid., Mar. 3, 1832.

[106] Ibid. Major Noah was the editor. There was a good-natured feud running between Mrs. Royall and Noah over many public issues.

[107] Ibid., July 21, 1832.

[108] Ibid., Dec. 1, 1832.

[109] Ibid., Oct. 5, 1933.

[110] Ibid., Nov. 19, 1836.

[111] *The Huntress*, July 24, 1854.

[112] Porter, *Life and Times*, p. 226. The paper from which the notice is taken is not identified, but it may be the *National Intelligencer*, which Mrs. Porter quotes in the next paragraph. On the other hand it may be the *Washington Globe*, which the *Montgomery Advertiser* copied.

[113] *Washington Evening Star*, Oct. 2, 1854.

[114] For example, *Montgomery Advertiser*, Oct. 11, 1854, quoting the *Washington Globe*. The issue for October 18 contains a longer notice about her which includes the story about her capture by the Indians.

[115] This quotation from the writings of Kendall, the "brains" of the Jackson administration, is given in Porter, *Life and Times*, without specific reference.

[116] "She was a Holy Terror," *Washington Post*, Feb. 22, 1891. The whole title to the article is "She was a Holy Terror: Her Pen was as venomous as a Rattlesnakes' Fangs: Former Washington Editress: How Mrs. Anne Royall Made Life a Burden to the Public Men of Her Day: Her Fight with The Presbyterians on Capitol Hill: With Indians Fifteen Years." Apparently the author of this

article had interviewed several elderly people who had known Anne Royall.

[117] "Poor Anne Royall," *Washington Evening Star*, Jan. 28, 1903.

[118] Porter, *Life and Times*, p. 231, quoting Ainsworth R. Spofford.

[119] Anne's grave in the Congressional Cemetery is in Range 25, Site 194 and marked with a granite stone on which is inscribed

Anne Royall
Pioneer Woman Publicist
1769–1854
"I pray that the union of these states may be eternal."
Erected in appreciative recognition by a few men of Philadelphia and Washington May 12, 1911

Notes to Anne Royall's Letters from Alabama, 1817-1822

N.B.: Mrs. Royall's footnotes, quoted from the 1830 edition, are identified as AUTHOR'S NOTES throughout. Other notes are by the editor.

[1] Cabell County, in the extreme western part of what was then Virginia (now, of course, West Virginia), is named for William H. Cabell, former governor; it was formed from Mason County in 1809. Its largest city is Huntington, some 50 miles west of Charlestown. Charles H. Ambler, *West Virginia, The Mountain State* (New York, 1940), p. 227.

[2] Mount Sterling, Kentucky, the county seat of Montgomery County, is some 30 miles due east of Lexington. An earlier traveler

had stopped here, Josiah Murdock. See his *Memorandums of a Tour made by Josiah Espy in the States of Ohio and Kentucky and Indian Territory in 1803* (Cincinnati, 1870), cited in Thomas D. Clark, *Travels in the Old South, A Bibliography*, 3 vols. (Norman, Okla., 1956), vol. 2, p. 24.

[3] Lord Selkirk does not appear in Clark, *Travels*. However, this must have been Thomas Douglas (1771–1820), fifth Earl of Selkirk, Baron Daer and Shortcleuch, of the Scottish peerage. Beginning in 1802, he was "drawn to the advantages offered to colonists by the fertile valley of the Red River" (now Manitoba) and began negotiations for a grant of land there. Changes in the grant and controversy within the ranks of both the promoters and the settlers caused him to move to Upper Canada. For information on Lord Selkirk see *Dictionary of National Biography* (London, 1917), vol. 5, pp. 1,255–1,258. An account of his travels is contained in "A Narrative of Occurances, etc. in North America, 1817." His papers are available on microfilm from the Public Archives of Canada. None of the usual travel bibliographies mention his presence in Kentucky. However, an article entitled "Selkirk's Return from Assiniboia via The United States to the Canadas, 1817–1818," ed. John Prichett, in *The Mississippi Valley Historical Review*, vol. 32, pp. 399–418, which contains correspondence between Selkirk and his wife, sheds some light on the matter. After visiting St. Louis and Vincennes, Selkirk journeyed toward Washington, D.C., taking the shortest route from Lexington, Kentucky (where he wrote his wife on Nov. 24, 1817) through the mountains of Virginia. Thus, he had made normal progress to meet Mrs. Royall on this date. As to Selkirk's reason for making a trip to Kentucky, which the innkeeper's wife considered suspect, he probably was looking for an asylum for his countrymen (the same motive that had prompted his endeavors in Canada). Selkirk was a frail man, and his wife, who worried constantly about his health, would have been distressed at his thin clothing. And perhaps with good reason; he died of tuberculosis in 1820.

[4] Doubtless residents of Kentucky called it a "city" because in 1815 between six and seven thousand "souls" lived there, according to *Niles Weekly*, Jan. 28, 1815. Three years later, in 1818, Timothy Flint called Lexington the "capital of Fashion in Kentucky." The

town exhibited "a well-dressed population"—several of its more genteel families kept coaches—and also boasted a university, a brick Masons' hall, several places of worship, three printing presses (where three weekly newspapers were published), a branch of the United States Bank and two other banking houses, seven mercantile houses, and some good taverns. This and much more about Lexington is contained in a long letter in Timothy Flint's *Recollections of the Last Ten Years* (New York, 1832), pp. 65–78. See also *Lexington and the Blue Grass Country*, American Guide Series (Lexington, 1938), pp. 8–19, and J. Winston Coleman, Jr., *Stage-Coach Days in the Blue Grass* (Lexington, 1935), p. 44.

[5] Licking River, which flows into the Ohio at Cincinnati, was the route pioneers followed on their way into central and eastern Kentucky. Thomas D. Clark, *A History of Kentucky* (New York, 1937), p. 20.

[6] See note 4 for population of Lexington. It was often called the "Queen City of the West." See Clark, *History of Kentucky*, p. 94 and passim.

[7] For Kentucky's hemp production and allied industries see Clark, *History of Kentucky*, pp. 240 ff.

[8] Bowling Green, now a thriving city, is the county seat of Warren County.

[9] Basic works on Andrew Jackson—though not free of error—are John Spencer Bassett, *The Life of Andrew Jackson* (New York, 1916), and Marquis James, *The Life of Andrew Jackson* (New York, 1938). *Author's Note:* "At this period the state of Tennessee and its high born sons, attracted universal admiration, and was the subject of conversation in all companies."

[10] Jackson resigned his seat in the United States Senate and accepted a judgeship on the Tennessee Supreme Court, a position that Bassett says suited his tastes better than did a place in the legislative body. Bassett, *Andrew Jackson*, p. 32.

[11] William Weatherford (1765–1824), known in early Alabama history as Red Eagle, was the son of a Scottish trader and Sehoy McGillivray of the Creek Nation. An outstanding horseman, athlete, and planter, he was very influential among the Indians and in the Creek War was leader of the Red Sticks, the war party. Born in what is now Elmore County, he lived later in Lowndes, Monroe,

and Baldwin counties, where he was widely known as a planter. Literature on Weatherford is somewhat fragmentary and often romantic. See James, *Andrew Jackson*, pp. 155–173; Bassett, *Andrew Jackson*, p. 119; "William Weatherford," *Dictionary of American Biography* (New York, 1936), vol. 19, pp. 567–568; G. C. Eggleston, *Red Eagle* (New York, 1878); J. F. H. Claiborne, *Life and Times of Sam Dale* (New York, 1860); J. H. Eaton, *Life and Times of Andrew Jackson* (Philadelphia, 1817); Albert J. Pickett, *History of Alabama* (Sheffield, Ala., 1851); H. S. Halbert and T. H. Ball, *The Creek War* (Montgomery, Ala., 1893). Weatherford also figures prominently in a recent novel, Bruce Palmer's *Horseshoe Bend* (New York, 1962). The massacre at Fort Mims (Aug. 30, 1813) in northern Baldwin County, Alabama, has been described as the "bloodiest in frontier history." On that day 517 of 553 residents of South Alabama who had assembled at the block house of Sam Mims were killed by the Red Sticks led by Weatherford, High-Head Jim, Josiah Francis, and other prominent Indian chiefs. For an account of the event by a survivor, see Dr. Thomas G. Holmes, "Fort Mims," in Lucille Griffith, *History of Alabama, 1540–1900, As Recorded in Diaries, Letters and Other Papers of the Times* (Northport, Ala., 1962), pp. 72–75. Jackson's description of Horseshoe Bend is contained in reports to Governor Willie Blount of Tennessee and to Mrs. Jackson; *Correspondence of Andrew Jackson*, ed. John Spencer Bassett (New York, 1926–1935), vol. 1, pp. 489–494.

[12] A comparison of Nashville and Lexington can be found in F. Gavin Davenport, *Antebellum Kentucky: A Social History, 1800–1860* (Oxford, Ohio, 1943), p. xvii.

[13] Author's Note: "A favorite dog of the *Author*."

[14] Modern authorities on American language have shed very little additional light on the meaning of the words "Tuckahoe" and "Cohee." Tuckahoe, however, seems to have an Indian origin since it was the name for a root from which the aborigines made a kind of bread; Cohee comes from a Scottish expression "Quo' he." It is interesting to note that the earliest mention in print of these two words is 1817, the year in which Mrs. Royall is writing. See Mitford M. Mathews, ed., *Dictionary of Americanisms on Historical Principles* (Chicago, 1951), vol. 1, p. 386, and vol. 2, p. 1,776.

[15] Author's Note: "I am obliged to retain the *r* in hear, fire,

&c, or not be understood; but she *sounded* it not in speaking, nor does any of her sort. *For* they sound like *faw* or *fow*, (light,) and *nor* like "naw," &c. as "naw you," "naw or na I," &c. and, "what *faw*," "you hea or he," &c. Also, *tha* for there, and *sharance* for assurance, &c. Nev'r or nev' for never—stars for stairs—mar for mare, &c."

[16] There are so many writers by the name of Park that it is virtually impossible to identify this one. John Ledyard, celebrated companion of Captain Cook, was later the subject of a multivolume book by Jared Sparks, *Memoirs of the Life and Travels of John Ledyard. . . .* (Cambridge, Mass., 1828). Isaac Weld, born in Dublin in 1774, but widely traveled in America, may have been the Weld Mrs. Royall cited here. *A Critical Dictionary of English Literature and British and American Authors*, ed. by S. Austin Allibone (Philadelphia, 1908), vol. 3, p. 2,636; and François, Duc de La Rochetoucauld-Liancourt, *Voyages to the United States* (London, 1799).

[17] Mrs. Royall is a classic example of the kind of woman who belittles and condemns her sex in general and yet rejects the "double standard" in morality, the business world, and politics. At the same time, she was trying to win a place for herself in a man's world.

[18] Author's Note: "I have conversed seriously with several of my female friends on this subject, and they tell me 'that the fear of being suspected, prevents them from showing compassion to this unfortunate class of females'. If I were to hazard an opinion, I would say, their want of charity to their own sex, ought, by no means to enhance our opinion of their virtue. I once heard a libertine say, 'he wanted no better sign for his purpose:' and all men of sense say the same thing. On the other hand, I am astonished those affected ladies do not spurn the men upon the same grounds. Abominable affectation!"

[19] The circuit rider was an important factor in the westward spread of Methodism. For accounts of their work see Anson West, *A History of Methodism in Alabama* (Nashville, 1893), passim; William Warren Sweet, *Methodism in American History* (New York, 1954), pp. 161–185; William Warren Sweet, *Religion on the American Frontier*, 1783–1840, vol. 4, and *The Methodists* (Chicago,

1946), pp. 202–260. The last work cited contains the journal of a circuit rider, Benjamin Lakin, who rode circuits in Kentucky and Ohio.

[20] AUTHOR'S NOTES: "The land is so rich, and never or seldom freezing in winter, and the want of good roads, makes the travelling unspeakably bad." "Cattle" is the "Yankee phrase for Horses."

[21] The number of Methodists was growing rapidly. In 1804, there were 3,560 white and 248 colored members of Methodist societies in the Tennessee Conference. Even after losing territory in the formation of the Mississippi Conference, the number of Tennessee Methodists in 1817 was 18,049 whites and 1,352 colored. John B. McFerrin, *History of Methodism in Tennessee* (Nashville, 1871), pp. 13, 459.

[22] Lincoln County was created by act of the state legislature in 1809; a hundred acres of land was set aside near the center for a seat of justice to be called Fayetteville. A century later the county seat had 3,629 inhabitants and was, as in earlier days, the trading center for a prosperous farming area. John Trotwood Moore, ed., *Tennessee, the Volunteer State, 1769–1923* (Chicago, 1923), p. 860, and Austin P. Foster, *Counties of Tennessee* (Nashville, 1923), p. 67.

[23] This fishpole cane grows in many parts of Alabama. The canebrake was a good winter refuge for livestock in the days before stock laws required owners to fence in their cattle.

[24] AUTHOR'S NOTE: "He pronounced it "sugh" for Sir. The low raised Virginians have a great aversion to r's, except where they ought not."

[25] AUTHOR'S NOTE: "Now Alabama."

[26] AUTHOR'S NOTE: "A lawyer, in one of the lower counties of Virginia, being in court one day, arose and observed to the court, 'my witnesses *is* come, and I *ar* ready for trial.' The opposite counsel, whom I believe was Mr. Wirt, rose up, and bowing, replied, 'am you, Sir?' "

[27] By 1816 Madison County was producing annually about 10,000 bales of cotton, more than any other county in the Tennessee Valley. Albert B. Moore, *History of Alabama* (Tuscaloosa, Ala., 1934), p. 271 n.

[28] The Northwest Ordinance of 1787 stated that the sixteenth

section of every township should be set aside for public education. This provision was later extended to the Southwest.

[29] Susannah Henry married Thomas Madison, "son of the long-time clerk of Augusta (John Madison) and relative of the future president." Robert D. Meade, *Patrick Henry, Patriot in the Making* (Philadelphia, 1957), p. 234; and *Virginia Magazine of History and Biography*, vol. 7, p. 253. Sarah Henry, mother of Patrick, willed to her daughter Suzannah Madison her Negro woman Fanny and to Susannah's son John Henry Madison, a Negro girl named Cloe. She also appointed Thomas Madison as one of the executors of her estate. The will, dated Mar. 12, 1784, was recorded in Amherst County Will Book, 2, p. 229, and is printed in *William and Mary Quarterly* Second Series, vol. 8, pp. 117–118. Thomas Madison was a brother of the Reverend James Madison, the first Episcopal bishop of Virginia. George McClaren Bryden, *Virginia's Mother Church* (Philadelphia, 1952), vol. 2, pp. 474–478; F. W. Kegley, *The Virginia Frontier, the Beginnings of the Southwest* (Roanoke, Virginia, 1928), p. 604. See also Griffith, *The Virginia House of Burgesses 1750–1774* (Northport, Ala., 1963), pp. 107, 131.

[30a] Sic.

[30b] Mrs. Royall was not the first to appreciate the situation of Huntsville, but she was a better prophet than probably she guessed. Huntsville maintained the lead among north Alabama towns through its history, and after World War II it became the fastest growing center in the state; it is now the fourth largest city in Alabama. See Edward Chambers Betts, *Early History of Huntsville, Alabama, 1804 to 1870* (Montgomery, Ala., 1916); and Erick Bergaust, *Rocket City, U.S.A.* (New York, 1963).

[31] AUTHOR'S NOTE: "When they were digging the vault for the Huntsville Bank, they found a vast number of snake skeletons."

[32] Leroy Pope (1765–1844), a native Virginian who moved to Madison County in 1809, became one of the pioneer leaders who did much to "further and encourage growth, stability and progress for the new frontier town." He purchased a large tract of land (one writer says a thousand acres) around Big Springs, and named the settlement "Twickenham" (after the English estate of the poet

Alexander Pope). Most residents found that name unsatisfactory, however, and in due course the place was renamed Huntsville, after the first white settler (John Hunt). Leroy Pope, the wealthiest man in the area, was public spirited and liberal, serving his county and state in a variety of roles—as a promoter of the Indian Creek Navigation Company, a founder of the Episcopal church in Huntsville, a commissioner to take subscriptions for the first bank in Alabama (the Planters & Merchants Bank of Huntsville), and chief justice on the first county court in Madison. Indeed, so often was Pope called on to serve his people in "many and varied capacities" that one historian was moved to call him the "Father of Huntsville," Betts, *Early Huntsville*, p. 20; and Thomas M. Owen, *History of Alabama and Dictionary of Alabama Biography* (Chicago, 1921), vol. 4, pp. 1,374–1,375.

[33] Madison County was created by the proclamation of Governor Robert Williams of Mississippi Territory on Dec. 18, 1808, becoming the second county in what is now Alabama. It was named for James Madison, then secretary of state in Thomas Jefferson's Cabinet. Willis Brewer, *Alabama: Her History, Resources, War Record and Public Men from 1540 to 1872* (Montgomery, Ala., 1872), p. 346; and Betts, *Early History of Huntsville, Alabama, 1804–1870* (Montgomery, Ala., 1916), pp. 11–27. Betts says that Madison is the only county in the state whose boundaries were ever extended after its creation.

[34] Author's Note: "The author had not seen Philadelphia, or any town east of the Alleghany."

[35] General John Coffee (1772–1833), a native of Prince Edward County, moved to Davidson County, Tennessee, in 1789, and worked as a surveyor. On hearing of the massacre at Fort Mims, he went to Alabama with some Tennessee volunteers and served under Andrew Jackson at Horseshoe Bend, at New Orleans, and elsewhere. When peace was restored he moved to Huntsville (and later to Florence), and became surveyor first for Mississippi Territory, and after statehood, for the state of Alabama. Coffee is described as being of "gigantic stature, fine proportions, and calm face." James Edmond Saunders, *Early Settlers in Alabama* (Tuscaloosa, Ala., 1961), p. 36; Dorothy Gentry, *Life and Legend of Lawrence County Alabama* (privately printed, n.d.), p. 36; Owen,

History of Alabama, vol. 3, p. 386; and James, *Andrew Jackson*, passim.

[36] Betts says that Neal B. Rose built a store on the east side of town square. *Early Huntsville*, p. 29.

[37] AUTHOR'S NOTE: "It was said that there was but two pans left with handles on them in Huntsville—one of these belonged to Mrs. T which she keeps under lock and key."

[38] AUTHOR'S NOTE: "Since this the author has been surprised at the difference of the Atlantic people from these—they do not, it is true, swear, but are as hard hearted as the flinty rock."

[39] Pope's house, which is still standing as this is written, was built on Echols Hill, overlooking the entire city. The estate has been much reduced but "the grounds are still broad in keeping with the house which they surround." Now considered Alabama's "most photogenic mansion," it was at the time it was built—around 1815—the "most magnificent dwelling of the entire Tennessee Valley region and by far and away the finest of its time." Its construction was supervised by George Steele, "a prominent architect who left a lasting imprint upon the architectural life of Huntsville" by introducing Greek Revival into the area. For a full description, see Ralph Hammond, *Antebellum Mansions of Alabama* (New York, 1951), pp. 52–54.

[40] William Patton (1778–1846), born in Londonderry, Ireland, emigrated to Virginia with his parents and later moved to Huntsville, where he became a planter and merchant and a founder of the Bell Factory, which is believed to have been the first cotton mill in the state. Patton had arrived in Monroe County, Virginia, in 1791. William Patton was the father of Robert M. Patton, the first governor elected under the Constitution of 1865. Owen, *History of Alabama*, vol. 4, pp. 1327–1328.

[41] Major General William (Billy) Carroll (1788–1844), who had come from Pittsburg to Nashville to open a hardware store, became Andrew Jackson's brigade inspector—a position that did not assure great popularity. He became involved in a duel with Jesse Benton and "plunged a bullet" into the seat of Benton's trousers, doing "far more injury to the spirit than to the flesh." He and John Coffee were among Jackson's mainstays in the Battle of New Orleans, and it was Carroll who urged Jackson to run for president in 1816.

James, *Andrew Jackson*, pp. 151, 211, 215, 216, 248, 270, passim. Evidence of the popularity Mrs. Royall speaks of is the fact that Carroll was elected governor of Tennessee six times (1821, 1823, 1825, 1829, 1831, 1833). *Dictionary of American Biography*, vol. 3, pp. 529–530.

[42] Carroll left an incomplete manuscript describing incidents of the trip down the river and the fighting around New Orleans. It is in private hands but is often quoted by James. See p. 820 n.

[43] John Henry Eaton, *The Life of Andrew Jackson* (Philadelphia, 1817), passim.

[44] Judge Kelley may be the Alexander Kelley who held many positions in Tennessee even before 1800. See J. G. M. Ramsey *Annals of Tennessee and Fain's Index* (Chattanooga, 1926), pp. 643, 658, 659, 688.

[45] Judge John Haywood was Jackson's choice for a federal judgeship in Florida. James, *Andrew Jackson*, p. 326.

[46] Felix Grundy (1777–1840), best known as one of the "War Hawks," was born on the Virginia frontier but lived in Pennsylvania and Kentucky before settling in Nashville in 1807. He became famous as a criminal lawyer and public figure, at times disagreeing with Andrew Jackson privately, but supporting the Administration publicly. In addition to serving in the United States House of Representatives (to which he was elected in 1811), Grundy sat in the Senate and later served as attorney general in President Van Buren's Cabinet. Nearly everything written about the political figures of this period—Jackson, Calhoun, Clay, or even the minor ones—contains references to Grundy, yet specific material about him is sparse. See, however, Joseph H. Parks, *Felix Grundy, Champion of Democracy* (Baton Rouge, 1940); *Dictionary of American Biography*, vol. 8, pp. 32–33; Henry McRaven, *Nashville, "Athens of the South"* (Chapel Hill, 1949), pp. 46–48.

[47] Counsellor Jenkin Whitesides was a United States senator and the most celebrated lawyer in Tennessee. Bassett, *Andrew Jackson*, p. 53; and James, *Andrew Jackson*, pp. 133, 137.

[48] Hayes—though this is not the spelling Mrs. Royall uses—is such a common name that it is practically impossible to identify the gentleman.

[49] Dr. James Priestley (d. 1821), a native of Rockbridge County, Virginia, was educated at Liberty Hall (forerunner of

Washington & Lee College) and had a distinguished career as a teacher of classical literature and school administrator in Kentucky and Maryland before becoming principal of Cumberland College—not "Columbia," as Mrs. Royall says—in Nashville (now George Peabody College for Teachers). Priestley was recommended to this position by a former pupil, Felix Grundy. *Dictionary of American Biography*, vol. 15, pp. 222–223.

[50] This is a period during which natural science was becoming extremely popular. See Brooks Hindle, *The Pursuit of Science in Revolutionary America, 1735–1789* (Chapel Hill, 1956); and Clement Eaton, *Freedom of Thought in the Old South* (Durham, 1940), passim. According to Eaton, most interest in the natural sciences was centered on the college campuses.

[51] AUTHOR'S NOTE: "At Huntsville, I saw *crickets* to put feet on, for the first time." Probably, crickets had meant "insects" to her instead of "small, low footstools."

[52] See below, note 55.

[53] The Rev. Gideon Blackburn (1772–1838), a Presbyterian missionary to the Indians, was born in Augusta County, Virginia, but spent his adult life in Kentucky and Tennessee, where he won considerable fame as a preacher. He is said to have exemplified "the best type of backwoods eloquence." In his later years he was president of several schools, including Centre College. *Dictionary of American Biography* (New York, 1929), vol. 2, pp. 314–315. James Edmonds Saunders says of him: "He was of commanding person, graceful manners, and a scholar of extensive learning," and—quoting a political figure—"Dr. Blackburn's eloquence as General Jackson's chaplain, inflamed the hearts and nerved the arms of the Tennessee volunteers, who carried the victorious flag of our country through the great campaigns of Jackson . . . , the most eloquent and powerful minister I ever heard." Saunders, *Early Settlers in Alabama*, p. 302.

[54] In 1817 the Cherokees ceded land enough to form three counties. Saunders, *Early Settlers*, p. 36. The process of eliminating Indian lands in Alabama has been mentioned many times, but there is no satisfactory and complete account. As good as any is that of Marie Bankhead Owen, *The Story of Alabama* (New York, 1949), vol. 1, pp. 102–116.

[55] AUTHOR'S NOTE: "Now called Marathon."

[56] Melton's Bluff, the seat of justice in Lawrence County while Alabama was a territory, was reportedly laid out by Andrew Jackson and his associates, and surveyed into 658 lots by John Coffee, and it was the first and largest town in the county for many years. It was situated at the head of Elk River Shoals on the south bank of the Tennessee River. Its first inhabitants were immigrants from Virginia and the Carolinas who settled the area rapidly, building their houses for more than a mile along the bluff facing the river. A county historian says that Isaac Brownlow was the leading citizen until his death in 1828. The town lost its importance when the county seat was moved to Moulton in 1820, and there is no trace of it left now. Dorothy Gentry says the place was named for one Melton, "a Cherokee Indian." Gentry, *Lawrence County*, pp. 29–30. In 1899 Melton's Bluff was the cotton plantation of Thomas Jones; today it is in the lake formed by Wheeler Dam. Saunders, *Early Settlers*, pp. 84–85.

[57] Mrs. Royall evidently refers to the treaty of 1806 between the United States and the Cherokee Indians, whereby the Indians ceded to the United States a tract of land "which lies to the northward of the Tennessee River, and westward of a line to be run from the upper part of the Chickasaw Old Fields. . . ." Article II mentions an island on which a "Moses Melton now lives," and which was to be reserved for him. The record does not reveal whether this was the Melton to whom Mrs. Royall made reference. The text of the treaty is given in Saunders, pp. 19–20.

[58] AUTHOR'S NOTE: "Such was the eagerness of the white people to possess these lands, that the camp fires were not extinguished when they took possession." There was a treaty with the Cherokees (1817) by which much of their territory in Alabama and Tennessee was ceded to the United States. Few authors, however, say anything about their removal until after the Treaty of New Echota in 1835. See, for example, *The Removal of the Cherokee Nation: Manifest Destiny or National Dishonor?* Problems in American Civilization (New York, 1962).

[59] Jackson owned not only farm lands but also town lots in the Tennessee River area. A shareholder in the Cypress Land Company, he (together with John Coffee) was "deep in Alabama speculations." See Andrew Jackson to Egbert Harris, Apr. 13, 1822, *Cor-*

respondence of Andrew Jackson, vol. 3, p. 158; *The Life of Andrew Jackson* (New York, 1938), pp. 277, 306, 335, 336, 349. It is interesting to note that James cites this passage from *Letters from Alabama* as his source about the Melton Bluff plantation. It is understandable, however, when one learns that his wife stopped work on a biography of Anne Royall (she never completed it) in order to help him finish his biography of Jackson. James, *Andrew Jackson*, p. 909.

[60] AUTHOR'S NOTE: "Pronounced Bias."

[61] For further scientific information about the topography of the state, consult *Alabama Geological Survey, Bibliography of Alabama Geology, 1935–1958* (University, Ala., 1960).

[62] Commonly called Spanish moss, its botanical name is *Tillandsin usneoides*. It grows in the proximity of water—near the seacoast or along streams—in the lower South. Its long shaggy, beard-like appearance often fascinated earlier writers. For instance, see William Bartram, *Travels*, ed. Mark Van Doren (New York, 1940), p. 92. Bartram calls it "a singular and surprising vegetable production."

[63] Neither Colonel Pettis—nor any other Pettis—is named by Dorothy Gentry in *Lawrence County*, so he remains unknown except for this reference.

[64] Major [Edward] Wyatt eludes further identification but the Wyatts and Bibbs, both from Virginia, were closely allied by birth and marriage. See Saunders, *Early Settlers*, p. 254 and passim. AUTHOR'S NOTE: "She has a daughter married to Mr. Pope, one of the wealthiest men in Madison." Thomas M. Owen says Mrs. Leroy Pope was Judith Sale of Amherst County, Virginia. See Owen, *History of Alabama*, vol. 4, p. 1,375.

[65] Patrick Foley was listed among some men of high standing who opposed certain measures adopted by the territorial Governor Winthrop Sargent. J. F. H. Claiborne, *Mississippi as a Province, Territory, and State with Biographical Notices of Eminent Citizens* (Jackson, 1880; reprinted by Louisiana State University Press, 1964), p. 209.

[66] Doctors Crabb and Rousseau may have died young or moved on to other locations—in any case they do not appear in the annals of the county. The others named in this section are likewise unidentifiable.

[67] Ditto's Landing, on the Tennessee River, was early a landmark on the Indian trail that ran from Huntsville to Mud Town on the Cahaba.

[68] This incident does not appear in biographies of Jackson.

[69] Robbery, such as that planned here, was common. For an account of some of the notorious gangs on the Natchez Trace see Robert M. Coates, *Outlaw Years* (New York, 1930).

[70] The Kenhawa River is in West Virginia, running northwest into the Ohio River at Point Pleasant. Originally—1738—in Augusta County, Virginia, the area has since been part of many counties. For its varied political evolution see Edgar B. Sims, *Making a State* (Charleston, 1956), pp. 191–211. For Washington's Lands see ibid., pp. 151, 157; and Charles Henry Ambler, *West Virginia, The Mountain State* (New York, 1940), pp. 108–112.

[71] Lencour [Lincoyer, Lyncoya] Jackson was reared at the Hermitage and apprenticed to a saddler in Nashville. Whether or not it was confinement in a shop that made him ill, he did contract tuberculosis and died in 1828. If a year old in 1813, he would have been a lad of sixteen at the time of his death. Notwithstanding his hatred of Indians, Andrew Jackson had great affection for this boy and often referred to him as his "son." See Stanley F. Horn, *The Hermitage, Home of Old Hickory* (Richmond, 1838), pp. 122–125; and James, *Life of Andrew Jackson*, pp. 159, 266, 288, 329, 344, 408, 450, 460. Horn says that John Coffee rescued the infant and sent him to Jackson's tent. The general then sent him to Mrs. Jackson by way of Huntsville, where he was cared for by the Leroy Pope family who, reportedly, gave him his name.

[72] This story does not appear in any of the standard biographies of Franklin. It may be a garbled version of his own account of his first visit home after an absence of seven months. Benjamin Franklin, *Autobiography*, ed. Leonard W. Labaree, et al. (New Haven, 1964), pp. 80–82.

[73] For the evolution of the counties in what is now West Virginia, see Sims, *Making a State*, passim.

[74] AUTHOR'S NOTE: "A pewter dish or spoons, in those days, were considered articles of opulence—two-thirds of the people of the frontiers eat with muscle shells; and I have had a great veneration for muscle shells ever since; for my sister soon broke or lost,

together, our half dozen spoons." The frontier cabin is familiar, but the person who wishes to learn more about it may consult C. D. Aldrich, *The Real Log Cabin* (New York, 1928); Thomas D. Clark, *The Rampaging Frontier* (Bloomington, Ind., 1964); Fletcher M. Green, *The Lides Go South* (Columbia, S.C., 1952); Clarence M. Babcock, *The American Frontier* (New York, 1965); Margaret Bell, *Women of the Wilderness* (New York, 1938); Stanton A. Coblentz, *The Swallowing Wilderness* (New York, 1961); and Everett N. Dick, *The Dixie Frontier* (New York, 1948).

[75] This is probably William Findley (1741–1821), representative from Pennsylvania who held many public positions, including membership in the Second and Third congresses. Mr. Findley, a native of Ireland, opposed the federal government's action in the Whiskey Rebellion. *Biographical Directory of the American Congress, 1774–1961* (Washington, D.C., 1961), p. 887.

[76] James Kirke Paulding and William Irving, *Salamagundi* (Harper & Brothers, n.d.; 1902 ed. by G. P. Putnam's Sons); *Speeches by Phillips* (Emmet, Curran, and Grallan, E. C. & J. Biddle, n.d.); Lady Morgan, *France*, 2 vols. (Harper & Brothers, n.d.); and *Bibliotheca Americana . . . , Catalog of American Publications, 1820–1852* (New York, 1939).

[77] The John Melish map of 1816 shows Fort Hampton on the south side of the Tennessee River, across from the mouth of Elk River.

[78] AUTHOR'S NOTE: "This renegade was apprehended three years afterwards, and lodged in Huntsville jail, where I saw him, and shortly afterwards he broke jail and made his escape with fifteen others, and was not heard of at the time of writing this note. The murderer, from the first, laid the murder on the two Indians. They being informed of this, assisted in taking him the last time, and came on with the guard to Huntsville. They were much enraged with him, and made him run before them on foot, and they on horseback. They made him wade all the creeks, and now and then gave him a cut with their whips, saying, "You kill white woman, and tell lie on Indian."

[79] AUTHOR'S NOTE: "A friendly phrase, quite common here."

[80a] This was definitely a political campaign, and yet according to the published journals Lawrence County did not have a repre-

sentative in the Territorial Assembly at this time. Flemming Hodges, elected in 1819, was the first state senator, and Lewis Dillahunty and Samuel Bigham were the representatives. William H. Brantley, *Three Capitals* (Boston, 1947), pp. 230–231.

[80b] AUTHOR'S NOTE: "In this country horses are called *critters*—In West Pennsylvania, and West Virginia, they are called beasts."

[81] A bit of rough horseplay on the occasion of weddings seems to have been quite common in this period. For a similar event see the account of an earlier wedding in St. Stephens in Griffith, *History of Alabama*, pp. 161–162.

[82] Dorothy Gentry says that an election to determine the seat of justice was held in February, 1820, approximately a year after Anne Royall was writing. Courtland was the keenest rival for the location. Gentry, *Lawrence County*, p. 30.

[83] Among the leading family names, as listed in Gentry, *Lawrence County*, were: Roberts, McDaniels, Hodges, Peters, Roddy, White. Ibid., p. 35.

[84] For convenient information about this period, see Harriette Simpson Arnow, *Seedtime on the Cumberland* (New York, 1960) and its sequel, *Flowering of the Cumberland* (New York, 1963); Wilma Dykeman, *The French Broad* (New York, 1955); and Donald Davidson, *The Tennessean, the Old River* (New York, 1946).

[85] At the beginning of this tale, Mrs. Royall said that the incidents of Mr. Burlison's life made a "complete novel." It is doubtful that at the time she intended to use it as the basis for a work of fiction, but later, in 1830, she did incorporate many of the ideas and episodes in *The Tennessean*. Even the name of the hero was only thinly disguised: Burlison becomes Burlington.

[86] AUTHOR'S NOTE: "The crime of horse-stealing is punished with death."

[87] Although the earthquake of 1811 gets frequent mention, there seems to have been no scientific description of it, and there are few circumstantial accounts of any kind. According to the best of them the quake began "Shortly after two o'clock on the morning of December 16, 1811, [when] the settlers [of New Madrid, Missouri] were awakened by the groaning and creaking of their houses and the falling of furniture. They hurriedly groped their way into the open where with the ground trembling in a succession of shocks,

they stood through the winter's night. Daylight brought other shocks, and for almost two years scarcely a day passed without a disturbance. The ground rose and fell, accompanied by loud rumbling noises and the discharge of gases. Great cracks formed in the earth, and trees were bent until their branches interlocked. Landslides swept down the bluffs and hillsides; areas were pushed up and still larger areas sank, in some instances as many as twenty-five feet. Great waves churned the bed of the Mississippi, washing boats high on the shore and sweeping thousands of trees into the river." *Missouri*, American Guide Series (New York, 1941), p. 458. The only contemporary mention recorded in Clark, *Travels in the Old South*, vol. 1, pp. 177–178, is that of one John Bradbury, who left New Madrid for New Orleans the day before the quake occurred.

[88] From his closing sentence it would appear that the narrator meant for this to be a tirade against the government. But the story itself contains one of Mrs. Royall's favorite themes—the unchristian acts of professedly religious people. AUTHOR'S NOTE: "Having inadvertently settled on the Indian lands, his house was burnt by order of the government."

[89] We cannot be sure to whom Mrs. Royall was referring, but it may have been either John Henry Eaton, *The Life of Andrew Jackson. . . .* (Philadelphia, 1817), or William James, *Full and Correct Account of the Military Occurances*, 2 vols. (Philadelphia, 1818).

[90] The story of the mutinies that plagued the general is given full treatment in Bassett, *Andrew Jackson*, pp. 99–106; Eaton, *Andrew Jackson*, pp. 63–71; and James, *Andrew Jackson*, pp. 160–170, passim. See also Wilburt S. Brown, *The Amphibious Campaign for West Florida and Louisiana: A Critical Review of Strategy and Tactics at New Orleans* (University, Ala., 1969), passim.

[91] Andrew Jackson was one of Mrs. Royall's prejudices—he could do no wrong! He was an exceedingly popular hero, to be sure, but he did have enemies. Most of them appeared after he became a political figure but even at the time of this writing he had made enemies by his duels, his Indian policy, and as events turned out, most of all by his actions in Florida where, John C. Calhoun declared, Jackson had exceeded his authority. See James, *Andrew Jackson*, pp. 302–332.

[92] It is not clear what Mrs. Royall did in the months between this last letter and Apr. 30, 1821, the date of the next one. The best guess—it is no more than that—is that she returned to Virginia to defend herself in the lawsuit in which she lost all her property.

[93] Flint River, famed as the location of the first Baptist Church in Alabama, is in Madison County.

[94] Mrs. Royall was interested in dialects which, since her time, have received much attention from linguists. See, for example, Cleanth Brooks, Jr., *The Relation of the Alabama-Georgia to the Provincial Dialects of Great Britain* (Baton Rouge, 1935); Lewis Herman and Marguerete Shalett Herman, *American Dialects* (New York, 1947); and *Word Lists from the South*, published by the American Dialectic Society, University of North Carolina, 1944.

[95] Literature on the Presbyterians includes: Walter B. Posey, *The Presbyterian Church in the Old Southwest, 1778–1840* (Richmond, 1952); Ernest Trice Thompson, *Presbyterians in the South* (Richmond, 1963); William Warren Sweet, *The Presbyterians, 1783–1840* (New York, 1936); and James H. B. Hall, "The History of the Cumberland Presbyterian Church in Alabama Prior to 1826," *Transactions of the Alabama Historical Society, 1899–1903* (Montgomery, Alabama, 1904), pp. 365–394. Hall quotes the Rev. R. D. King, a field officer, about the work in North Alabama (p. 380): "In April 1821, I was ordered by the presbytery to form a circuit on the south side of the Tennessee river, in the counties of Morgan, Lawrence, and Franklin, in Alabama. I had to hunt my own preaching places, and make my own appointments. The country was all newly settled, having been lately purchased from the Indians. I formed a circuit of four weeks' extent, with regular daily appointments. I succeeded in getting up three camp meetings, one in Morgan County [then Catoca County]. Here I was assisted by the Rev. James Stuart, the Rev. James Moore, and my father [Rev. Samuel King]. . . . The results of those three campmeetings were one hundred and fifty professions. Besides these, there are a good many professions on my circuit appointments. . . ."

[96] The Rev. John C. Burress was named the Presiding Elder of the Cahawba District, Methodist, in 1822. Marion Elias Lazenby, *History of Methodism in Alabama and West Florida* (n.p., 1960), p. 159.

[97] The Rev. William McMahon, appointed Presiding Elder of the Tennessee River District, 1822, had some churches in Tennessee, ibid., pp. 159–160. The Rev. James A. Butler was a Campbellite preacher. Gentry, *Lawrence County*, p. 76.

[98] Three modern works on this phase of frontier religion are: Charles A. Johnson, *The Frontier Campmeeting* (Dallas, 1955); William G. McLoughlin, Jr., *Modern Revivalism* (New York, 1959); and William Warren Sweet, *Revivalism in America* (New York, 1944). McLoughlin's work is most valuable for the period since 1830.

[99] This antireligious sentiment grows as the years pass, and Mrs. Royall becomes very caustic in her remarks about the Church. There is hardly an issue of *Paul Pry*, the weekly newspaper she began publishing in 1831, without a tirade against it. Her general dislike and suspicion crystalized in her attack on what she believed was a plot to form a union of Church and State.

[100] Dorothy Gentry lists many early settlers and office holders, *Lawrence County*, pp. 30–35.

[101] These songs do not appear in Byron Arnold, *Folksongs of Alabama* (University, Ala. 1950) or in any other available anthologies of folk music.

[102] Clement Comer Clay (1789–1866) was at this time one of four circuit judges in the state. Born in Halifax County, Virginia, in 1789, he went with his parents to Tennessee, where he grew to manhood in Grainger County. He read law with Hugh Lawson White and was admitted to practice in 1809. Two years later he moved to Madison County, Alabama, arriving with "one Negro manservant, two horses, his law books in his saddle bags" and only enough money to last a few days. However, blessed with good looks, charming manners, and ambition, he soon built up an extensive law practice in Huntsville and held several important offices. He was elected to the only territorial legislature Alabama had, and he was a member of the Constitutional Convention (1819), serving as chairman of the Committee of Fifteen that drafted Alabama's first constitution. After the date Mrs. Royall is writing, Clay was elected to both houses of Congress and to the office of governor of Alabama. Ruth K. Nuermberger, *The Clays of Alabama* (Lexington, 1958), pp. 1–93; Owen, *History of Alabama*, vol. 3, pp.

342–343; and Royall, *Letters from Alabama*, appendix, p. 226.

[103] Literature on the fur trade of this period is extensive. The person who wishes to know more on this subject should consult Dale Van Enery, *The Final Challenge* (New York, 1964); Hiram M. Chittenden, *The American Fur Trade of the Far West* (New York, 1902); Paul C. Phillips, *The Fur Trade* (Norman, Okla., 1961); and Bernard DeVoto, *Across the Wide Missouri* (Boston, 1947) or one of many others. There was more interest in western mining later but even at this date the lead mines were attracting prospectors. Edwin C. McReynolds, Missouri, *A History of the Crossroads State* (Norman, Okla., 1962), pp. 66–67.

[104] The court house in Lawrence County burned some time after this trial and there is, of course, no record of it.

[105] Coffee's Trace does not appear on any of the early maps. Mrs. Royall may have been referring to a wagon road, designated merely as the Huntsville Road, that led north into Tennessee. It extended south to Ditto's Landing on the Tennessee River. Olin Dee Morrison, *The American South,* Historical Atlas (Athens, Ohio, 1965), vol. 3, pt. 1, pp. 23–24.

[106] It is interesting that the theme of the lone, wandering woman appears again and again. This King family may have lived outside the county—at least the King families that Mrs. Gentry mentions in *Lawrence County* do not seem to fit the description.

[107] Yet another instance of Mrs. Royall's anti-church sentiment.

[108] Author's Note: "A small coin current in those days."

[109] Courtland, established in 1818 and incorporated in 1819, is about 15 miles north of Moulton in Lawrence County. Owen gives the Bynum, Shackelford, Sherrod, Gilchrist, Harris, Sykes, Perrine, Saunders, Swope, Watkins, Jones, and Pointer families as being among the earliest settlers. Owen, *History of Alabama*, vol. 1, p. 427; Saunders, *Early Settlers*, passim; and Gentry, *Lawrence County*, pp. 36–27.

[110] Carolina Pink, according to Webster, is the wild pink, *silene pennsylvanica.* The Colomba root remains unidentified. The sensitive brier is any "trailing, prickly plant of the genus *Schrankia* but especially a perennial irritomobile herb with pink flowers which many a youngster called a "shame vine" because one could say

"shame, shame" and wave a hand over to make it fold up in "em barrassment."

[111] The jointed snake, also known as the glass snake, is really a limbless lizard whose tail breaks easily into small pieces. There are many local tales about this jointed snake and its equal, the hoop snake, which is often reported to have swallowed its tail to form a hoop and to have then rolled down a hill!

[112] Mrs. Royall had to wait until a later visit to the state to see a chameleon. The reptile is only a few inches long. Royall, *Southern Tour*, vol. 2, p. 197.

[113] Sugar cane was tried in many parts of the state and is still grown in some areas. There seems to have been little attempt to produce it commercially.

[114] Since Mexico's independence from Spain did not become effective until July 6, 1821, what the author was saying about the terms of the Spanish was still true. The terms that Moses Austin made are given in Euguene C. Barker, *The Austin Papers*, Annual Report of the American Historical Association for the year 1919 (Washington, D.C., 1924), vol. 2, pp. 389–390. See also Alfred B. Thomas, *Latin America, A History* (New York, 1956), pp. 258–259.

[115] Mrs. Royall's comment makes one think "C.C." was a national figure. Since no president had these initials, the man may have been a governor or other local figure, or perhaps a legislator.

[116] This is one of the longest passages about her husband, but in her other writings she mentions his hospitality.

[117] For a brief survey of Florence, county seat of Launderdale County, see Owen, *History of Alabama*, vol. 1, pp. 595–596.

[118] AUTHOR'S NOTE: "This was literally fulfilled. He actually delivered the property as stated above; had his house burnt twice to the ground, with all its contents, and died a wretched death. Thus the Lord avenges the widow's wrongs."

[119] The Florence–Muscle Shoals–Tuscumbia–Sheffield area has become one of the great industrial centers in Alabama, thanks in large part to the power supplied by the Tennessee Valley Authority.

[120] This part of Mrs. Royall's prediction did not come true for nearly a decade. In 1828 the little *Atlas* steamed across the shoals at high water to ply the upper Tennessee and the Holston Rivers. Steamboats could go *down* to the Shoals or *up* to the Shoals but not

through them—a situation that gave rise to a great deal of agitation in favor of a canal around them. Residents of the area, through their congressmen, persuaded Congress to donate four hundred thousand acres of "relinquished lands" in the Huntsville area for its construction. With the proceeds of this land the state built a canal around Big Muscle Shoals, fourteen and a quarter miles long, sixty feet wide and six feet deep. This, however, was usable only during high water and was soon abandoned. Moore, *History of Alabama*, p. 303; and Betts, *Early History of Huntsville*, pp. 66–70.

[121] AUTHOR'S NOTE: "Now a Senator in Congress from Alabama." John McKinley (1780–1852), was United States senator from Alabama from 1826 to 1831. He was born in Culpeper County, Virginia, and resided in Kentucky and Tennessee before moving to Huntsville in 1819; later he moved to Lauderdale County, of which Florence is the county seat. McKinley held many public positions, including a seat on the Supreme Court of the United States. Owen, *History of Alabama*, vol. 4, p. 1,124. James Jackson, unlike many of the settlers in North Alabama, was Irish and not a Virginian. Born in County Monoghan, Ireland, 1782, he migrated to Philadelphia and then followed relatives to Nashville. In 1814 he became an important member of the Cypress Creek Land Company and bought extensive lands in Lauderdale County. His home, "The Forks," built on his plantation at the forks of Big and Little Cypress Creeks, was one of the show places of the area and stood until 1966 when it was consumed by fire. The two-story house was completely surrounded by Ionic columns. Jackson (no kin to Andrew Jackson) was a horse fancier, and descendents of his stock have won many Kentucky Derby races. Owen, *History of Alabama*, vol. 3, p. 891; Hammond, *Antebellum Mansions*, pp. 33–36.

[122] Mrs. Coffee was Mary Donelson, sister to Emily Donelson, mistress at the White House during the Jackson administration. Henry McRaven, *Nashville*, p. 54; Marquis James, *Andrew Jackson, Portrait of a President* (New York, 1937), p. 206; and Owen, *History of Alabama*, vol. 3, p. 368. Owen is in error, however, when he says that Mary was the sister of Mrs. Jackson.

[123] AUTHOR'S NOTE: "This amicable man I lament to hear, is now dead." She probably added this note at a later date as she readied the letters for publication.

[124] Judge Ellis and Attorney Fulton may have been prominent people in their day, but they left no available record of themselves.

[125] AUTHOR'S NOTE: "Fine pickings for the blue skins."

[126] Compare Mrs. Royall's description of Huntsville in 1817 (in her letter of January 1, 1818).

[127] The most complete account of social activities in Huntsville is in Hammond, *Antebellum Mansions*, pp. 33–68. Also see Betts, *Early History of Huntsville*, pp. 73–76.

[128] Evidently Mrs. Royall made this trip, because on July 1, 1823, she left St. Stephens, Alabama, for Virginia. *Sketches*, By a Traveler, p. 2.

[129] One wonders why she loved to dwell on such hardships as these.

[130] AUTHOR'S NOTE: "The land where it happened being poor, was settled by poor people generally."

[131] AUTHOR'S NOTE: "He was the first man (or woman) I ever saw hand the tracts about. He was from Philadelphia."

[132] A mad-dog stone, or simply madstone, was a "stonelike object obtained from the stomach of a deer, popularly believed to be efficacious if placed on the wound caused by the bite of an animal that has hydrophobia." Mitford M. Mathews, ed., *A Dictionary of Americanisms on Historical Principles* (Chicago, 1951), vol. 2, p. 1015.

[133] Sentiment was not uniform throughout the state, but in the Tennessee Valley it seems to have been. See map showing vote "On motion proposing Jackson for President, *House Journal*, 1823." Thomas P. Abernethy, *Formative Period in Alabama* (University, Ala., rev. ed. 1965), p. 131; Moore, *History of Alabama*, p. 159–161.

[134] For Leroy Pope, see note #32 above. Dr. Thomas Fearn was among the commissioners to open the bank in Huntsville in 1816. Dr. Henry H. Chambers (1790–1826), another of the many native Virginians who came to Madison County, was surgeon on the staff of Andrew Jackson during the Creek War. Active in politics, he was on his way to Washington to take his seat in the Senate when he died. Chambers County is named for him. Owen, *History of Alabama*, vol. 3, p. 310. Thomas Bibb, native of Amelia County, Virginia, came to north Alabama by way of Georgia. Merchant, planter, politician, he became the second governor of Alabama at

the death of his brother, William Wyatt Bibb in 1819. Ibid., vol. 3, p. 147. His beautiful Greek Revival home, Belle Mina, which was finished in 1826, is still standing. Hammond, *Antebellum Mansions* (New York, 1951), pp. 46–51. Dr. James Manning came to Huntsville from Elbert County, Georgia. He was accompanied by other prominent citizens and thus "stripped the town of its vital forces." Dr. Manning was described as a man of "great wealth and modesty." His wife was Sophia Watkins, sister of Mrs. William Wyatt Bibb. Betts, *Early History of Huntsville*, pp. 22–23.

[135] Dr. Alexander Erskine, a native of Monroe County, Virginia, located in Huntsville in 1817, and was for many years president of the medical examiners, Alabama Medical Association. The leading hotel in Huntsville at this writing bears the name of his son, Russell Erskine. Owen, *History of Alabama*, vol. 3, p. 543.

[136] AUTHOR'S NOTE: "This was the first Missionary I ever heard; and it was amusing to hear the women next day passing severe reflections on Colonel Pope, because he put only 25 cents in the hat. 'Such a man—a man of his wealth—to give a quarter—Did you ever see the like! *They* would have given *all* they had!' It was, beyond doubt, the worst laid out quarter he ever spent."

INDEX